INTELLECT and SPIRIT

The Life and Work of
Robert Coles

INTELLECT and SPIRIT

The Life and Work of Robert Coles

BRUCE A. RONDA

CONTINUUM · NEW YORK

1989

The Continuum Publishing Company
370 Lexington Avenue
New York, NY 10017

Printed in the United States of America

Library of Congress Cataloging-in-Publication Data

Ronda, Bruce A.
    Intellect and spirit : the life and work of Robert Coles / Bruce
  A. Ronda.
    p. cm.
    Bibliography: p.
    Includes index.
    ISBN 0-8264-0436-7
    1. Coles, Robert.   2. Authors, American—20th century—
Biography.
    3. Psychiatrists—United States—Biography.   4. Educators—United
States—Biography.   I. Title.
    PS3553.047456Z84   1989
    818'.5409—dc19
    [B]   88-27458
                                                                  CIP

"Speaking," A black mother, Boston, 1971, in Robert Coles,
A Festering Sweetness: Poems of American People
(Pittsburgh: University of Pittsburgh Press, 1978), quoted
by permission of the author.

For Priscilla Inkpen: spouse, companion, friend

I realize that, with even so much involvement in explanations as this, I am liable seriously, and perhaps irretrievably, to obscure what would at best be hard enough to give its appropriate clarity and intensity; and what seems to me most important of all: namely, that these I will write of are human beings, living in this world, innocent of such twistings as these which are taking place over their heads; and that they were dwelt among, investigated, spied on, revered, and loved, by other quite monstrously alien human beings, in the employment of still others still more alien; and that they are now being looked into by still others, who have picked up their living as casually as if it were a book, and who were actuated toward this reading by various possible reflexes of sympathy, curiosity, idleness, et cetera, and almost certainly in a lack of consciousness, and conscience, remotely appropriate to the enormity of what they were doing.

If I could do it, I'd do no writing at all here. It would be photographs; the rest would be fragments of cloth, bits of cotton, lumps of earth, records of speech, pieces of wood and iron, phials of odors, plates of food and excrement. Booksellers would consider it quite a novelty; critics would murmur, yes, but is it art; and I could trust a majority of you to use it as you would a parlor game.

James Agee, from *Let Us Now Praise Famous Men*

Speaking

I'm not speaking for myself
I'm speaking for my children.
I'm speaking for Joseph and Sally and Harry
and Stevie and Benjie and Mary,
I'm speaking for them,
They enter my dreams,
in the night I see them grown older.
So I get the words out,
Do my complaining, hollering and
do my scolding
do my begging and pleading.
I'd better, don't you think.

A black mother, Boston, 1971, in Robert Coles,
A Festering Sweetness: Poems of American People

Contents

Acknowledgments

This book began as a Winterterm course at Skidmore College in 1981. My friends and colleagues there—Mary Lynn, Joanna Zangrando, Benjamin Berry, Wilma Hall—encouraged me to offer such a course; in this, as in so much, I am grateful for their support. Friends in upstate New York were equally interested and supportive; they include Bryce Butler, Marilyn Mowry, Faye Harvey, and Sharon Carter. Much thanks to them.

I delivered a small part of this work to the first meeting of "Revisionings: Religion and American Life" sponsored by the Center for American Studies at Indiana University/Purdue University at Indianapolis, and benefited from much insightful comment and criticism there. Several passages from my review essay "Robert Coles: Psychiatry and the Life of the Spirit," *The Christian Century*, 103 (June 18–25, 1986), 583–587, Copyright 1986, appear here, and are reprinted by permission of The Christian Century Foundation.

Here in Boulder, I have engaged in many conversations on Coles and Coles-related themes. Many of the insights here, especially in the later chapters, grow out of such conversations. I am particularly grateful to the "Marx-Gandhi" reading and reflection group, of which I am privileged to be a part—LeRoy Moore, Larry Tasaday, Dick Counihan, Caroline Hinckley, Cathy Comstock, Anne Sellar, and Brian Mahan.

At the University of Colorado, Marcia Westkott provided helpful background in psychological theory. Other colleagues—Ericka Doss, Fred Anderson, Virginia Anderson, Steven Epstein—were steadily encouraging and supportive. I want particularly to thank Anna Vayr, administrative assistant in Women's Studies, for her help in deciphering the mysteries of computer printing, and in general for her kindness and generosity.

Finally, I want to thank Robert Coles for spending time with me, for being so open and informative, for not putting limits or restrictions on what I could write. I have tried to respect his willingness of spirit in the book that follows.

These pages are dedicated to the one who provided the most steadfast encouragement, care, and love.

Boulder, Colorado
February 1988

Introduction

Robert Coles is depositing his huge collection of tapes, transcripts, children's drawings, and notes in the library of the University of North Carolina. This announcement, made in the pages of *The Moral Life of Children* and again in *The Political Life of Children* (both 1986 publications), probably comes as a shock to those whose image of the rumpled child psychiatrist sitting cross-legged on the floor drawing with his young subjects is virtually untouched by the passage of time.

In fact, Coles has been listening to and reflecting on children (and youth and adults as well) for more than twenty years. Best known for the *Children of Crisis* series, for the two-volume *Women of Crisis* (coauthored with Jane Hallowell Coles) and for his conversations with Daniel Berrigan, *The Geography of Faith,* Coles has also written literary criticism, reviews, poetry, social commentary, several children's books, and regular columns for *The New Republic, New Oxford Review,* and *American Poetry Review.* We can expect many more books and essays from Coles, but the establishment of a Coles archive provides the occasion for reflecting on the work of this remarkable man.

Who is Robert Coles? In the introductions to the several volumes of *Children of Crisis,* Coles variously identifies himself as a doctor, child psychiatrist, social anthropologist, teacher, friend, busybody, and nuisance. He is also a contributor to popular magazines, a public speaker in great demand, a professor at Harvard University, a husband and father. No single professional or personal label even hints at the range of Coles's accomplishments; none captures the essence of his work.

His gentle refusal to be pigeonholed professionally, together with the great variety of his work, makes tremendous demands on the reader. Simply finding the threads of continuity in the life and work of Robert Coles is no easy task; commenting on them requires at least passing familiarity with the many different issues and bodies of material that Coles has taken up.

To call Robert Coles a "translator," as I do throughout this book, is to suggest that he stands between a partially hidden text or experience and an expectant public. The translator is faithful to the original, but

1

also brings to the work of translation an intuitive, sympathetic spirit, trying to capture the inner life that the words of the original convey. Translation is an act of intersection, in which text or experience crosses with and enlivens translator and is brought to life through that act of translation. For the audience unfamiliar with the original, there is no original without translation. Much of the lifework of Robert Coles is a work of translation or crossing, in which the words and experience of children and adults in crisis, often in hard-pressed circumstances, are given shape and form through Coles's interviews and commentary, and cross over to a larger, more empowered audience.

How that translation is carried out, and how Coles became such a "translator," is the subject of this book. Here in the introduction we can only hint at how this mediating stance came about. In the late 1950s, after medical school and an internship in psychiatry, Coles was rapidly coming to distrust psychiatric language, method, and assumptions. "Everything was 'interpreted,' given a name, and attributed derivatively to the 'oral' or the 'anal' stage of libidinal development," he recalled.[1] As he encountered children and adults engaged in the desegregation struggle in the South, he looked instinctively for signs of pathology or maladjustment in these people who were so obviously violating social customs of long standing. Much to his astonishment, Coles found that many of these early activists were psychologically normal, even remarkably healthy, given the stressful circumstances they encountered. "I was looking for 'psychopathology' in those early years of my residence in the South." What he discovered instead was "remarkably little psychiatric illness . . . despite their trials."[2]

As Coles grew more dissatisfied with orthodox psychoanalysis as a means of narrating and explaining the civil rights struggles of the children and their parents in New Orleans and Atlanta, he was also growing more suspicious of the quantitative method used by social scientists. Of the method in *Children of Crisis* and subsequent books, Coles commented:

> I am not a survey social scientist. I claim no definitive conclusions about what any "group" feels or thinks. . . . One can only insist on being as tentative as possible, claiming only impressions, observations, thoughts, reflections, surmises, speculations, and, in the end, a "way of seeing." . . . I aim essentially to evoke, to suggest, rather than pursue a more cognitive approach or a psychopathological orientation.[3]

Lacking, or rejecting, an explicit agenda from either psychoanalysis or social science, Coles has acted instead as a translator, bridging the gap between readers and his often ignored, stereotyped, ridiculed, or simply little-known subjects. Though he does occasionally offer comparative, historical, and theoretical observations on the lives of his "subjects," these are secondary to his main purpose. "The whole point of this work," he wrote in 1977, "has been to put myself in a position, with respect to a number of children, that offers them a chance to indicate a certain amount about themselves to me, and through me, to others. But each life . . . has its own authority, dignity, fragility, rock-bottom strength."[4] Through Coles, these adults and children are made real to an audience of strangers; through Coles, a large readership encounters people whose lives and circumstances are sometimes as strange as an untranslated novel. Throughout his work, Coles has insisted that his subjects' stories, not his own theories and preoccupations, are the central matter. The essence of Freud's "talking cure," the young psychiatrist had been taught, is that the patient cannot and will not recall the past, dodging and evading the truth. The analyst patiently, cooly, works like a detective to uncover and reconstruct the authentic, or a plausible, situation. In sharp contrast, Coles "has tried primarily to convey or evoke the thoughts and feelings of others. . . . "I have tried to describe the circumstances, the conditions of life, that they as particular individuals must come to terms with."[5]

To act as a conduit for the reflections and observations of one's subjects, with minimal commentary, can easily lead to the stance of disinterested observer. But Coles is deeply suspicious of any attempt to stand aloof from the people he, or any investigator, studies. The work of translation requires not only fidelity to the original, but sympathy, even participation, in recreating that original. "As a child psychiatrist I had to learn how important it is not only to 'detect' something going on in a child's mind, but to go through a certain experience with the child in order to be of help. . . . Long ago Freud urged all of us who would know how others think and feel to look at our own reactions and responses and styles of thought or feelings."[6] The translator's tension between desire to efface oneself and let the subject speak, and awareness that all "observers" are deeply implicated in the very work they do and the questions they ask, run as a leitmotif throughout Coles's lifework. The great irony, perhaps the greatest, in Coles's work is that these hard-pressed children and adults, whose stories he so desperately wants us to hear, may have no other public identity than that which he imparts to them through his words. The human material is there, in all its richness and subtlety; but we require a Robert Coles to convey those lives to us through his shaping, designing, mediating consciousness.

As Coles listens to people talk about their lives, he has been impressed and moved by their moral sensitivity, by the ways in which people reflect on their lives in moral terms. He has been astonished by the moments of sudden insight that quite "ordinary" folk experience. In *The Moral Life of Children*, Coles reflects on the life of Ruby Bridges, the six-year-old heroine of the first volume of *Children of Crisis*, with whose story he began almost twenty years of work. Her mother told Coles in 1960 that every night the child prayed for those in the mob that threatened and harassed her. "I think of the many black children my wife and I came to know, in Arkansas and Louisiana and Georgia and Alabama and Mississippi—and of white children too, who braved awful criticism to befriend them. . . . Whence that moral capacity, that moral spirit, that moral leadership? How are we to make sense of such moral behavior in psychodynamic terms?"[7]

The persistence of moral character, the lifting of the self beyond daily drives and needs, the achievement of moral insight in the midst of the most trying circumstances—these are issues that have preoccupied Robert Coles throughout his career. As he tells these stories of moral sensitivity, Coles is acutely aware that no general principle can be drawn from the narratives; suffering does not invariably elicit moral awareness, nor does prosperity necessarily preclude it. Nonetheless, with George Orwell in *The Road to Wigan Pier*, Coles is struck by the inverse relation between comfort and ethical insight; as Orwell put it, "the truth is that many of the qualities we admire in human beings can only function in opposition to some kind of disaster, pain, or difficulty; but the tendency of mechanical progress is to eliminate disaster, pain and difficulty."[8]

In his work of mediating the lives and words of scores and hundreds of the "nonelite," wondering at their psychological healthiness and moral acuteness, Coles finds himself most critical of intellectuals. Too often, Coles feels, learned and articulate people try to label, describe, and reduce complex human lives. All technical languages fill him with disgust. Rather, like his mentor Erik Erikson, he prefers a simpler, more "old-fashioned" vocabulary, employing words like trust, virtue, morality, insight, perseverance. Most of all, Coles prefers a language that honors the spiritual and religious sensibilities of the people he interviews. Throughout his life's work, Coles has returned continually to the central role religion plays in the lives of his subjects. While social scientists seek alternative explanations for religion, or advertise a "secularization theory" in which religion is gradually fading away, Coles insists that religion is not a smoke screen for other, unconscious motives, nor is it vanishing from social and personal life. Intellectuals may be contemptuous of religion, seeing it as an illusion or crutch for the weak-minded. The people Coles studies find in their faith both solace for their hard-pressed lives and an inspiration for a better life.

I have touched here on some of the main themes explored in this volume: Coles as translator, mediating between the lives of people in crisis and a reading public; Coles's desire to be faithful to the words and experience of his subjects without being a dispassionate observer; his acknowledgment of the power of religion in their lives; his disdain for jargon and his suspicion of intellectuals. To these should be added his preference for fiction, history, poetry, and philosophy over all quantitative discourse; his awareness of the complex ironies that accompany acts of civil disobedience and resistance; his attention to the tensions between a pastoral care for the spiritual and ethical lives of the many and a prophetic call to be among the heroic few. The reader may expect these themes to emerge in a variety of ways in the chapters that follow.

Chapter 1 deals with the main events of Coles's life: the influence of his parents, his undergraduate years at Harvard, his medical school training at Columbia and residency at Massachusetts General; his dissatisfaction with professional training and his "alternative education" at Union Seminary, the Catholic Worker hospitality houses on New York's Lower East Side, and at Harvard Divinity School; his assignment, courtesy of the doctors' draft, to a hospital near Biloxi, Mississippi, and his subsequent involvement in what was to become his lifelong project of describing the intersection of personal life with social change. Subsequent chapters describe other events in Coles's life: his role in the civil rights movement; his nearly ten-year sojourn in the South, interviewing people, testifying on behalf of antipoverty programs; his return to Massachusetts to teach with Erik Erikson at Harvard; his departure again to live among Hispanic and Native American people in the Southwest and among Eskimos in Alaska; his return to Harvard in 1974; his current intense involvement as teacher in several of the schools of Harvard University, and his continuing research and writing.

Chapter 2 considers the *Children of Crisis* series that emerged from the intersection of Coles's own vocational crisis with the larger social turmoil of the 1960s. As Coles begins to listen to the adults and children who are drawn into social change, he adopts the method of "participant-observer" that had earlier been recommended to him by Anna Freud. As

Coles is led from one region to other, following hints, leads, and invitations, he experiences a growing tension between recording words and shaping those words into narratives.

During the years Coles was interviewing a great variety of people and writing the *Children of Crisis* volumes, he was also writing literary criticism, reflecting on texts and ideas that seemed particularly relevant to his work in the field. His criticism is the subject of Chapter 3. Much as Coles experienced a tension between absence and presence in his documentary work, so he revealed a tension in his preference for two very different kinds of fiction and philosophy. William Carlos Williams exemplifies the first, in which the writer avoids "symbolic" language or the heavy imposition of meaning on experience, but rather works to allow meaning to emerge from the material itself. On the other hand, Coles is attracted to a writer like Walker Percy. Writing for a select and professional audience, Percy explores issues in existentialism, phenomenology, and the philosophy of language. Like his predecessors Kierkegaard, Heidegger, and William James, Percy is drawn to those moments when we step out of the ordinary round of experience, moments he calls "rotations," in order to gain new perspective and regain authentic selfhood. Typically, such moments of rotation are associated with the existentialist stance of alienated intellectuals and seem far removed from the concerns of the ordinary folk William Carlos Williams champions. But in the hands of Robert Coles, themes like rotation are powerfully relevant to adults and children in crisis, as they find themselves face-to-face with survival or oblivion. Often, Coles finds, these socially marginal people experience moments of intense insight, moral epiphanies that are explicable in the terms Percy offers.

Most of all, Coles is drawn toward those writers—Dickens, Tolstoy, Agee, George Bernanos, Flannery O'Connor, George Eliot, and again Williams and Percy—whose work reveals a moral sensibility. Here is fiction, Coles would insist, that is not an elaborate artifice, a clever game between deceptive writer and suspicious reader. Rather, he meditates upon, and teaches, a "personal reading list" (as he once put it) whose authors use fiction to raise to consciousness the moral dilemmas, choices, paradoxes, and ironies that are part of the human condition.[9]

Coles's relationship to the psychoanalytic community and the nature of his own social psychiatry are the subjects of Chapter 4. A resident in psychiatry at Massachusetts General Hospital in Boston, Coles underwent psychoanalysis himself there and again while on military assignment in Mississippi. Even as a young doctor in preparation for a career as one of a handful of child psychiatrists, he was disenchanted with psychoanalytic orthodoxy, feeling constrained by what he perceived as its mechanistic and reductive theory and language. Exposure to the work of Anna Freud and later to that of Erik Erikson made Coles aware of the contribution of ego psychology. Rather than focusing on pathology, ego psychologists like Anna Freud and Erikson, among others, emphasized psychic health, flexibility, growth, and development. Out in the field, Coles found these theories corroborated by the psychic normality of those who were desegregating Southern schools, churches, and politics. He became convinced that the Freudian emphasis on the unconscious, buried life simply could not account for such remarkably resilient behavior.

Like Anna Freud, Coles was coming to see, in the early 1960s, that long-term, in-depth observation was required in order to grasp the rich life experiences of his subjects. Human behavior is never completely determined by "intrapsychic forces," he argued, although these are surely powerful, as are the immense social forces of class, race, and region. Notwithstanding all those shaping pressures, each person combines and recombines these inner and outer forces differently, making generalizations suspect and inadequate. At the core of each person is mystery, unpredictability, twists of paradox and irony. Nothing less than a recreation of the total being-in-the-world can capture the subtlety of such lives, Coles insists. One cannot lift lives out of their social and regional contexts and expect to understand them. Long sections in the *Children of Crisis* series and other volumes are therefore devoted to establishing the contexts in which these lives have meaning.

Given his long personal history of listening to and reflecting on the situation of some of America's and the world's most impoverished and hard-pressed people, is Coles also committed to political and social activism? How does the demand for justice for these people square with his desire to be a good, and therefore silent, listener? These questions are some of the most anguished and recurrent for Coles, and form the subject of chapter 5. His political sympathies in the early and mid-1960s were obvious: He worked on the staffs of the Student Nonviolent Coordinating Committee and the Southern Christian Leadership Conference; he helped train student volunteers for the Mississippi Freedom Summer of 1964; he wrote scores of essays describing and defending the moral and physical courage of civil rights workers. He testified before Robert Kennedy's Senate Subcommittee on Employment, Manpower, and Poverty on the medical and nutritional impact of poverty in the South, traveled with Kennedy to Mississippi and Appalachia, and wrote the senator's last speech. Yet even in the midst of such advocacy and involvement, Coles wished not to lose sight of the essential humanity of white Southerners, even of members of the Klan, nor of the beauty of the land, nor of the exquisite and powerful literature that the South's social arrangements have so bitterly and ironically produced—Faulkner, Welty, Shirley Ann Grau, Robert Penn Warren.

As Coles sees it, politics and political analyses all too quickly become abstractions; people become numbers, "voters," "the people." "Maybe it comes to this," he wrote in the second volume of *Children of Crisis:*

> As a citizen I am appalled by the injustice I see about, injustice that is consolidated, injustice that is handed down as a birthright over the generations, injustice whose continuing presence disgraces all human beings everywhere; but as an observer intent on seeing what exactly goes into making up these lives . . . I would only be adding to the injustice just mentioned, were I to translate clear-cut economic and political wrongs into the same kind of psychological alternatives, and paint for you portraits of brutalized and desperate workers, set upon daily and viciously by rich, savage, heartless plunderers or their lackeys.[10]

So it will not do, Coles thinks, to interpret public wrongs as functions of psychological disorder; that amounts to the worst sort of reductionism. In fact, simply too much generalization and too much commentary are equally problematic. Intellectuals in particular risk substituting their words and analysis for the original, thereby losing the pith and bite of original experience:

> I have wanted all along to remain true to something I can only try to get at, something I can only try to describe with a series of warnings to myself: do not come up with a lot of brittle, pretentious generalizations that explain everything and anything; do not smother with sticky sentiment lives already weak and open to attack; do not refuse those lives their tenacity or shirk from pointing out the price that has to be paid for just such tenacity, for all that goes into remaining, bearing up, continuing, and lasting.[11]

This habit of mind, of seeing complexity, ambiguity, and irony, or saying "yes, but," is most strikingly evident in Coles's most anguished and heartfelt book, *The Geography of Faith.* There, Coles records his conversations with Daniel Berrigan, the activist priest then in hiding from the FBI. Two Christians, educated, articulate, sensitive, Coles and Berrigan dialogue deeply about the tangled issues of social protest, resistance, and violence. At first simply playing the interlocutor, Coles is drawn into the conversation more actively when Berrigan gently puts the questions back to him: How can one be an observer at times of social catastrophe, be a scientist studying people about whose lives one cares deeply? Does not the Christian message contain the seeds of radical resistance to unjust institutions and practices?

Coles's desire, even obsession, to see "the other side" of political and social arguments, and not to rest easily in conventional liberal pieties is most evident in *The Middle Americans*, a 1971 piece of photojournalism/ interview that Coles calls his "most controversial book," and in recent columns on gay rights and abortion in *The New Oxford Review*.[12] In the former, Coles sympathetically portrays working-class people who supported the Vietnam War, and feared and distrusted blacks, students, and intellectuals. Like his much-beloved Robert Kennedy, Coles hoped in those years that working-class people, white and black, would find that they had much in common. In *The New Oxford Review* columns, Coles takes issue with the way liberation struggles often become demands for more middle-class privilege. "Politically I don't like a lot that goes on in both parties," he said recently. "I don't like the Right and I don't like the welfare state, either. I am very skeptical about the government and what it can do. I think I am a conservative on moral issues, which separates me from a lot of people on the left. . . . I have grave worries about abortion regarded as a kind of casual right."[13]

Questions of politics impinge on matters of religion, in Coles's life and work, and it is to religion and spirituality that we turn in Chapter 6. From the very beginning of his work he has been impressed with the way his interviewees draw on religion as solace and challenge, providing often astonishing mental and moral health in the face of sometimes staggering adversity. In his own intellectual life from undergraduate years to the present, Coles has been drawn to thinkers and writers who have themselves been gripped by the reality of the spirit—Kierkegaard, Augustine, Pascal, Dostoevsky, Walker Percy, Flannery O'Connor.

Still, Coles's turn toward overtly religious themes, his willingness to be articulate about his own preferences and commitments, have become more pronounced in the 1970s and 1980s, as he grew more suspicious of the secular political agenda of the left. Irritated at the ridicule that secular academics heap upon religion, Coles has become more and more convinced of the truth of Saint Paul's words to the Corinthians, "Divine folly is wiser than the wisdom of man, and divine weakness stronger than man's strength. . . . To shame the wise, God has chosen what the world counts folly, and to shame what is strong, God has chosen what the world counts weakness. He has chosen things low and contemptible, mere nothings, to overthrow the existing order." Coles is attracted to people like Dorothy Day, Simone Weil, and Daniel Berrigan, and to writers like George Bernanos and Ignatio Silone, who speak of moral witness. For these Christian heroes, life is not meant to be happy, or fulfilling, or successful. Embracing suffering and rejecting security, they live self-emptied lives for the sake of others and out of love of God. Powerful in their weakness, so easily dismissed as suffering from false consciousness or from masochism or other psychotic breakdowns, these lives haunt and inspire Robert Coles.

Finally, we touch on themes in Coles's life yet unexplored: his role as teacher, his work in progress. Here, as much as is possible for such a maverick, we seek a place for him in certain traditions of American thought. Like Emerson and William James, Coles presses for a recovery of "experience" as a central category in knowing. Distrustful of abstraction, like his predecessors, Coles has stressed "unlearning" as a way of learning. To share in the lives of others, to listen, to resist abstraction and judgment—in these ways Coles has become the vehicle for an extraordinary human document, a collection of accounts of people in crisis that ranks with the work of WPA field recorders in the 1930s. Here, too, we return, with the help of psychiatrist and author Donald Spence, to the tension between recording and creating. Are these tendencies always in opposition? Might not we see them, in the work of Robert Coles, blending into a lovely and powerful synthesis?

I first encountered the writing of Robert Coles in the mid-1960s, as an avid reader of *The New Republic*. He quickly became part of my intellectual landscape, although as that time I only knew his journalism. I relished his distinctively folksy, informal style, his combination of moral fervor and scholarly mastery. Here was a man who could reproduce the speech rhythms and metaphors of Appalachian whites in one paragraph, speak knowledgeably about Orwell, Zola, and Faulkner in the next. This was a synthesis of human sympathy and intellectual skill that I also aspired to, as an undergraduate and a graduate student. I began to read Coles's books: *The Geography of Faith, Irony in the Mind's Life*, returned to the *Children of Crisis* series, then (in the late 1960s and early 1970s) still appearing, followed his columns in *The American Poetry Review* and his memorable review-essays in *The New Yorker*.

Emerson once said that "in every work of genius we recognize our own rejected thoughts; they come back to us with a certain alienated majesty." For many years now I have felt drawn to Robert Coles and his work because he has often been able to articulate my own inner life and experience better than I could. I feel deeply in sympathy with his lifelong struggle to integrate the competing claims of head and heart. Like Coles, I feel myself to be an anti-intellectual intellectual, a skeptic among the religious, a person of faith among the skeptics.

Most of all, I feel drawn toward Coles's love of irony. More than a literary device, irony is another word for the unexpected, the unpredicted, the mystery of life that confounds personal plans, social ideology, religious dogma. The banana peel on the road of certainty, irony is a modest reminder of life's incalculable dimensions. If irony can paralyze the self-conscious intellectual, keeping him or her from being fully committed to a cause or a person, it is also the healthy stance of irreverence. Neither skepticism nor despair, irony forbids the activist and the analyst from taking their ideology or system as the last word for this complex and contradictory human reality.

· 1 ·

The Autobiographical Impulse

*R*obert Coles seems everywhere on the intellectual landscape: featured at the recent Harvard three-hundred-fiftieth anniversary, reflecting on the impact of the Challenger shuttle disaster on American children, commenting on the quest for happiness for readers of *Vogue,* disputing the views of Allen Bloom (author of *The Closing of the American Mind*) on the MacNeil-Lehrer Report.[1] A prolific writer, conference keynoter, teacher at Harvard College and the Law, Medical, Business schools, Coles appears to be an established figure in the American intellectual community.

For all that, Robert Coles is also an oddly marginal figure, as he himself acknowledges. "I've always been a wanderer . . . an odd man out," he observed. Although *Time* magazine once labeled him "America's most influential psychiatrist," Coles believes that his "influence on my own profession of psychiatry is probably minimal."[2] He belongs to no Harvard department, goes to no faculty meetings. "I'm a loner, wandering around without any companionships other than my family and students and these books." Coles's readership is drawn not from the ranks of his fellow professionals and academics but from those of clergy, social activists, students, and the body of "educated readers."[3]

Robert Coles has attracted such a large following outside his profession of psychiatry principally *because* he defines himself and his work as marginal. For the reader who is suspicious of or unfamiliar with the special language of psychiatry, social science, or literary criticism, for the reader who wonders how all the theory and abstraction so common in academic discourse can possibly connect with the daily, gritty, often unpleasant life that most of us lead, Robert Coles offers a powerful and appealing alternative.

In one way or another, Coles's many books and essays strikingly reveal the author's rational and emotional forces at work. Repeatedly, Coles discloses the often anguished conflict between his desire to record, without much editing or commentary, the words of the often hard-pressed people he has encountered, and his simultaneous awareness that he is deeply involved, implicated, in the stories he tells. This tension, between the self as conduit and the self as narrator, leads Coles to the central tension of his professional life: the adequacy of the life of the mind. Is it enough to be a concerned citizen, a successful academic (in his case), while so many suffer? Is reflection, the life of the intellect, sufficient? On the other hand, is it possible to turn off the doubts and qualifications, the love of irony, in order to become passionately involved in a cause? Engagement and reflection, passion and intellect: these are the polarities, intensely personal in nature, between which Coles's work has so creatively oscillated over the past thirty years.

This book is a reading of Coles's work to date in light of his biography. I intend to show how the central themes of his work reflect and in part arise from the central themes and currents of his life. Coles's work is intensely personal; he continually wrestles with his passionate care for the people he encounters and his equally passionate desire to be transparent for their words and experiences. In the pages that follow, I argue that Coles's many essays and books, while not generically "autobiography," spring from an autobiographical consciousness.

Saint Augustine's *Confessions* provided a model for scores of spiritual autobiographies in England and America in the seventeenth and eighteenth centuries, and continues to offer a powerful, though now perhaps more indirect, influence on personal writing. The center of Augustine's narrative is his conversion to Christianity: the dissipated, self-indulgent young man, weeping at the foot of the fig tree in his Christian mother's garden, hears a child singing unfamiliar words and pauses to listen. "Tolle, lege; tolle, lege," he hears; "take up and read." Going indoors, he finds a copy of the New Testament, and opens it to these words in Romans 13: "Not in rioting and drunkenness, not in chambering and impurities, not in strife and envying; but put you on the Lord Jesus Christ, and make not provision for the flesh in its cravings." Augustine's resistance to God collapses, and his sorrow and bitterness at his debauched life dissolve. "Instantly, in truth, at the end of this sentence [in Romans], as if before a peaceful light streaming into my heart, all the dark shadows of doubt fled away."[4]

The light of this experience casts forward and back as Augustine relates his life story. The rest of his life is shaped by that decisive event, with prior events taking on new significance as precursors of the crucial moment. Drifting through a life of aimless pleasure or mindless conformity, the self is confronted, seized, possessed, in such a way that the entire life is reshaped and redirected. In the light of this conversion, the narrator can look back and see the prior life as pre-text, as unredeemed folly or the bitter but necessary preparation for the great event. Texts as otherwise disparate as Darwin's *Autobiography,* Jane Addams's *Twenty Years at Hull House,* and *The Autobiography of Malcolm X* owe something to the influence of the fifth-century North African and his encounter in his mother's garden.

For Robert Coles, the garden of his destiny was a stretch of beach along the Gulf of Mexico near Biloxi, Mississippi; the voice of the child in Augustine's narrative became the anguished outcry of a black woman barred by a gang of whites from swimming at a public beach. This moment, like Augustine's conversion, takes place not at the beginning of the chronological life, but at the beginning of the "new life"; it reorients, reshapes the whole life, and provides a way of interpreting all that went before and all that has happened since. For Coles, this moment on the beach was an "identity crisis" in the sense intended by Erik Erikson: a shift in the developmental level of an individual, occasioned by changes both in the person's moral and psychological condition and in the situation of the surrounding culture.[5]

Coles recounts this moment in the first volume of *Children of Crisis.* He was cycling near the beach on a Sunday morning in early spring of 1958, returning from church. This was an idyllic moment, a much-needed break from his relentless duties as physician at the nearby Air Force base hospital. The calm is broken by sounds and sights of conflict: "For a few seconds, I suppose, my lifetime—and I don't think only mine—was recapitulated: its innocence, its indifference, its ignorance, its sheltered quiet, its half-and-half mixture of moral inertia and well-intentioned effort."[6]

That evening, taking his turn in the hospital's emergency room, Coles struck up a conversation with two local policemen who had been called to the scene on the beach. Heretofore indifferent to the South's racist folkways, Coles found himself stunned by the vehemence of the officers' racism. Over the next few days he found himself reading newspaper accounts of the efforts to desegregate the schools of New Orleans and Jackson, stories he earlier would have ignored.

> Somehow that news didn't manage to slip by me the way some news does, out of the impossibility of keeping totally abreast. It wasn't simply my reading that was being affected. I started noticing where Negroes lived, where they didn't; where they were in evidence, where they were not; how they behaved with white people, and white people with them.

> This new consciousness took root over several months. I find it hard
> to do justice to whatever growth and consolidation of feeling may
> have occurred during those months, because to think about that time
> often invites in myself a certain scornful disbelief—that I could have
> lived so long under such a clearly oppressive social, political, and
> economic system, only to have been so blithely, so innocently un-
> aware of its nature. Yet I was.[7]

Coles's shock of recognition was not his alone. Other Americans, including the Southern white liberals he interviewed for *A Study in
Courage and Fear* (the first volume of *Children of Crisis*) were also
experiencing similar crises of conscience in the late 1950s: "I think most
people of the South—Negroes and whites alike—have experienced some
of that same surprise I did, a jolting flash when one kind of world begins
to collapse, another begins to appear, and it all becomes apparent."[8]

As the foundations of segregation began to give way in the late
1950s, so did Coles's own professional assumptions, nurtured by a
Harvard and Columbia education. He appeared destined for the comfortable future of a psychiatric private practice among the "privileged
ones" whose lives he would later describe by that name and critique in
the fifth volume of *Children of Crisis*. Instead, he was drawn into
investigations of the people caught up in traumatic change, first in the
Deep South, then in the North, in Appalachia, the Far West, the
Southwest, and the Arctic. In the late 1970s and early 1980s, he
extended his investigations beyond the United States, looking at the
lives of children in crisis in Central and South America, Northern
Ireland, South Africa, and Poland.

Coles insisted, particularly early in his career, that his books are about
the many children and others whose stories and observations fill their
pages. He is not using them to illustrate a favorite theory or to provide
background for the life story of Robert Coles:

> In writing about my work, I have tried primarily to convey or evoke
> the thoughts and feelings of others; I have tried to describe the
> circumstances, the conditions of life, that they as particular individu-
> als come to terms with and (such is their fate) try somewhat desper-
> ately to overcome. I still feel no inclination to go on an ego trip . . .
> nor do I wish to go on and on about the hang-ups my work causes.[9]

Even as late as 1977, in the last volume of *Children of Crisis*, Coles testily
defends a certain amount of "academic objectivity." In response to an
apparent criticism that he should have shown more outrage at the

enormous gulf between the "privileged ones" who are the subject of that book and the desperately poor whom he featured in earlier volumes, Coles wrote, "I am not about to allow my social, political, and economic views to distort a presentation of the lives of a number of children. . . . One has to distinguish between social criticism and psychological observation."10

Nonetheless, Coles's work has shown a growing awareness of the autobiographical dimension, of the ways in which his own assumptions, preferences, prejudices, have informed that work. Indeed, from the very beginning of his professional career, Coles has rejected the neutral observer pose of classic psychoanalytic method, in which the therapist stands in distant and objectivist judgment on the patient. In a 1972 essay, "The Observer and the Observed," he wrote, "In five years [since the first volume of *Children of Crisis* appeared] a lot has happened to make me more willing to discuss candidly and at some length the difficulties that go on between an observer like me and those he hears and watches, and, hopefully, learns from."11

What, after all, *was* his position, his role, in all these interviews, these hundreds of hours of listening and conversing and observing that eventuated in *Children of Crisis, Women of Crisis,* and his more recent international work? Reflecting on his early work in New Orleans and Atlanta, Coles wondered,

> Was I, then, running some kind of part-time college—in which I went back and forth, to and fro, furnishing one set of individuals information about another set? To be less grandiose, was I a messenger, maybe—or a mediator? Was I suspect, a spy or double spy? Did they suspect . . . that I was really at loose ends, torn by conflicting purposes and ideals?12

Few passages in all of Coles's writing reveal so poignantly and powerfully the tension between involvement and observation. The answer to all Coles's questions in that passage, with the possible exception of the one about being suspect, is, of course: Yes. He was indeed "torn by conflicting purposes and ideals." He was, and is, a messenger, a mediator, a translator.

If the beach near Biloxi turned around an already restless Robert Coles and launched him into a lifetime of social psychiatry, child advocacy, and social commentary, then his encounter with Daniel Berrigan in 1970 is another watershed experience.

Published as *The Geography of Faith,* the Coles-Berrigan conversations powerfully disclose Coles's struggle with the conflicting values of objectivity and involvement, the tension between self-emptying and self-revealing. Having witnessed the collapse of the civil rights movement and the increasing polarization of American society over the Vietnam War, Coles found himself unable to embrace wholeheartedly the progressive politics then popular on American campuses. Opposed to the war yet distrustful of the left, Coles was confused and disheartened as he began his conversations with Berrigan.

Coles had not wanted to interview the fugitive priest, who was in hiding from the FBI after conviction for defacing selective service files in Harrisburg, Pennsylvania. Coles was afraid of alienating the working-class Bostonians he was then interviewing for the third volume of *Children of Crisis*. His reluctance to get involved had surfaced earlier when a group of young doctors asked him to join their protest against the harsh treatment of Berrigan's brother Philip, then in prison in Lewisburg, Pennsylvania. Coles replied,

> I was spending day after day with policemen and factory workers who do not easily give their trust to one of my ilk—and who would (I feared) react strongly to any mention in the newspapers of my involvement with those who condemn the government and its foreign policy. I said that I simply can't have it both ways; that is, I can't join a group of upper middle class liberal-to-radical intellectuals and expect even so to be welcomed unreservedly by already suspicious and troubled men and women, who feel ignored and insulted by the "left-wing college crowd," to use one expression I so often hear.[13]

Coles and the young doctors agreed that he would raise the question with the people he was then interviewing. To his surprise, they encouraged Coles to meet Philip Berrigan. In their own way, these workers were as confused and ambivalent as was Coles himself. To one service-station attendant, professional people were much more likely than workers to trim their attitudes to circumstances. Politicians were deceptive and self-serving, and fronted for the "big industrialists." Father Berrigan, said this worker, was "probably an idealist, that's what. And let me tell you, the world doesn't like idealists." Berrigan and other dissenters simply could never triumph over the "fat cats."[14]

Encouraged by these conversations and shocked by the self-serving attitude of the Lewisburg prison officials whom he met when he visited Philip Berrigan, Coles agreed to meet Philip's brother Daniel. Coles began these conversations, as he had his many conversations with children and adults over the years, with a few comments, but mostly by allowing the subjects to range widely over the topics that engaged them. Much of the first half of *The Geography of Faith* is dominated by Berrigan, Coles playing the occasional questioner. But gradually Coles was drawn into dialogue with Berrigan: "As we talked, I became more and more 'involved,' as it is put these days. Daniel Berrigan is a strong-minded but not particularly self-centered person. He wants to talk with people rather than at them."15

Coles was fascinated by Berrigan's complex personality, his blend of Jesuit logic, political acumen, fierce devotion to radical discipleship, and lack of personal ambition. Most of all, he was deeply attracted to the intensely personal quality of Berrigan's political commitment, his will-ingness to live "at risk," as Berrigan put it. As for himself, Coles wondered if "perhaps I am a coward, pure if not so simple; that is, perhaps all the complexity and ambiguity I can't stop calling to mind enable me to hedge my bets ever so carefully in the face of any serious and threatening risks."16

Later I will have more to say about the moral landscape of *The Geography of Faith,* but for now let the book suggest another biograph-ical element in the lifework of Robert Coles: Is being a "concerned and involved citizen" enough? Judging by the written record, Berrigan forced Coles into a deeper awareness that not choosing, that preserving a stance of objective observer, is a form of choosing. But Coles is unable, or unwilling, to allow his work to become wholly auto-biographical, nor does he want to be transformed into a single-minded advocate for this or that cause. He is suspicious of excessive introspec-tion; he wants to hear and to enable us to hear the distinctive voices of his informants, with a minimum of background noise. But Berrigan presses him with a question already familiar to the introspective Coles: To what extent are we implicated in our work?

For nearly thirty years, Robert Coles has been following the lead of Anna Freud and Erik Erikson in investigating the intersection of indi-vidual lives with historical circumstances. As he put it in the first volume of *Children of Crisis,* "I have aimed to find out how individual minds (with all their past history) engage with contemporary change as it makes future history."17 As his career has developed, Coles has come to realize that what he studies in others, that intersection of self and culture, is precisely what he finds most compelling in his own life. Early in *A Study in Courage and Fear* he wrote,

> Before I went South my interest was in the stress exerted by severe physical illness upon the minds of children. I was in psychiatric

training during a severe epidemic of poliomyelitis in Boston, just before the Salk vaccine came into widespread use. I became interested in how a group of paralyzed individuals managed such a cruel strain suddenly thrust upon them. . . . All these interests I left to go to Mississippi, and all of them, as I look back, I picked up again while there. I began to realize that right before my eyes human beings were facing severe stresses, this time caused not by a virus but by a society going through a hard time of change and conflict. Would it somehow be possible to learn about the lives—the attitudes, hopes and fears—of those human beings?

In sum, my life interests intersected with a situation that freshly stimulated them.[18]

This intersection of professional and personal interests allows us to call Coles's work "autobiographical" without constituting autobiography. From the very beginning, or rather the new beginning on the beach, he was intensely aware of the personal dimension: "I pedalled faster; I almost had the scene out of sight; but I can remember today slowing down, hesitating, only able to stop by lifting my body from the seat of the bike, by using my dragging, scuffing feet. I let the bike lie on its side, and stood still."[19]

A few years later, Coles suggested that society wants to evade the struggle against injustice by resorting to labels and jargon, much as he wanted to avoid the beach struggle in 1958. But the issue both for himself and for American society is not so much therapeutic as moral in nature. "For years in the South I heard those words ['masochistic,' 'crazy,' 'self-destructive'] hurled at civil rights workers. . . . The line goes as follows: What's the matter with them? What kind of people do things like that?"[20] There were those, of course, who genuinely needed clinical care; the pressures and dangers of social activism intensified the psychic problems of some workers. But in general, Coles concluded, they were not sick, not psychically disturbed. Instead, they were identifying those structures and values in the dominant culture which were themselves inhumane and destructive. "Perhaps these students challenge our assumptions, our concepts, our language. . . . They make us aware of our limitations."[21] These words echo Coles's description of the scene on the beach as a confrontation with his own moral apathy: "I can still feel myself standing there, benighted, frightened, seized with curiosity, suddenly quite restless. I was not morally outraged. . . . Eventually, I simply wanted to go away; and I did. . . . I am not now very proud of those minutes. Yet if I forgot them, I would be even more ashamed."[22]

Perhaps all this seems rather obvious. Coles wants to explain how he got involved in his particular kind of research and writing. Yet more is at stake than mere explanation, for we are working toward an understanding of the peculiarly autobiographical nature of Coles's work. In being autobiographical without constituting an autobiography, Coles's work exists on the margin, the boundary between personal revelation and professional presentation. Indeed, the very success of his books, articles, and speeches over the decades hinges on his audiences' willingness to suspend the rules of genre. Neither psychiatry nor sociology, neither conventional literary criticism nor predictable social commentary, Coles's work exists in a richly ambiguous liminal realm, in between established methods and disciplines.

To call Coles's work "autobiographical" rather than "autobiography" suggests an even larger insight about the spiritual life, a dimension of human reality Coles presses the reader to acknowledge and honor. As he sees it, the life of the spirit is not synonymous with "self-actualization," or becoming one's own best friend, or deciding that we're "ok" or pursuing any of the myriad of recent therapies. There is great danger, Coles believes, in confusing the work of religion with that of psychology or of psychiatry. These latter, with their therapeutic efforts, lead "to a concentration, persistent, if not feverish, upon one's thoughts, feelings, wishes, worries—bordering, if not embracing, solipsism: the self as the only form of existential reality."[23] Coles resists the notion, fashionable in some circles, that all writing is covert autobiography. Nonetheless, he would acknowledge that we are deeply implicated, most of all as spiritual selves, in all we do. For Robert Coles, the question of how to acknowledge the mystery of the self without indulging in narcissistic self-preoccupation is at once a personal, a professional, and a spiritual question.

Robert Coles was born in Boston in 1929. His father, Philip, was an Englishman of Jewish ancestry who came to the United States to study engineering at MIT; his mother, Sandra, a native of Sioux City, Iowa, was an artist, booklover, Episcopalian, possessing a "mystical bent." One does not have to indulge in psychologizing to see in this parental couple an early and powerful instance of the observer-participant, scientist-humanist dialectic so evident in their son Robert.

In an essay in *Katallagete*, Coles reflected on his parents and their very different visions of life. Philip, Coles recalled, "always wanted to analyze: chemicals, which he did for a living and out of love; words, which in the form of etymological excursions was a hobby; and even people, whom he would call 'basically' this or that." He had no use for large-scale theorizing, for abstractions and systems of thought. "To him it was all either simple or ineffable: man seeks after food and love and money and power, after concrete people and concrete things." To this "worldly scientist," religion and philosophy were implausible and imponderable. That an important part of the Western world's religion and philosophy came from Jews, from people of the same ancestry as Coles's father, was part of the puzzle of this family living in Boston in the 1930s and 1940s. His father, Coles remembers, "had not been brought up Jewish," and had no interest in claiming his Jewish identity. Nonetheless, the particular danger experienced by European Jews facing the Coles's English cousins began to enter into family conversation. After all, heritage is not something one chooses, Philip Coles began to realize; it is something that one is, part of the mystery of human life.[24]

Coles's mother was a "warm, emotional, and very religious woman. She was brought up on the Bible, the Book of Common Prayer and the Apocrypha and she knows them all well. She has a mystical bent, never out of control, but always there. She makes a point of questioning 'worldly' things—but at the same time has had no apparent trouble enjoying them." Sometimes, Coles recalls, the obvious tension between his parents was too much for him: the conflict "between my father's chemistry and his kind of resignation, not unlike the kind Kierkegaard described, and his affection for Robert Taft and his denied Jewishness on the one hand; and on the other hand the Holy Ghost and 'faith and faith alone' my mother talked about so much and her expensive, catholic, artistic tastes and her passion for Jeremiah and Isaiah."[25]

Coles's parents did agree on one thing at least: they distrusted "too much thought." His father feared he would become " 'too brainy,' hence a Jewish intellectual, and my mother feared I would forget the 'more important things,' " a phrase that revealed, besides her devotion to spiritual, nonrational truth, her "midwestern anti-intellectualism."[26]

Coles attended Boston Latin School and Harvard College, where he majored in English and earned admission to Phi Beta Kappa. His parents did not want Robert to study business or law, or earn a Ph.D. They preferred that he study "something that required work and dedication and thought, but not too much thought; and something a good distance away from the suspect and tainted 'commercial' world." At Harvard Cole studied classic Christian writers and texts with the late Perry Miller: Augustine, Pascal, Kierkegaard, the Bible. Later we will have occasion to consider Coles's particular angle of vision on these authors; for now let us linger over his recollections of Perry Miller.

In *Irony in the Mind's Life*, which Coles dedicates to Miller and to William Carlos Williams, he describes Miller as "a professor of English who might well have been called a historian, a moral philosopher, a man all taken up with theological interests, as opposed to convictions."[27] This rather harsh judgment is softened somewhat later in the book. "Perry Miller taught in classrooms, received visits in his Widener Library study from dozens and dozens of students. But he also wrote books that gave new point to the Puritan divines."[28]

Along with Samuel Eliot Morison, Herbert Schneider, and a handful of others in the 1930s, Perry Miller had rescued New England Puritanism from popular contempt and scholarly disfavor. Himself an atheist, Miller introduced into American intellectual life a new respect for the chiaroscuro spiritual outlook associated with Augustine, Paul, and Calvin. At first, almost single-handedly, Miller insisted that the core of the New England experience, which was so influential on much of subsequent American culture, was religious.

For Miller, the distinguishing mark of those seventeenth-century pioneers was the creative tension they maintained between the conflicting claims of piety and intellect. In the words of Robert Middlekauf, another scholar of the Puritan experience,

> Piety implied the exaltation of the divine; it connoted unending worship of God's power and mercy and justice; it involved the surrender of the self to the most high. Intellect urged the claims of man, who was after all created in the image of the divine; it enjoined recognition of human powers and capacities; it counseled control of the spirit lest inner promptings lead men to an ecstatic anarchy.[29]

Having dismantled the edifice of the liturgical church—the Roman Catholic Church, the Church of England—Calvinist reformers like the Puritans were now faced directly with the experience of the divine, the searing, blinding confrontation with perfection that drives humanity into a profound sense of its own unworthiness and an intense desire to be reconciled with that perfection. Miller describes this encounter in his influential book *The New England Mind: The Seventeenth Century* (1939) with the phrase "the Augustinian strain of piety." For him,

> The heart of this piety was its sense of the overwhelming anguish to which man is always subject, and its appeal to anguish-torn humanity has always been its promise of comfort and of ultimate triumph. The Augustinian strain of piety flows from man's desire to transcend his imperfect self, to open channels for the influx of an energy which

pervades the world but with which he himself is inadequately sup-
plied. . . . It was an inward experience in which the disorder of the
universe was righted, when at least some men were brought into
harmony with the divine plan.[30]

Sin, alienation, reconciliation—these themes marked other texts Coles
studied with Miller. In the work of Blaise Pascal, for example, Coles
encountered another seventeenth-century writer like the New En-
glanders, one who addressed not unbelievers but church members,
believers. It was precisely these smooth and comfortable folk, argued
Pascal, whose spiritual lives were the most misshapen, for they had
substituted a safe and coolly rational faith for the original, radical
message of Jesus. For Pascal, religion was ultimately of the heart, not of
the mind:

> And that is why those to whom God has given religion by feeling of
> the heart are very happy and legitimately persuaded. But to those
> who have it not [in this way] we cannot give it except by reasoning,
> while waiting for God to give it them by feeling of the heart, without
> which faith is only human, and useless for salvation.[31]

Søren Kierkegaard, whom Coles likewise read under Miller's guidance, also stressed the limits of intellect in matters of faith. The religion
of Jesus was an affront to comfortable, reasonable people, argued the
Danish philosopher, and consequently it must either be tamed and
denatured, or ignored. For Kierkegaard, possessed of a powerful intellect in a crippled body, "a Christian must be an exile, a wanderer not
only tormented from within but hounded from without."[32]

Here then was the young Robert Coles, already experiencing from his
home life the contrasting emphases of intellect and emotion, now
exposed to that same tension in the work of some of the masters of
Western religious and philosophical thought. Studying their insights
under the guidance of a master teacher, whose own life was, it appeared,
in considerable disarray, and who bore no obvious signs of considering
these matters as relevant for his own life, brought home to Coles just
how momentous this tension was, how easy it was to gravitate to one
pole or the other, how difficult the task of maintaining a creative
balance.

In the early 1950s the Harvard undergraduate encountered another
figure who would exert considerable influence on him, New Jersey's
doctor-poet, William Carlos Williams. Coles had written his senior
thesis on Williams's *Paterson* and had visited him several times. Williams

took Coles on his rounds and impressed the young man with his ability to integrate his professional and artistic commitments. "Dr. Williams spent hours taking care of patients, helping them (and himself) live out a life. . . . But he also wrote poems, stories, essays."[33]

Both Miller and Williams revealed to the young Coles that the powers of the rational and of the nonrational can exist, even flourish, within the same self. After all, Miller was a powerful intellectual whose most influential work was to insist on the experiential nature of religion (though not experiential for *him*), and Williams was a tough old doctor who wrote some of the most lyrical verse in modern American poetry. In short, these men, with varying degrees of completeness, saw that duality was not the same as dualism, that oppositions can find a higher synthesis within an integrated system or an integrated self. For his part, Coles has inveighed for thirty years against what he sees as the modern tendency to reductionism, to explain the spiritual life of humanity as a function of biology, sociology, economics, or false consciousness.

The young Coles had assumed, throughout his undergraduate years, that he would be an English, or perhaps a classics, teacher on the secondary level. Once, when visiting William Carlos Williams, Coles identified his interests as "theology and moral philosophy and American literature, all of which, in a way, I was studying with the brilliant and inspiring Perry Miller."[34] Besides Miller, the Harvard classicist Werner Jaeger had also been a stimulating teacher, moving Coles with his lyric presentations of the Greek poets and playwrights.[35] But how would such diverse interests translate into a career? "I was beginning to wonder what the devil I'd be doing with this uncertain stretch of time given each of us, called a life to live. In that regard, I seemed by my junior year badly adrift."[36]

Williams cut through Coles's undergraduate angst with advice that was "characteristically quick, sharp, concrete, specific, and yes, impatient: 'Try medicine, why don't you! Lots to keep you busy, and lots to make you think. The great thing is—you get to forget yourself a lot of the time.'"[37]

His parents were surprised at his career choice. Philip remembered the terrible burden that medicine had placed on his surgeon brother, who died from the strain. His mother thought Robert might "'study history and then teach it,'" but neither stood in his way.[38]

What was much more problematic about this about-face for the undergraduate English major was the need to take pre-med courses: biology, chemistry, physics—courses that "bored me to no end." He was appalled by the competitiveness of his fellow students, and found himself scorning them, in a kind of reverse arrogance, for their narrowly professional, careerist mentalities. But Coles persisted, largely because of the powerful role model of Williams, who was, after all, not an ordinary doctor, but a remarkable combination of general practitioner and leading American poet.[39]

After graduation in 1950, Coles entered Columbia College of Physicians and Surgeons, in part through the intervention of Williams. He was interviewed there by Philip Miller, a "grey, gaunt, laconic biochemist." Coles confided his doubts about medical education to this Miller. Surprisingly, the interviewer said that "he knew how I felt." In any event, said Miller, "'We ought to take someone like you, even if you're not sure you want to finish medical school.'" Perhaps Coles would even "'find something half interesting here in medical school.'"[40]

Those were "four hard, troublesome years" for Coles. He did poorly at Columbia, having, as he put it, "no aptitude for dissecting the corpse or spotting things under the microscope, though I loved looking at the forms and colors the slides offered the eye."[41] A "borderline" student, Coles felt himself in "an alien world. . . . I was a non-scientist; I had no interest in organic chemistry, physics; I had no real competence in those fields."[42] The medical school dean suspected that that was all too true:

> He would tell me that I had done very well at college, at a good college, and now they were all unable to figure out why I couldn't do equally well at medical school. I would murmur something about my woeful literary and historical interests, and each time he would take that as a serious challenge: medicine requires culture; medicine requires a "whole man"; medicine requires a "broad knowledge of the humanities and the social sciences"; and finally, each doctor must be an "alert, informed citizen." I could not argue, only feel amused or at loose ends. But his brief lectures invariably had the effect he must have desired. I studied just harder enough to stay in school—and in the fourth year, at long last, I came to the clerkship in pediatrics.[43]

But it had all been a tremendous, wrenching struggle; "it was very fragile, the whole enterprise."[44]

During those years at Columbia, Coles sought out people and situations that would nurture his literary/historical/philosophical interests. He visited Williams across the river in New Jersey, in order to be reminded that it was possible to combine the life of a physician with that of a "writer/social observer of sorts." He attended Riverside Church. He was a member of a three-person Bible study group. In his restless, questing way, Coles even sought out a world immensely distant from

Harvard Yard or the scrubbed-down labs and lecture halls of Columbia. In his recent book on Dorothy Day, Coles recalls his first encounters with the Catholic social activist and subsequent involvement with the Catholic Worker Movement, one that persists to this day.

> In the spring of 1952, I was a medical student ready to abandon the idea of medicine. On the day that classes ended, I took the downtown subway at Broadway and West 165th Street, hard by the Columbia-Presbyterian Medical Center, where I was going to school. I wasn't quite sure where I was going—only glad to be getting away from where I was.

On that particular day, Coles rode the subway down to the Bowery, and found himself at Saint Joseph's Hospitality House, drawn by a memory of his mother's passion for Dorothy Day and the *Catholic Worker*.[45]

Coles's restlessness at Columbia also led him to Reinhold Niebuhr, then teaching at Union Theological Seminary. Already put off by an education that treated people as equivalent to their symptoms, Coles was attracted to the ironies and paradoxes that equally fascinated the intense and passionate Niebuhr. The theologian would ask: how do we explain the depths and motivations of people, the frequently unexpected breakthroughs or resistances, the sudden bursts of insight? Niebuhr told his students about Dietrich Bonhoeffer, whom Niebuhr encountered at Union in the late 1930s. When Bonhoeffer, a leader in the anti-Nazi Confessing Church movement, "decided to return to Germany in 1939 to fight Hitler, a number of people wondered whether he might not need psychiatric help. A problem, a conflict of sorts? A masochism at work?—the need to suffer? Some neurotic guilt in search of exorcism through exposure to the risk of punishment?"[46] Resisting the easy dismissal of inexplicable, especially self-sacrificial, behavior as maladjustment or neurosis was the lesson Niebuhr meant to convey; Coles would later reflect his teacher's point in his own refusal to label as psychically disturbed those civil rights activists who persisted in their work despite imprisonment and physical abuse.

Meanwhile, Coles was not yet finished with his medical training. He had been relieved to reach the study of pediatrics, in which he imagined he would have some aptitude. "For two days I was genuinely excited as a medical student. . . . I loved helping [the children], and loved getting to know their parents. I found my mind again its old self." But talking with the young patients was an insignificant part of the requirements. Instead, he was obliged to draw blood from their tiny arms, analyze urine samples, treat them, in short, like any other patients, a collection of symptoms. The moment of truth came, he later recalled, when he needed to take a blood sample from a toddler whose arm was simply too small to evidence a usable vein.

> "You'll have to use the neck," she [the nurse] said, and for a second or two I must have thought she had lost her mind. I stared at her, and she stared back. Then she moved toward the child, to hold his head and body so that we both could be done with the job.

But Coles was unable to perform this task. He did go back later and do the venipuncture. "But I had finally realized what I should have known all along, that I was not meant to work on children."[47]

That left the last clerkship, the one in psychiatry, conducted at the New York State Psychiatric Institute at Columbia-Presbyterian Medical Center. This experience was a nightmare for Coles. His teachers were "anxious to prove they were scientists." His mentor in particular was "an arrogant, vain, dogmatic, parochial man." He recalls it as a kind of parody of education, in which clichés and jargon substituted for deeper insight: "'It doesn't make any difference whether you do it while hanging from a chandelier, so long as the penis is in the vagina. Remember, P in V.'" To conclude, as several of his friends had on the basis of his medical education thus far, that Robert Coles was destined for psychiatry was to condemn him to a particularly noxious corner of Hell.[48]

"Restless, bored, and confused," Coles decided to extend his tour of hell by enrolling in the internship program at the University of Chicago. It was an extremely difficult program, requiring the interns to be on call virtually twenty-four hours a day, insisting that they do lab work as well as rotate through the services.

As that difficult year came to a close, Coles found himself experiencing a kind of spiritual crisis, wondering what to do next in his life, wondering if five years of grueling graduate education had been worth it. He visited the Trappist monastery in Kentucky where Thomas Merton lived; he contemplated working at Albert Schweitzer's hospital in Africa. Perhaps he would return to Harvard for graduate work in literature, or maybe just travel. Then there was the doctor's draft to be considered, the requirement that each doctor serve two years in the military.

More fragmentary experience drifted by, to add to his confusion. The theologian Paul Tillich lectured at the University of Chicago. Coles remembers dashing away from his internship duties, white coat flying, to catch part of a Tillich lecture. Tillich combined psychotherapy and religion, an intriguing possibility. Then a friend recommended Freud's *A General Introduction to Psychoanalysis,* and another suggested Erik Erikson's *Childhood and Society.* So, yes, perhaps a residency in psychiatry.[49]

Entry into medical school required pre-med courses, and entry into psychiatric residency required interviews. Probing, confronting, challenging, these "interrogators" submitted Coles to "stress interviews," another nightmarish experience. But he survived, and was accepted as a psychiatric resident at Massachusetts General Hospital.

Coles's brief experience at New York Psychiatric Institute was the merest foretaste of the sophisticated psychoanalytic training he would receive in Boston. But the ideology was the same. "I learned to call [my patients] 'phobics' and 'hysterics' and 'psychotics,' people whom I learned to diagnose more quickly, more correctly, more authoritatively. . . . I learned a whole new language": castration anxiety, negative transference, instinctual aggression.[50]

While at Massachusetts General, Coles underwent psychoanalysis. Several of his most prominent teachers and supervisors were also undergoing this therapy, following Freud's insistence that psychoanalysts themselves be analyzed. These influential people thought of analysis as the exposure of repressed material that powerfully affects current behavior, and the correction of behavior on the basis of that new self-understanding. "I remember the most erudite and prominent of those teachers—his long silences, his wariness with words when he did choose, finally, to use them. I remember, too, a paper he delivered at a psychoanalytic meeting—the emphasis he put on the 'value free' stance we ought to take as we do our work." For this leader in the movement, "science now demanded rigor, established procedure, controlled behavior. The buzzwords were 'neutrality' and 'value-free'—an impersonality marked occasionally by one's subdued interpretive remarks."[51]

Not all of Coles's teachers and mentors in Boston sounded like that "erudite and prominent" figure. One of his more sympathetic supervisors at Massachusetts General, Paul Howard, encouraged him to audit courses at Harvard Divinity School. There Coles sat in on a seminar taught by Paul Tillich. Coles clearly preferred the instruction, advice, and outlook of Tillich to that of his own medical professors and supervisors.[52]

Tillich was fond of bringing in current articles, Coles recalled, that bore on the topics they were discussing. A Walker Percy essay, "The

Man on the Train," came from an issue of *Partisan Review*, although Tillich did not identify the author.[53] It was only later that Coles recognized this famous Percy essay as the same one he had read for Tillich. But in a sense, authorship did not matter. "I would have read anything Tillich recommended, no mind if the suggested author were a garbage collector, a madman, a theoretical physicist,"[54] for Tillich offered the young doctor insights beyond the narrow professionalism of medicine. The theologian was "full of passion and ready to insist upon the mystery of things, the strange and fateful 'moments,' he often called them, that make such a difference in our lives."[55] In any event, Tillich put Coles on the trail of Walker Percy. Coles would later repay the favor by writing a *New Yorker* profile which would become a long book of criticism and commentary on the novelist. They have indeed maintained a close relationship since the early 1970s; Percy dedicated *The Thanatos Syndrome* to Robert Coles.

At the end of his psychiatric residency, Coles was liable to the doctor's draft measure then in effect. He became chief of the neuropsychiatric unit of the military hospital at Keesler Air Force Base near Biloxi, Mississippi. Every weekday, Coles drove to New Orleans in his white Porsche with red leather seats (purchased in memory of James Dean), "in order to attend medical and psychiatric conferences and pursue psychoanalytic training." It was a second analysis for Coles, this time at the New Orleans Psychoanalytic Institute. "Since I was in psychoanalysis at the time, I was perhaps given to more ruminations than usual—efforts to figure out not only how I had come to be the kind of person I was, but what I ought to do with my life, and, not least, what 'meaning' there is in that more than generic use of the word life."[56] On a beach near Biloxi, Coles encountered that group of Southern blacks who were breaking in on the customs and complacency of a way of life, and found them equally breaking in on his own way. Already restless, unhappy, and self-preoccupied, Coles was lifted out of his introspection and out of his comfortable career-in-the-making as a child psychiatrist in private practice.

As Coles recounts, in several places, his story up to that "conversion experience" on the beach, several themes emerge and take shape, themes that link Coles's early life and education with his work in the 1960s and later. One is the tension between character and intellect. One of his mentors, William Carlos Williams, demonstrated profound respect for people unhindered by their educational attainments, rooted in an understanding of common humanity. Thirty years after first encountering

Williams, after more education and much distinguished achievement, Coles still wonders if it is possible to be a bright, creative person, even an intellectual, and still "become [a] personally more decent and honorable human being, meaning of higher character than was the case before?"[57] American writers like Emerson and Walker Percy, themselves no mean intellectuals, share with Pascal and Kierkegaard a keen sense of the difficulty of reconciling intellectual achievement with admirable character traits: love, decency, honor, fidelity, compassion. "In his 'American Scholar' address Ralph Waldo Emerson insisted to his audience that 'character is higher than intellect'; and in our time the novelist Walker Percy has reminded us that one can 'get all A's and flunk life.'" Is it possible, Coles wonders, to bring together these two dimensions? Or are we limited to the choices so graphically expressed by Yeats: "The intellect of man is forced to choose/Perfection of a life or of the work,/And if it take the second must refuse/A heavenly mansion, raging in the dark?"[58]

Though Coles resists romanticizing the poor, poorly educated, marginal, and dispossessed people in this or any country, he sees far greater danger to one's soul in intellectual attainment than in its absence.

> When I see my kind (after years and years of clinical training and supervision and personal analysis) torn by angry disagreements and splits; when I see grown men and women, well-educated and supposedly well aware of the reasons for their conflicts, nevertheless demonstrating nasty, envious, rude behavior toward others . . . then I realize yet again that "aggression" is not only something postulated by eager theorists, but is part of everyone's life, including theirs—no matter the education, the accumulation of credentials, the recognition.[59]

Yet this is the same person trained in America's premier educational institutions, who became one of a handful of child psychiatrists, who has written hundreds of books, papers, essays, introductions, and reviews. This assault on the character deficiencies of intellectuals comes from one nurtured in the bosom of privilege. Perhaps when Coles recalled that Perry Miller was a man "taken up with theological interests rather than convictions" he was suggesting that, even in his undergraduate days, he sensed that intellectual mastery easily led, not to understanding and self-understanding, but to denial of one's own weaknesses and an inability to empathize with others. Accounting for this gap between intellect and character and working to bridge it constitute major life themes for Robert Coles.

A second theme evident in Coles's early life is the relationship of intellect and emotion. His parents, we have seen, embodied the two distinct emphases of head and heart, but maintained a loving, if also conflicted, marital bond. Quite likely Perry Miller suggested to Coles the delicate balance American Puritans tried to maintain between reason and the irrational, and William Carlos Williams provided a splendid role model in living out that delicate balance.

So head and heart are not mutually exclusive, not unalterably opposed means of knowing and being, and Robert Coles should not be understood simply a champion of heart over head. As an intellectual, Coles is not about to forswear the use of language, reason, research, linear thinking, historical investigation, social and psychiatric scholarship. Rather, he is intent on showing how *involved* our intellectual life is with our emotional and affective life. In this sense, Coles echoes the insights of his fellow Bostonian Richard Sennett. In *Authority,* Sennett argues for a recovery of Aristotle's understanding of emotion as feelings we have thoughts about; they are "interpretations people make of events or other people."[60] As interpreted feeling, emotion is at the very center of personal identity and should be understood as intrinsic to intellectual life.

Coles wishes to expose the intellectualist fallacy that one can reason without feeling, that value-free cognition exists and is a good thing. His effort to explode the notion of the objective, rational observer puts Coles in company with a distinguished, or notorious, crew that includes Marx, Nietzsche, Freud, and the Frankfurt School. Like them, Coles criticizes a way of knowing that seeks lawlike, impartial regularity in personal and social life: "Social scientists, taking their cue from the natural scientists who are valued so highly in our Western industrial world, insist upon banishing ironies with all possible dispatch, if such can be done. The point is exploration. . . [:] find out why, and having done so, change the set of circumstances. Irony thus regarded becomes a kind of fanciful illusion of a decidedly reactionary character."[61]

In contrast, Coles, like the "masters of suspicion" named above, does not forswear use of critical reason or abstraction, but proposes that critical thought is itself shaped and influenced; there can be no such thing as the autonomous rational self. Knowing is never separated from knower, nor knower from the complex web of society and culture in which s/he is embedded. The intellectual product is never totally distinct from the interpretive method that produced it. To appreciate this "postmodern" spirit is to appreciate the irony present in contemporary life. Our pretensions to control, to knowledge, to power, to success, are continually undercut by forces, internal and external, quite unexpected and beyond our control. "Often enough," writes Coles,

> the presence of irony provides a reminder or signal, if not an important warning. Irony may offer us the best hint we may get of vulnerability of jeopardy. . . . When Thomas Hardy gave us the phrase "life's little ironies," he had in mind, of course, the continuing distance, in all of us, between intention and actuality—between our stated intentions . . . and the manner in which fate and circumstance, chance and accident and incident, end up shaping the particular destiny that is ours.[62]

Finally, in Coles's early years we can identify a third theme which persists throughout in his career and written work, dissatisfaction with conventional professions, a preference for living and working at the boundaries. An English major, Coles studied with a professor of literature who had gained international prominance as an intellectual historian. A student of the humanities, Coles was deeply influenced by William Carlos Williams, a doctor who was also a major American poet. Despite his major, Coles pursued a career in medicine, but once at Columbia was repelled by the competitive and overspecialized atmosphere. He sought refuge at Union Theological Seminary, where he studied with parish clergyman-turned-theologian and culture critic, Reinhold Niebuhr. Back in Boston, Coles did a two-year residency in psychiatry at Massachusetts General, followed by two more years in child psychiatry at Children's Hospital, but felt more comfortable taking his charges to the galleries of the Museum of Fine Arts than subjecting them to analysis.[63] Drawn once again to theology as a means of expanding his powers of reflection, he studied with Paul Tillich, who once defined himself as a man on the boundary: "When I was asked to give an account of the way my ideas have developed from my life, I thought that the concept of the boundary might be the fitting symbol for the whole of my personal and intellectual development. At almost every point, I have had to stand between alternative possibilities of existence, to be completely at home in neither and to take no definitive stand against either."[64]

In his subsequent career, Coles has combined psychology, history, sociology, literary criticism, natural description, autobiographical fragments, conversation, and long transcriptions from his subjects. Like his mentors Tillich and Erikson, Coles has been both observer and observed, both the social scientist who seeks to generalize and abstract from experience, and the artist who wishes to convey the full richness of human experience in all its infinite particularity. Reflecting on what attracted him to Paul Tillich, Coles noted that Tillich's combination of intelligence and compassion resonated with "a certain tension in me":

> a tension between a belief in the letter and a search for the spirit; between a search for facts and an ear for speculations; between an interest in history, in its bulky and coercive weight, and a desire to recognize the possibilities that come with each ("existential") moment; between a recognition of the "inner" life of the mind and an awareness of the power that the "outer" life of the world exerts; between a wish for analysis and a longing for action; between the hunger for abstract explanations and interpretations on the one hand and the need to confront emotions . . . and experiences and events and happenings.[65]

Although Coles's interdisciplinary approach, both in the life and in the work, has been extraordinarily fruitful, it has also laid him open to the charge of vagueness and shallowness. Joseph Epstein, for example, has accused Coles of being the typical liberal doctor, embracing all the right causes, but spread so thin and feeling compelled to speak on so many topics that he ends up saying nothing of substance.[66] Elsewhere, Epstein has accused Coles of simply being too nice, of being, for example, too generous a book reviewer. "Generosity, like humility, can be carried too far. Doris Grumbach, Robert Coles, and Robert Towers are three people who review too generously. Their liking a book carries no weight—they like so many."[67]

These criticisms—of being spread too thin, of feeling compelled to speak on too many subjects, of liking too many texts and arguments and people—seem inevitable for a person like Coles. A liminal person himself, dwelling on several professional and personal boundaries, Coles is also generous, warm, and sympathetic. Thus it is not surprising that he should be attracted to those, particularly children, who live on margins of age, race, gender, economic survival, or cultural acceptability.

· 2 ·

Children of Crisis:
Style and Method

As of this writing, Robert Coles has published or contributed to forty-five books and written more than 1,000 articles and reviews. Our investigation of his work will take into account a fair number of these publications, but Coles's widest fame has come through the *Children of Crisis* series. The reasons for the popularity of those five volumes are several: The earliest were written at a time when many Americans were paying attention to ethnic and racial minorities, migrant workers, and other oppressed people; the books, in their use of narrative and of personal experience, reflected a broad public impatience with theory and abstraction and a preference for experiential knowing. Coles's efforts to practice psychiatry in the field and in the midst of explosive social conflict won him a kind of guru status among many young people in the 1960s and early 1970s.

We need to pay extended attention to *Children of Crisis* not only because the series is central to Coles's work and outlook, but because the methodological chapters in each volume provide some of the best evidence regarding Coles's intentions in this work and throughout his career.

The busy reader, faced with the prospect of reading five five hundred- to six hundred-page books, is tempted to concentrate on the chapters labeled "The Method" and forgo the rest of the text. The stories, after all, do begin to blur into one another after a while, whereas "The Method" gives us authentic Coles, struggling with the tensions and conflicts outlined in the previous chapter. The interpreter of Coles is faced with a similar temptation. Why not generalize from those very chapters where Coles is most general and theoretical? After all, interpretation is a series of abstractions about particulars, and in Coles's case, where so much of the evidence is particular and anecdotal, we can use all the help we can get to make sense of these stories.

But Coles warns his readers strenuously against allowing the chapters on method to replace the narrative core. "If those more abstract remarks are the essence of what the reader ends up taking away from this book, then I will have, by my lights, failed miserably."[1] So the interpreter of *Children of Crisis* is in something of a bind: If we accede to Coles's demand, then we can only point to the narratives themselves, retell the stories, or, better, ask the reader simply to read and ponder the originals. If we neglect Coles's warning and reach for the generalization, then we are in danger of distorting the very nature of his work. Our dilemma in reading Coles is heightened when we realize that these stories, thus selected, arranged, introduced, printed, bound, and sold, constitute interpretation, a re-presentation of the original. To turn the screw once more: For all his insistence that we focus on the narratives of people in crisis, it is *Coles* who brings these stories to our attention and thus, in a very real way, to life.

Robert Coles has very little patience with talk about method, and so is at odds with a central preoccupation of much of current American and European academic practice. Studies in literature, for example, are dominated not by practical criticism of individual texts but by exercises in literary theory, with occasional use of texts as illustrations. The scholarly journals are filled with dense language borrowed from French criticism, semiotics, feminism, and Marxisms of various types. In historical circles, narrative has fallen into disfavor, and theory, often quantitative in basis, is supreme.

Coles himself is often asked about his method. "Students in various universities where I've lectured repeatedly ask me *what* my work is: please give it a name, or a series of names, so that it can be put into a category, defined. Have I been doing social science research, fieldwork? Have I been a participant-observer? Do I write nonfiction novels? Am I practicing oral history? And so on and on."[2] Repeatedly in *Children of Crisis,* as if in response to such insistent questions, he denigrates method, distances himself from conventional approaches and tools of sociologists and social psychologists:

> This is not an "attitudinal study." I do not pretend that any assertions made here, by the people quoted or by me, have any "statistical significance," any general or large-scale "validity." I have used no questionnaires. I have not tried to determine whether the people I met and grew to know are in any way accurate reflections of this or that "group" or "segment" of the population. It is all impressionistic, this kind of work, all tied to one person's mind and body.[3]

Nonetheless, there are these chapters called "The Method," and for all his qualifications and reservations, Coles does have a method, more or less. He announced his approach in the first volume of the series, *A Study in Courage and Fear:* "I have aimed to find out how individual minds (with all their past history) engage with contemporary change as it makes future history." He is intrigued by "how private lives affect and are affected by world events."[4] He is drawn to those individual lives embedded in times and places of profound (sometimes acute, sometimes chronic) social change, without pretending that they are a "representative sample" or "statistically significant."

Ironically, the New Orleans and Atlanta public school boards selected Coles's first sample for him when they initiated school desegregation in the fall of 1960. In New Orleans, that process began when four black girls entered white elementary schools. Through the efforts of a "very kind and maternal" black woman, Leontine Luke, Coles met the families of these girls. Over a period of several visits, he gained their permission to talk with them and their children about the desegregation effort and its effects of them, but these conversations, at least at first, were rarely easy or comfortable: "There was . . . quite enough uncertainty and awkwardness—television sets kept on and tuned at high volume, people hiding but listening in nearby rooms, nervous ingratiation or unrelenting silence similar to the long familiar behavior felt to be white people's due while working in their homes or offices."[5]

Coles remembers those as very difficult, painful days. He knew he did not want to go into private practice in child psychiatry. But what would he do? "I was trying to get my bearings," he noted. Returning to Boston after his tour of duty was over, he had married a Radcliffe graduate, Jane Hallowell. Having had some experience observing children in clinical settings in Boston hospitals, he thought perhaps he would study these black children undertaking to integrate Southern schools. "But I didn't quite know what I was going to do with this, other than maybe write mythical articles for the *American Journal of Psychiatry,* which was sort of the thing that kept me from thinking I'd had a nervous breakdown."

Driving into the South with their few possessions, the Coleses settled into an apartment in Vinings, Georgia, outside Atlanta. They lived on $4500 a year borrowed from Jane Coles's grandmother and Robert Coles's parents. They applied for grants, but were "rejected by every foundation. . . . They all turned me down. . . . It was all amorphous, our research plans. . . . It must have seemed like a psychiatric deterioration of some kind." "What would your results be?" the foundations asked. Finally the New World Foundation accepted a proposal, and offered $7500 a year, still no princely sum given the immense commuting the Coleses were doing.

From those first four New Orleans children and their families, Coles extended his scope to five of their white classmates and families, then to the classroom teachers. From the crowd that gathered outside the schools to taunt and threaten the children, Coles interviewed "die-hard segregationists." In Atlanta, he was also presented with his initial sample, the ten black high school students chosen to integrate schools there. He interviewed these young people and their families, as he had the primary sample in New Orleans, on a weekly and sometimes daily basis. Similarly, he came to know white students and their parents, teachers, those reluctantly or silently in favor of integration, and those desperately opposed. From Louisiana and Georgia, Coles expanded his work to other Southern states, to interviews with white liberals, with civil rights activists, with yet more segregationists. All these interviews form the substance, much edited and rearranged, of the first volume of *Children of Crisis*.

Subsequent volumes follow this pattern. Coles meets with a small group of people, and intensive weekly conversations ensue. From these folk, often with their encouragement and guidance, Coles is led to others whose lives are also implicated in social change. His conversations with Southern blacks lead him to their kinfolk in Northern cities, to which the civil rights struggle had also moved in the mid-1960s, and thence to working-class and suburban whites caught up in social change. In interviewing Chicano migrant workers in Florida, Coles realizes he needs to talk with their relatives in the Southwest. There, he encounters native Americans, also struggling against poverty and discrimination. And while in the Southwest, Coles meets an Eskimo sent there to study, and through him is drawn into a lengthy series of conversations with native Alaskans. The expanding universe of Coles's informants is not only racially and ethnically diverse; it is marked by vast disparities of wealth and poverty. In the last volume in the series, *The Privileged Ones*, Coles interviews children of affluent families upon the insistence of several hard-pressed people: "Ask them what they've done to us. You can't really know about plain working people like us, unless you go find out about the big shots. It's their decisions that end up making us live our lives the way we do."[6]

Crisscrossing the nation over a period of almost twenty years, Coles has amassed thousands of interviews, which he has edited and shaped into the narratives in five volumes. What kind of interviews are these? What did Coles set out to discover? In practically every volume Coles reminds the reader that he is simply trying to listen, and thus has no particular agenda. He does, of course, have some broad concerns that motivate him, to "observe not only how people participate in a social revolution or how others oppose such changes, but also to observe how people live and conduct their affairs and try to make do—those who live out from day to day their own version of history by trying to deal with particular burdens: historical, social, political and awful economic burdens."[7]

But again, how does Coles observe? What questions does he ask? How does he proceed? Readers of *Children of Crisis* are sure to note in each volume a section of children's drawings, which have become something of a hallmark of the series. Coles notes that the use of drawings in psychological work with children has become standard procedure. Asking children to describe what they see in a series of pictures, or asking them to draw certain people and places constitutes one way to "appraise growth, development, intelligence, and in some cases a patient's psychological status."[8] But Coles's approach is somewhat different. "To ask a child to draw whatever he wishes to draw in order to learn about his racial attitudes, or even to request from a series of children that they each draw the same person, place or thing for such a purpose, is to court the subjective and individually variable."[9] This may be a dubious method for those committed to the statistically significant, but it is precisely what Coles admires in these drawings: "I value these pictures for what they have told me about individual children, rather than children in general or one race or another."[10]

With older children and adults, Coles can listen and converse, but younger children are often bored or baffled with talk, and their drawings thus become a crucial means of communication. On many occasions, Coles draws alongside the children, each working silently and diligently on his/her creation. Interpreting the art work, he sees suggestions of the dense life circumstances of the child: "I am saying that each child's particular life—his age, his family, his neighborhood, his medical and psychological past history, his intelligence—influences what and how he draws. I am also saying that the way these children draw is affected by their racial background, and what that 'fact' means in their particular world (society) at that particular time (period of history)."[11]

Six-year-old Ruby Bridges, one of the pioneer New Orleans integrators and heroine of the first part of *A Study in Courage and Fear,* was the first Southern child who drew for Coles. "Over the years she has drawn and painted during most of our talks, so that I now have over two hundred of her productions."[12] Ruby's drawings reflect her own ambivalent feelings about being black at a time when she was regularly reviled and threatened. She drew white figures more solidly, with bodies taller and more intact; black figures lacked eyes, ears, fingers, toes, limbs.

Studying these drawings, Coles is careful not to interpret Ruby as suffering from a psychological deficiency. Indeed, he is astonished at the normal behavior of Ruby and the many other children facing these unusual and even life-threatening situations. "With only one or two exceptions, these children were in no sense 'sick.' They had no symptoms, gave no clinical evidence of serious trouble with eating and sleeping, with nursery school or regular school, with family and friends. They did not come to see me in a clinic; it was I who sought them out because of their role in a social struggle."[13]

As for the pictures: It should not be surprising that Ruby and the others should draw pictures of blacks threatened, dismembered, lacking in full human stature, for that was the message they were daily receiving from the mob of angry whites.

Children's art can be collected and duplicated; we are, presumably, looking at unaltered copies of the children's original work. How does Coles treat the stories of those he interviewed? What are his interpretive methods? Each volume contains an explicit warning of what not to expect:

> No statistics are offered here, no graphs or charts, no surveys of attitudes or beliefs, nor is a "representative sample" with respect to this or that "variable" to be presented or analyzed. I have not used a questionnaire. I have no percentages of anything to give anyone. I have no idea how accurately the children discussed here, and indeed the children who speak in this book, reflect the way various other children . . . think and feel and talk. I have no "conclusions" or "findings" to offer, either.[14]

Without an explicit agenda, then, Coles simply wants to be present to the people he interviews; as he puts it, "to try, most of all, to *be* there." He wants to establish a relationship with them, not simply to observe them. This lesson was a difficult one to learn, he recalls, for he approached his early work in a "scientific" and dispassionate manner.

> Once upon a time (a long time ago, it now seems) I desperately wanted to make sure that I was doing the respectable and approved thing, the most "scientific" thing possible; and now I have learned, chiefly I believe from these people in this book [*Migrants, Sharecroppers, Mountaineers*] that it is enough of a challenge to spend some

years with them and come out of it all with some observations and considerations that keep coming up, over and over again.[15]

From that early and false "scientific" start, Coles gradually became aware that his work required not simply studying, but also befriending, those whose lives he wish to comprehend and record. "As a child psychiatrist," he wrote in *Sharecroppers,* "I had to learn how important it is not only to 'detect' something going on in a child's mind, but to go through certain experiences with the child in order to be of help." Thus, there is a "back and forth movement of ideas and impressions, a shared earnestness and eagerness."[16]

The point of these volumes, he reminds us, is not to "discuss the complexities of my relationships with the various people I have inter-viewed."[17] Nonetheless, he is the filter, the organizer, the conduit for this material. More than that: he molds and shapes it into prose that is reminiscent of the fiction and journalism of the writers he most admires: Orwell, Agee, Williams, Percy, O'Connor, Bernanos, Weil.

From the hundreds of interviews he has taped or recollected, from hundreds of transcripts of conversations, Coles has worked to bring shape and order to *Children of Crisis.* It is precisely at this point that we feel the great tension in his work. On one hand, he wishes to be faithful to the lived reality, the inviolable selves of the people he has encountered and who have confided in him. He seeks to be faithful to "the sounds of those voices, the rhythms and cadences, the pauses, the hesitations that suddenly are overcome, the hurry that is shown, followed by a relaxed stretch."[18] On the other hand, though he wishes his intervention to be minimal, his is after all the shaping hand, the mediating consciousness. "I had to read and edit the statements of others, and make sense of my own. . . . I had to extract what I thought to be the significant part of the material. . . . I had to weave together fragments and cut away at long monologues or dialogues."[19] The words are not his, "but the order of the words, or whole sentences and paragraphs and days and days and days of conversation has definitely been my doing."[20] The result is a complex and subtle interplay between Coles the participant-observer and the people whose lives he engages: "Much of the narrative . . . comes across as a mixture of what I heard others declare and what I hear my own mind speak."[21]

Coles takes pains to explain his editorial stance in *Children of Crisis.* He has altered names, places, family situations; he has put "some (by no means all) of these interviews into familiar (middle-class) grammar and sentence structure."[22] He has combined the insights of several different people into one narrative, and has taken a series of interviews with one person and condensed them into one or two paragraphs. Despite all this restructuring, this shaping and reshaping, Coles insists that he has been faithful to the tone, the mood, the characteristic gesture of his subjects.

> The aim of all these trips and visits can be put like this: to approach certain lives, not to pin them down, not to confine them with labels, not to limit them with heavily intellectualized speculations, but again to approach, to describe, to transmit as directly and sensibly as possible what has been seen, heard, grasp, felt by an observer who is also being constantly observed himself.[23]

Ultimately the reader must decide if the project of *Children of Crisis* is persuasive, if it is faithful to the gestures, speech rhythms, and life patterns of Coles's subjects as we know them from other sources. Does Coles's work match what we know of migrants, native Americans, urban blacks, affluent suburbanites? For this reader as for many others, Coles's re-presentation of the reality of these children and adults in crisis is persuasive and compelling. Despite all the changes he has made in the organization of the material—changes in names, situations, number of interviews, changes in the logic and coherence of speech—his devotion to the full and authentic humanity of these people is powerfully evident.

Like James Agee, whose documentary *Let Us Now Praise Famous Men* inspired and guided him, Coles embraces an artifice that seeks to make nature more natural. Like Agee, Coles has worked to highlight the crucial words or gestures, to pare away the repetitious, to bring out the naturally luminous comment or aside. "I do offer some comparative remarks," Coles notes in a manner strikingly like Agee's,

> that move beyond the individual children I know; but I am, or at least I have wanted to be, exceedingly wary about categorical, over-inclusive descriptions and, certainly, causative links. . . . What I can offer is my "direct observation" to use Anna Freud's much favored words. . . . The whole point of this work has been to put myself (body, mind and, I pray but cannot at all be sure, heart and soul) in a position, with respect to a number of children, that offers them a chance to indicate a certain amount about themselves to me, and through me, to others. But each life, as we ought to know, has its own authority, dignity, fragility, rock-bottom strength.[24]

Here, then, is the young child psychiatrist Robert Coles embarking on a project that was still unclear to him. His "method," what method there was, lay simply in listening to and recording the stories of people, especially children, in situations of social and cultural change. As he listened, transcribed, arranged, and compiled each successive volume, he found inspiration from a few social scientists like Anna Freud and Erik Erikson. Even more, he found corroboration of his efforts in the work of novelists, poets, and historians.

As he labored to become an archivist, a genealogist for the voiceless, he had to learn to quiet other voices that had been clamoring for attention: the voices that urged success and prestige as the chief goals of professional life; the voices of his medical school professors who urged on him a medicine of objectivity and distance; the voices that urged him to an intellectual mode of theory and abstraction. What was required, Coles discovered in the course of writing *Children of Crisis,* was something truly daunting for intellectuals, namely the "turning off" of the abstracting power of intellect in preference to a sensitivity to the rich and particular life of experience. Even more, it is not just any experience that Coles has attended to. He has been drawn to the words and lives of the "others": racially and ethnically marginal people, working-class whites, women, children, maids and servants, native Americans. Coles has engaged in a vast project of recovery and reclamation: to bring to the attention of literate, educated America the thousands whose voices and stories are rarely heard, people caught up in immense social forces beyond their control and yet whose lives demonstrate remarkable sanity, coherence, and dignity.

At the same time, Coles is engaged not just in recovery but in, to use a fashionable literary-philosophical term he would disdain, a *hermeneutics* of recovery. We have in *Children of Crisis,* as in *Women of Crisis* and his more recent work, not just archives, not just genealogy, but interpretation. To use the term we have been preferring here, Coles is a translator, taking the text (here, the lives and words of his subjects) and rendering it intelligible to another audience. Translators, as we noted earlier, need to be faithful to the original, and cannot compose their own texts. Nonetheless, they draw on their own knowledge of the language, culture, and biography of the original author in order to convey the inner meaning of the original. Since language is inherently metaphorical, translators in part transmit, in part create, the text at hand.

Coles acknowledges his creative role in shaping these narratives. To an interviewer's comment that "reading *Children of Crisis* is like reading a novel," Coles responded, "that's what I aim at. *Children of Crisis* is made up of stories based on real people. I view myself as an observer of people. . . . I try to catch the everyday drama and also the complexity. There is a lot of complexity." Later in the interview, he notes, "In the course I teach at Harvard, the writers I choose are almost all novelists. They have a sense of what is going on. That's missing in too many textbooks."25

Scattered throughout the method chapters of *Children of Crisis* are further acknowledgments that Coles has shaped his raw material into narrative form. In *The South Goes North*, he comments: "It has seemed to me wise to avoid turning this book into a word-for-word tapescript, or even a slightly or heavily edited version of the same thing. If I am to bring alive as best I can the presence of certain people . . . then I myself had best assume the responsibility of speaking." Having assumed such a responsibility, Coles feels obliged on some occasions to alter names, places, number of speakers: "I have changed the names of counties and states, and changed dozens and dozens of other details. Often I have drawn composite pictures; that is, I have combined two or three people into one to make the particular individuals I know unrecognizable and also to emphasize and highlight the issues for the reader." Despite all his editing, abstracting, condensing, and reshaping, Coles has tried to remain faithful to the "essence . . . of particular lives."26

We should note, however, that on at least one occasion Coles rejected the label "translator." In the same passage from *The South Goes North* cited earlier, in which Coles takes on responsibility for presenting certain lives to a reading public, he also makes the following claim: "I therefore do not speak for particular people, nor do I speak as a translator; essentially I am speaking to the reader as an observer and writer."27 I take Coles here to mean something like "mouthpiece" or "direct pipeline." In the sense of "speaking for particular people," a translator would simply pass on the words he has been given. But I mean something more complex and creative than that in using the word "translator," something indeed closer to "observer and writer."

Having identified Coles as a translator in our understanding of the word, simultaneously transmitting and creating, we need now to look at some of the particular ways he goes about translating the lived reality of his informants into the scores of narratives in *Children of Crisis*. Like any good writer, Coles employs several narrative strategies as he shapes the thousands of hours of interviews, tapes, and transcripts into these stories.

Perhaps the most typical narrative in the series combines extended quotation with commentary from the interviewer. "George and His Lois," from *A Study in Courage and Fear*, begins with the narrator's voice, giving us some information on George's frame of mind at the time of school integration, and an early comment on the white boy's stability and normality: "He and all like him were being punished. He wasn't sure why, but he knew the time had arrived, a time of suffering. When he talked about it he emphasized his despair with a firm shake of his head. . . . He was a bright and ambitious boy. He did well in school and he played football well."[28]

Then follows some biographical information on George's father. The narrator combines what critic Wayne Booth calls the "telling" and "showing" dimensions of narrative. Some insights we gain through the words and actions of the characters; others are presented through the author's commentary. We still do not know exactly why Coles, the narrator, is interested in these people, except that presumably they have something to do with the struggle over integration. Our understanding deepens as the narrator turns to the words of George Simmons's father. An insurance agent, he collects premiums from black families as well as white. Of the blacks he says, "They're fine. I don't have anything against them. I know them. I've been in their homes. Every day I go and talk with them. They trust me."[29] No commentary is offered on Simmons's words, but it would be an unperceptive reader who does not feel that these words make the man suspect in our eyes—he is an authority figure, a collector of revenues, complacent and lacking in self-knowledge. In addition, the reader may begin to feel, although not obliged to feel, a compensatory closeness to the narrator; perhaps his point of view is more trustworthy.

But then complexity sets in: We may find Simmons's perspective on his black clients shallow and unreflective, but we are led by the narrator to have a more sympathetic view of this man than of his wife. Simmons refuses to have anything to do with the Ku Klux Klan, and wants his son sufficiently educated so that he will not have to "ride about in white robes." Mrs. Simmons is a whole other matter. She is "breezy, amiable, plump," but her amiability masks a self-preoccupied, rigid, angry person. "She storms into a room, taking it over with an improbable walk, toes always pointing outward and other parts of her body revolving around several axes. While sitting she fastens her hands upon her chubby arms, often pinching or rubbing them as she talks. Her voice has a forceful high pitch to it—perhaps she was meant to be a Northern dowager—as well as the inevitable drawl."[30]

Springing from a family that dates its presence in Atlanta from the Civil War, Mrs. Simmons seems unsure upon whom to cast the blame for the disaster of integration, but knows that "most of them [black

Atlantans] didn't want to do what a few of them were now planning to do: threaten her and her son and others." Here the narrator returns to the family theme of threat, punishment, and suffering, with which George was preoccupied at the story's outset. The narrator highlights this theme with an aside: "I could not fail to notice his genuine sense of being victimized." Failing to notice the irony between his sense of being victimized and his victimization of blacks, the teenager willingly admits his plan to harass the two black students who will come to his high school next month: "People say we have no choice, but we do. We can make sure those two don't have a picnic. They've got a few surprises coming."[31]

Here, then, in the space of a few pages, Coles has combined narration, characters' voices, and the reader's assumptions into a complex pattern. The narrator provides background information and some commentary, but in general he relies on the interplay between reader and character to provide the movement and drama of the story. The father, a white-collar worker seeking security and respectability; seeing in his son the means of social advancement; the mother, a veritable fortress figure, her high, forceful voice belying her seeming graciousness; the son, absorbing his parents' sense of victimization and their distinction between "our Negroes" who must surely oppose integration and the outsiders who agitate for it—these are the characters, thus far, with whom the reader is called upon to interact. They are portrayed sympathetically, not as stereotypical racists, and yet critically. We are led through their own words to see them as willfully ignorant of who is victim and who is victimizer in the racial situation. For all that, Coles does not reject their feelings, only seeks to put them into a larger social and cultural context.

Despite George's hostility toward the two black students, he is forced to admit by the end of the school year that he had come to admire them for their courage and persistence. Particularly, he admired Lois. "She was 'our nigger' as against the other girl, whom he judged less attractive and intelligent. . . . When Lois made the honor society, George was both pleased and scornful. She certainly didn't deserve it. How could anyone ever compare the high marks she received in a Negro school with those given in a white school?" But, "he did not want to deny Lois her membership in the honor society. Let her have it—to help her keep going."

Then, in the narrator's voice, comes this passage:

> One day in April she dropped her lab notebook in the corridor and before he could think about it he had picked it up. . . . George tried

> hard to explain the unexplainable. He hadn't wanted to do it; he had just done it, without a thought, a plan, or a wish. If he had it to do over, he would not—though he had to admit a certain affection and pity for Lois. She was a lonely girl; white or black, she was lonely. He reminded his friend what it was like for her every day of the year. Shouldn't they go easy on her, even try to be nice to her? Negroes and whites are different, whites superior and Negroes inferior; but Lois—she should be allowed to finish the school year in peace.[32]

Here Coles the narrator is helping the reader identify what is happening in George—the growth of a sense of compassion, the development of a more complex moral universe. George's insistence that he and other whites were the victims was giving way to a more accurate assessment of the situation; he was beginning to see that in fact the black students suffered and endured infinitely much more than he. In paraphrasing George's words, rather than substituting his own, Coles stays close to the boy's own growth of consciousness.

Later that spring, George tells his parents that Lois would attend a local black college. This scene is conveyed using some authorial language, some paraphrasing and some direct quotation. This combination of points of view allows Coles to maintain distance from his subjects while still remaining faithful to their views, insights, and changes. Note particularly the gradual shift from "niggers" to "nigras" to "Negroes."

> They approved of her choice, and of her for making it. . . . George's parents sometimes became angry at all niggers, but they didn't really mean "the good ones" who worked well, or the bright ones who wanted to educate themselves, or their "real" leaders, who understood Southern ways. Now Lois, she is a leader. One day she will lead other nigras in their struggle for learning. She was no integrationist, no agitator. She had made a mistake by letting herself be "used" by them, but all in all she had held her head up, and not caused any trouble. She was going to finish the year successfully, and they were proud of her, and glad she had chosen a first-rate Negro college. . . . George did not disagree with the praise lavished on Lois, but he did have the final word on the subject. "I think we've probably learned how she feels too." After he said that, his mother asked whether anyone wanted a Coke. Then his father wondered what kind of summer job George could find.[33]

Clearly the author intends the reader to be critical of the parents for these comments, for their racial slurs, their easy and complacent patronizing of blacks. Just as clearly, we are meant to see by the story's end, the moral distance between George and his parents measured in his ability to acknowledge Lois's feelings after a difficult year and in his parents' unwillingness to respond and eagerness to change the subject.

In this typical "story" from *Children of Crisis*, the narrator's voice is that of the author Coles. He is the transcriber and reporter of words, but also the shaper of the scene and consequently of our responses to it. Coles has his moral agenda, and urges our responses to fit that agenda. In that gentle manipulation, he is, of course, like virtually all other writers. As Wayne Booth has shown, even writers who pretend to an objective stance regarding character and action have in fact a distinctive point of view that is itself revealed in the claim to objectivity. Coles makes no such claim. But in such stories as "George and His Lois" he is not intimately involved in the action, and so must move the reader through a more subtle strategy involving his own words, his paraphrasing, and quotations.[34]

In a story like "To Hell with All of You," from the third volume of *Children of Crisis, The South Goes North,* Coles is much more intimately involved in the action. Indeed, in this kind of story, the "action" consists of conversations between narrator and subject. We find here the same combination of description, analysis, and extended quotation so typical of stories throughout the series. The additional element is the deep involvement of the narrator himself. Consider the opening:

> Curses, threats, diatribes, oaths, warnings, one indecent or coarse word after another. They all come easily to James Lewis, who is *only* fourteen, someone like me cannot help thinking to himself. He talks and talks, and if a listener who hears him does not look at the young man's extraordinarily expressive face, the temptation is to surrender or flee immediately to whatever sanctuary can be found.[35]

Here the educated and cultured narrator confronts his own fear in talking with this tough, street-smart kid. James's language is crude, vivid, and intentionally shocking, and forms a striking contrast, at least in Coles's eyes, with his youth. Perhaps later readers, inured to earthy language in the young, would find that contrast less remarkable. In any event, the narrator notes another contrast, that between James's language and demeanor and his age. If his vocabulary seems to Coles too advanced for his tender youth, his expressive face reflects a far more thoughtful person than either his language or his age suggest.

Indeed, so great is the youth's power of reflection that he readily identifies a similar disparity between outward appearance and inner reality in whites, including in the author himself.

> It's the white man who has dirtied up everything; he's ruined the air and the water; he's exploded atomic bombs; he's killed the Indians and made us slaves. He's been murdering and stealing for hundreds of years. . . . The white man lives off the black man and the brown man and the red man. That's the truth. I don't hold it against any one white man; it's all of them—all of you.[36]

Coles is stunned by James's words, and admits as much to the reader. He is also grateful for James's sense of humor, since it manages to disarm the intensity of some of his comments. "That is to say, he can tell me things I will later think about with a great deal of sadness or apprehension or anger or whatever—while at the time his quick eyes and sardonic tone of his voice and the smile, at once charming and challenging, all seem to soften somewhat remarks spoken in utter seriousness." Coles is grateful for the personal dimension of these conversations, so that "we will not once again end up talking about racist America, racist America—to the point that he himself is exhausted and at a loss to know what can be done."[37]

Indeed, Coles is so challenged, so threatened by James's words that he debates with him, the doctor with the street kid. James distinguishes between "Negroes" and "blacks" and asks Coles if he sees the difference. He does not. "Patiently and generously he will try to show me: 'I can understand. You're you. I'm me. You try to know the black man, but you're lost before you ever start. You're looking through a white man's eyes. Here in America the black man is just being born.'" Later, Coles suggests that James sees the racial situation in "too conspiratorial a fashion." James responds, his words passing through Coles's paraphrase:

> I [that is, Coles] can afford not to look underneath and see all the ugliness and meanness and treachery which really do exist in this world. He doesn't quite say it that way; indeed, he speaks eloquently and sharply: "If you have an easy time; if you're rich; if you're on top; if the world is always waiting on you—then sure you can look around and say everything is going fine, and what's the matter with all those people who keep on digging up trouble all the time. But if you're down, way down on the bottom, then you either learn the score or you're a slave. If you want to be a black man, a free man, you have to keep awake, wide awake."[38]

Coles's judgment is that this youth "has a highly developed political sensibility." In James, the street tough, Coles has met his match: They volley back and forth across the immense divide of race and class. "He looks directly at me and tells me how sorry he is that I am deceived, but how he understands, he understands." Coles ends his account thus: "Sometimes as I listen to him I remember those moments when I as a doctor, a psychiatrist, have told a troubled, confused patient that yes, I understand, I understand."[39] Here a number of shifts in perspective and role are at work. The repetition of "understand" established a link between James and the narrator, and the narrator and his patients. If Coles's patients are occasionally troubled and confused, then, the repetition suggests, in this situation Coles is equally confused and troubled. Social class and educational distinctions between Coles and James are reversed, the poorly educated youth becoming the mentor of the uncomprehending white man.

But such is the complexity of this brief account that we may not simply leave it there. Coles, we recall, is not interested in reversing head and heart, nor is he a soft-minded romantic champion of the poor. His respect for people like James is too great for the easy gesture of heaping guilt and blame on himself and letting it go at that. When he says that he as a doctor "understands, understands" his troubled patients, we are meant, I think, to conclude that he really does not understand, that out of haste and preoccupation he is dismissing their difficulties with a verbal formula. In the case of James, the youth is professing to understand, even sympathize with Coles's race- and class-limited perspective. But in using the formula "understand, understand" Coles shows how both educated professionals and street-smart kids may resort to verbal formulas ("black power," "Power to the People," "transference," "projection," "reaction-formation") rather than engage in the much harder effort to understand each other's full humanity. By the end of the story, this foul-mouthed teenager, who clearly threatens Coles (intellectually and emotionally at least, perhaps physically as well), has become his colleague and peer. What began as an effort to understand an exotic and dangerous ghetto dweller has become a recognition of their shared humanity.

A third kind of narrative, one that removes all overt signs of Coles's presence and yet which is suffused with his mood, language, and concerns, occurs occasionally in all volumes of *Children of Crisis* but is especially prominent in the fourth volume. In the introduction to *Eskimos, Indians, Chicanos,* Coles writes,

> Apart from those first few pages and these here that make up this chapter, this book is quite free, I believe and hope, of the vertical pronoun. More than that, I think there is a certain tone in this book

(if I may become my own critic) that distinguishes it from its predecessors. . . . It is a tone I learned from the Indian, Chicano and Eskimo children themselves, as well as from their parents and grand-parents: a certain detachment toward the world and themselves, a tendency toward ironic self-effacement.[40]

We can better understand this mode of narration by referring to recent "reader-response" theories in literary criticism. In engaging a text, the reader enters into a dialectical relationship that looks something like this: The reader begins with his/her own historical situation, the assumptions that situation generates, together with the personal con-text. Then the text confronts these preunderstandings with its own claims, its own mode of "being-in-the-world." Third, reader and text engage in their own conversation, making and testing claims about truth, behavior, values, plausibility, and so on. Finally, the entire com-munity of readers, to which this particular reader belongs, is drawn in, as the communal assumptions are challenged, deepened, or qualified through encounter with a text.[41]

Readers of the fourth volume will have already gained considerable insight into native American life in the Southwest before they reach the story discussed below. Three previous chapters describe Hopi children in the pueblos of Arizona and New Mexico. Equally, readers bring some foreknowledge; some may be preoccupied with native American pov-erty and social disadvantage; others may recall the bitter history of white-Indian interaction, and look upon these folk as a conquered people, victims of imperialism and racism. Still others may know some-thing about native American folkways and be prepared to see in their lives a vital reminder of a more mystical and holistic worldview than one finds in the U.S. cultural mainstream.

Whatever assumptions readers may have, they find in Coles's account of Miriam and her family a remarkably transparent and indeed self-effacing story. Here is no passionate debate with an angry minority person, as in "To Hell with All of You," no clever interweaving of authorial comment and paraphrase to help us see both the poison of racism and the possibilities of moral growth. Here Coles stays as close as he can to the felt reality and experience of these particular Hopi, and to whatever larger conclusions that arise, he implies, from the rich par-ticularity of their lives.

In the opening paragraphs, the nine-year-old Miriam and her mother watch and play with Miriam's baby sister, who is just learning to walk. Older child and mother work together, guiding, encouraging but never intruding, allowing the baby to fall and learn from her mistakes. Like her mother and grandmother did with her, Miriam sings and speaks to the little one: "Do not run/do not run before you walk/ do not walk/ do not walk before you stand/ when you stand/ you will be one of us/ the Hopis."[42]

In the middle section of the narrative, Miriam draws several pictures for Coles, one of the entire reservation, another of a nearby valley with its single tree on a hillside. This picture reminds the child of an exemplary story she heard from her father. It seems that once whites came looking for gold. They dug near the tree and considered cutting it down. The Hopi came and encircled the tree, standing their ground despite threats of death from the prospectors. Just then, a powerful wind and hailstorm came up. The whites were terrified by this completely unexpected shift in the weather and fled. The Hopi saw it as the timely intervention of the spirit world.

All creation is animated, Miriam and her people believe, and the spirits of the dead linger nearby. The child tells of her first sight of a local landmark, Three Fingers Rock, as she sketches this place for her visitor. A story from her father links this place with the still-present spirits of the dead: Three Hopi men once left their homeland to join some whites in the search for gold. Regretting their disloyalty, they asked to be allowed to return to the village. After much debate, the Hopi agreed, but before the men could return they died. More debate followed before the Hopi permitted their remains to be buried at Three Fingers Rock, where their spirits still restlessly move about. Coles phrases Miriam's explanation for their restlessness this way: "They express the regret they feel for wandering so far and for abandoning in their minds the conviction that they were and wanted to be Hopis. The glow of the Rock [when backlit by the moon] is the result of the intensity of their sadness, their self-accusations, their fervently spoken remorse."[43]

To these two life-patterns—participating with her mother in child-rearing and accepting the reality of the spirit world—Miriam adds a third, a deep sense of loyalty to and rootedness in the land. Although her teachers commend her as a bright child deserving of further training, her parents wonder what good white education will do for her. The child echoes their judgment. "My mother says that at school we learn a lot, but what we learn doesn't help us here on the reservation. The teachers want some of us to leave and try to live someplace else, in a city maybe. My father says this reservation of ours is the whole world, and he never wants to leave it; he never wants to go live in another world."

To the casual observer, this Hopi land may appear barren and useless. To the child, nurtured in its subtleties and convinced of the presence of spirits, the landscape is vibrantly alive:

> My mother tells us to look very closely because each time the Rock looks different. I like to look from far away: the three fingers practically touch the sky. . . . My mother says tumbleweed is the wind's hand; if the tumbleweed comes after you and hits you, that means some spirit is telling you something and you've done wrong; but if you're walking and the tumbleweed gets out of your way, then you've been doing good, and you deserve an easy walk.[44]

This kind of narrative, in which Coles interjects no commentary, no authorial presence, is remarkably effective: The child, the landscape, the whole feel of life in the Hopi Southwest come vividly alive through description and monologue that sticks close to the lived reality of Miriam and her family. Of course we are aware that Coles has written the words that bring the scene alive. But unlike the two previous kinds of narration—the first in which the narrator's voice is intertwined with quotation and paraphrase, the second in which the narrator is actively involved as a character in the story—he is virtually invisible here. The result is that the reader is drawn much more immediately into the narrative than in the other kinds. Here there is an invitation, a space to enter, an opportunity to cocreate a new reality in the space between our assumptions and lives as readers and those of the people here described. Some readers will conclude that the child occupies a primitive, magical world that will inevitably be demolished. Coles himself anticipates that response, and later in the volume writes,

> They have acquired a sense of proportion about man and his prowess that distinguishes them from other American children. An Indian child at work drawing is like a Chinese or Japanese artist of several centuries ago—less impressed by man and his artifacts than bound by the spell of trees, shrubs, waterfalls, hills, terraces, mountains. . . . The white man and his artifacts are, perhaps, dragons that Indian children must learn to subdue psychologically. One ought to stay skeptical of those who, though they have prevailed in many ways, may get destined to failure on the grandest scale."[45]

Our dialogue with this "open" text goes on: Why would parents actually encourage the child to stay on the parched, rocky reservation rather than follow the teacher's advice and go to the city? The text speaks: The child's eye, like that of an Impressionist painter, is being trained to see and appreciate nuances of color and texture, the changing play of light over form. Would she lose this gift when faced with the sensory overload of the modern American city? What is valuable and worth preserving? More dialogue: Is Miriam a victim, a member of a defeated and oppressed face? Yes, surely. But she is also heir to a coherent and even impressive way of viewing and living in the world, one that many whites envy or admire as science and technology deliver only material goods, not spiritual happiness.

We have described several narrative strategies at length in order to show that Coles is not simply transcribing some of his many interviews, but rather deliberately shaping this material into different kinds of stories. These strategies reveal through their method some of the life-themes that preoccupy Coles. Outraged by the self-delusion and complacency of "nice people" like the parents in "George and His Lois," Coles guides the reader's response toward a recognition of the insidious nature of racism. On the other hand, he is struck by the often unexpected signs of moral growth and change, the often unpredicted moments when people break free of their conditioning and assert moral freedom. George's recognition of fellow-feeling for the black girl Lois was such a moment.

In "To Hell with All of You," Cole struggles with his own ambivalence toward the black teenager James. Does his social, racial, and intellectual stature make him incapable of understanding the depth of James's anger and alienation? Can one simultaneously be a successful white professional and a person of compassion? These questions and more torment Coles, both in this narrative and in general, and make such stories both profoundly autobiographical and deeply disquieting for readers who share Coles's sense of inner division.

The transparent nature of the accounts in *Eskimos, Chicanos, Indians* springs, Coles suggests, from the witness of these minority people themselves, who encourage a certain reticence and self-effacement. Such silence is difficult for a person who relies on talk and therefore self-disclosure: "I must say that the Pueblo and Hopi children I worked with most closely were an enormous challenge to me. As a child psychiatrist I have long since learned to expect weeks, months, even, of silence, suspiciousness; then the feigned indifference that masks growing curiosity" and then gradual expressiveness. But Indian children are remarkably reticent. "I wish that a writer could convey the long stretches of stillness that take place—when an Indian child not only sees fit to say nothing, but seems strangely, wondrously, unnervingly disinclined to speak."[46] But in the silence, in the spaces of these lives are opportunities for readers to enter deeply. Less deliberately crafted or less passionately autobiographical than other narrative forms, the stories in Volume 4, like the narratives in *Women of Crisis,* simply *are.*

We have seen something of Coles's method in *Children of Crisis.* We have explored some of his narrative strategies in the belief that the accounts there are not simple transcriptions but careful reconstructions of a few of the many hundreds of encounters he has had. Perhaps the most obvious question still remains unanswered: What *is Children of Crisis;* what is it all about?

Parts of our answer will necessarily be repeated in subsequent chapters when we consider Coles's view of his profession, his attitude toward children, toward religion, toward social change. But we can begin to construct an answer here, relying mostly on the "Method" sections in the five volumes. Influenced by writers like James Agee and William Carlos Williams and by his professional mentors and friends Anna Freud and Erik Erikson, Coles wishes to grasp and convey the *lives* and *life-circumstances* of America's children. These are not people suffering from classic psychic disorders, he insists. Their problems are malnutrition, poverty, oppression, lack of hope and opportunity, the indifference of America's white majority and power structure. As he listens and observes them over long periods of time, Coles is struck by the immense dignity of both children and adults, their good humor and affection, their determination and unflinching realism. Most of all, he is impressed with their intense spirituality, their belief in a power and an order larger than this visible and often untrustworthy one.

In order to gain these insights, Coles believes, one must be immersed in these lives; theorizing about people is valuable but insufficient. "I speak as a physician and as a child psychiatrist, and as one who has tried to study not only the illnesses and problems that people have, but also their *lives.* . . . Lives, as opposed to problems, may puzzle the fixed notions of theorists, while at the same time adding confirmation to what has been revealed by such keenly sensitive (if 'methodologically untrained') observers as Dostoevski or Zola, Orwell or Agee."[47] Social scientists, Coles goes on to say, are fond of systems-thinking whereby complex human realities are classified and organized. Like the novelists he so greatly admires, Coles prefers, indeed feels compelled, to approach his subject experientially, to try to grasp the total life of the people we (but not he) call his subjects.

> And there does come a time, after a few years of visits and more visits, talks and more talks, good talks and rather dismal ones, when some-

thing seems to have happened, "clicked," come about, developed; when, that is, on both sides some reasonably reliable and trustworthy impressions begin to congeal and become something else, so that a mountaineer can say: "Well, I guess I know you a small bit and you know me the same, and I sure hope you go and tell those people out over beyond those hills what we're *really* like."[48]

So it is not pathology that Coles is interested in, despite his medical background. In *Varieties of Religious Experience,* William James was likewise uninterested in whether or not religious people could be labeled "sick." Rather, he was fascinated with their religious experience. It did not matter, he said, whether Theresa of Avila was disturbed or whether "she might have had the nervous system of the placidest cow," which she certainly did not; her insights and her behavior are what counts. "Immediate personal experience" is what fascinated William James, and Robert Coles as well.[49]

Further: Coles is uninterested in writing "sociological description" or "anthropological analysis" or "political discussion." Like James, he is drawn to individual experience, but wants to embed that experience in the full, dense richness of all that surrounds it.

My job, at least as I see it, is to bring alive to the extent I possibly can a number of lives, and especially to bring alive the "innerness" in those lives: the expectations and assumptions, the vacillations and misgivings and scruples, the rhythm—as it engages with the outside world, with social and political events, with our nation's history; as it takes place in thoughts and feelings, in a child's drawings or games, in a man's imprecations, his casual remarks, his offhand jokes, his private beliefs.[50]

In this effort, Coles echoes the work of theologian H. Richard Niebuhr. Each person takes on identity within history and society, Niebuhr observes in *The Responsible Self.* This matrix represents our fate, the givenness of our lives. For the theologian, the great human paradox was learning to accept the givenness in order to find the freedom within it.[51] Despite lives of hardship, Coles finds "moments of satisfaction, accomplishment and self-respect" among the mountaineers of Appalachia and the ghetto-dwellers of Boston.

Finally, like James Agee, Coles is deeply aware of the limitations of his words to capture the sheer fact of human existence. The "Method" chapters are filled with confessions of the inadequacy of language in the face of these lives: "I only hope that [my] work has measured up, in breadth and subtlety, to the day-by-day growth the children in this book have demonstrated, the awareness and discretion and humor and seriousness and common sense they continue to possess, and learn to exercise, often enough against great odds indeed."[52] In his monumental documentary of tenant farmers in the 1930s, James Agee phrases a similar insight this way: "In a novel, a house or a person has his meaning, his existence, entirely through the writer. Here, a house or a person has only the most limited of his meaning through me: his true meaning is much huger. It is that he *exists,* in actual being, as you do and as I do, and as no character of the imagination can possibly exist." It is outrageous, Agee goes on, that these farmers among whom he lived were in fact being spied on, and are now captured in the pages of a book for the "sympathy, curiosity, idleness" of strangers. Nothing should detract us from the simple, signal fact: that these people exist. "The one deeply exciting thing to me about Gudger [one of Agee's tenant farmer subjects] is that he is actual, he is living, at this instant. He is not some artist's or journalist's or propagandist's invention; he is a human being: and to what degree I am able it is my business to reproduce him as the human being he is: not just to amalgamate him into some invented, literary imitation of a human being."[53]

So despite our efforts to talk about "method" in *Children of Crisis,* to abstract Coles's research technique and narrative styles, we are forced back, by the internal logic of the volumes, to Coles's original intention: direct observation, over a long period of time, of children and adults many of whom are caught up in traumatic social and cultural change. What we remember, then, of *Children of Crisis* is the sharply drawn characters, their quirkiness and complexity, their unexpected depth and humor:

—The black crew leader, from *Migrants, Sharecroppers, Mountaineers,* who cares for "his people" like an overbearing parent. He prefers bringing the migrants food himself to paying them wages: "They have the money and they feel thirsty and they're tired, and they think to themselves that a bottle of wine would be good, so they go and get the wine and they drink it. Soon their money is gone, and if I get mad and tell them they're fools, they say yes sir, like always. . . ." Caught between his own desire for comfort and his genuine care for his workers, this man, Coles says, is "more tormented and anguished, more rocked by the awfulness of his life as well as the fate of his people than he can ever possibly realize."[54]

—The white Boston mother, watching her children's school undergo integration, struggling to understand social change. "Who gave my husband a chance? He made a chance for himself. He works so hard that I worry for him. He even does carpentry on the side. We've got to meet those bills. . . . Now, all of a sudden, our kids have these strangers in school with them. I don't know what the colored kids are actually learning here that's so much better than what they could be learning where they live, in their own school."[55]

—The Eskimo child in an Anglo school. "An uncle lies ill, for example. His niece is in school. . . . Suddenly, the girl turns her eyes toward the window, then back to the desk in front of her, then down toward the floor. She mutters a word or two." Asked to be excused, the child returns home to find that her uncle has died. "The girl, in a matter-of-fact manner, tells her mother that she 'heard' her uncle dying; a wind brought her the message, and another wind seemed on its way to carry off the uncle's spirit."[56]

·3·

Literary Criticism

The tension in Coles's early and educational life between self-revealing and self-concealing, between intellect and character, is reflected in the very structure of *Children of Crisis*. There, Coles is at pains to record the words and experiences of children and adults in situations of social and personal trauma. He insists that neither theory nor his own personal predilections should obscure this record of human survival. Impatient with abstraction, Coles insists on the full, particular, and unique humanity of the people whose stories he recounts. Nonetheless, as we discover through Coles's own admissions and through closer scrutiny of the stories themselves, he is not simply an archivist, a compiler of case histories. Like the novelists Agee, Orwell, Dickens, Percy, and O'Connor and the poet Williams, all of whom Coles claims as kindred spirits, he works to shape his material into art without losing the authenticity of the accounts. This same tension between archive and art, between recording and re-creating, is present in his literary criticism, and it is to a consideration of that material that we now turn.

Perry Miller, Coles's undergraduate mentor at Harvard, suggested that Coles write his senior thesis on William Carlos Williams. Coles should write the poet and ask him to read the essay, Miller went on. Coles remembers:

> Professor Perry Miller kept insisting—a response to my fearful hesitancy, an attitude which surely (I now realize) protected me from realizing how much of my pride . . . had been put into that research and writing effort. This particular poet, Mr. Miller reminded me several times, was hardly a favorite of many college professors, and might well enjoy readng what a student writing in an ivy-covered dormitory library managed to say about *Paterson,* where in no huge flowering of ivy is recorded.[1]

Attracted to Williams the poet, Coles found Williams the doctor equally attractive, and shifted his career goal away from teaching and toward medicine, particularly pediatric medicine, Williams's specialty.

Much as Perry Miller introduced the young undergraduate to Williams and to a host of other writers and thinkers, Coles the medical student was led by another master teacher, Paul Tillich, to the work of Walker Percy. Williams was instrumental in shifting Coles's career direction toward medicine without abandoning literature, and Percy's novels and essays confirmed for Coles his subsequent choice of psychiatry (and then, child psychiatry) as his preferred branch of medicine. Coles, we recall, had been assigned to an air force hospital in Mississippi in 1958 and was undergoing psychoanalysis in New Orleans during that time. When Percy's first novel, *The Moviegoer,* came out in 1960, Coles realized that he had in fact been driving back and forth through the very landscape Percy describes in his book. More deeply, Coles identified in his own life the same need that Percy's hero Binx Bolling feels, to break through the screen of the ordinary and experience life more intensely. He had had that same feeling several years earlier as a medical student in New York, riding the subways aimlessly, until brought up short by an encounter with a dying woman.[2] Here, in the South, Coles suffered from that same anomie, that hunger for depth: "Walker Percy's novel gave hope to me, helped me feel stronger at a critical time, when I was somewhat lost, confused, vulnerable, and, it seemed, drifting badly. . . . I read *The Moviegoer* over and over again; I would be embarrassed to list the number of times. To be honest, I lost count. On each reading I discovered something new that was amusing or instructive."[3]

During his work on the volumes of *Children of Crisis,* Coles read intensively in fiction, philosophy, history, and some sociology to provide horizon and depth for his interviews. There are few references in either the texts or the notes of *Children* to the canonized theorists in sociology and cultural anthropology: Parsons, Merton, Berger, Mannheim, Durkheim, Levi-Strauss, Boas, Mead, Geertz. Rather, imaginative writing, and philosophy, notably Christian existentialism, together with the work of Anna Freud and Erik Erikson, form the critical underpinning of Coles's efforts to understand psyche and society.

In addition to *Children of Crisis,* Coles also demonstrates his interest in literary texts and ideas in reviews, essays, and several books of criticism. He has published four such volumes (*Irony in the Mind's Life, Walker Percy: an American Search, William Carlos Williams: The Knack of Survival in America,* and *Flannery O'Connor's South*), an introduction to Williams's *The Doctor Stories,* and scores of essays on literary topics in *The New Yorker, The New Republic, American Poetry Review, Daedalus,* and most recently, in *The New Oxford Review*. What attracts Coles to certain authors and texts? What kind of criticism does he offer? What are the links between his work as literary critic and his career as child psychiatrist and social commentator?

"No ideas but in things," said William Carlos Williams. This aphorism suggests Williams's poetic theory, an insistence that poetry be descriptive of the concrete and lived reality rather than indicative of "states of mind." As a great admirer of Williams, Coles also admires his poetic theory, writing criticism that draws attention to literature of reality.

How does "no ideas but in things" shed light on the way Robert Coles reads literature? The author of the line gives us the first answer. Coles once mentioned to Williams that he would like to write about the New Jerseyite's fiction. Williams was pleased, not so much for himself, he said, but for the kind of people he portrayed in his stories, *Life Along the Passaic*, or in the trilogy devoted to the Stecher family. "He [Williams] added: 'I mean novelists are ignoring them; the sociologists and psychologists have taken over. At least someone cares.'"[4] This notion, that fiction resembles the work of sociology (particularly that of people like Herbert Gans and Richard Sennett) is deepened and solidified later in Coles's work on Williams. Coles links Williams's prose with other examples of "sociological fiction," efforts from the end of the nineteenth century through the 1930s to render the social and psychic effects of immigration, industrialization, and urbanization. In this company Coles places George Linhart, John Cournos, Abraham Cahan, Theodore Dreiser, Stephen Crane, Jack London, James Sullivan, Edna Ferber, Fannie Hurst, Isaac Friedman, and Upton Sinclair. They "wrote at a time when sociological studies had yet to gain the dominance they now have—as the almost matter-of-fact way that readers choose for access to the lives of others."[5] With the growth of sociology in this century, such "slice-of-life" fiction began to recede before "the notion that with a questionnaire, or a spell of 'field work' followed by the extended resort to theoretical formulations, the various and complicated thoughts and experiences of many different kinds of people can be quite adequately presented."[6]

The writers Coles mentioned are not the only ones confronting the situation of the self in a complex and dynamic industrial society. The realist movement in literature and art in the mid- and late nineteenth century, in both Europe and America, grew in response to dramatic social and economic changes. What Coles admires in Williams—his attention to detail, his refusal to moralize, his focus on neglected people and insistence on accurate rendering of their lives—is also applicable to the great realists of the previous century.

The work of Erich Auerbach enables us to single out those traits of nineteenth-century realism that make it most relevant to Williams and hence to Coles. In *Mimesis: The Representation of Reality in Western Literature* (1946), Auerbach argues that realism has had two flowerings. The first, manifested in the Torah and the narratives of the life of Jesus, is energized by the Judaeo-Christian conviction that serious, tragic, momentous things can happen to quite ordinary people. In the stories of Abraham and Isaac, of David, of Ruth and Esther, of the life of Jesus, the Hebrew and Christian writers are concerned to give depth, motivation, and universality to the lives of people who, in many cases, were socially marginal or undesirable: nomads, peasants, vagrants, women, conquered people. Of the illiterate fisherman Peter, Auerbach writes, "He is the image of man in the highest and deepest and most tragic sense." Unlike classical literature, which generally reserved tragic or extraordinary events for noble characters, biblical literature came out of an entirely different worldview. Its mingling of styles—tragic, comic, noble, base—is not artistic clumsiness. Rather, "it was rooted from the beginning in the character of Jewish-Christian literature; it was graphically and harshly dramatized through God's incarnation in a human being of the humblest social station, through his existence on earth amid humble everyday people and conditions, and through his Passion which, judged by earthly standards, was ignominious."[7]

What distinguishes this literature, Auerbach goes on, is not simply the complexity it attributes to ordinary people, but its insistence that events of cosmic importance are being incarnated in human reality without that reality losing any of its pithiness and grittiness. "What we see here is a world which on the one hand is entirely real, average, identifiable as to place, time, and circumstances, but which on the other hand is shaken in its very foundations, is transforming and renewing itself before our very eyes. For the New Testament authors who are their contemporaries, these occurrences on the plane of everyday life assume the importance of world-revolutionary events, as later on they will for everyone."[8] Auerbach labels "figural" that version of reality in which events are portrayed simultaneously as themselves in their complex facticity and as gesturing toward a larger, transhistorical reality.

The second realist movement was a revolt launched against the classical French drama of the late sixteenth and seventeenth centuries, and eventually spread out to include the new forms of the novel and the photograph in the nineteenth century. Like the old, the new realism focused on ordinary folk in daily life, and had its fullest expression in the social novel of which Stendhal was the great original. Says Auerbach, "Insofar as the serious realism of modern times cannot represent man otherwise than as embedded in a total reality, political, social, and economic, which is concrete and constantly evolving—as is the case today in any novel or film—Stendhal is its founder."[9]

Nonetheless, there is an immense gulf between the realism inspired by the biblical vision and that which triumphed in revolt against neo-classical artifice. The biblical vision is figural realism, whereas modern realism acknowledges no metaphysical reality as foundation for human reality. Ironically, says Auerbach, biblical realism leads to its own undoing in its very devotion to a faithful rendering of the human scene. The Jewish and Christian notion that God is at work in human history opposed any special sacred realm. If God is present throughout history and creation, then it is only one step, as Nietszche saw, to say that God is in effect nowhere present. An increasing number of Western people, after the Enlightenment, could interpret events without recourse to a transcendent realm of meaning.[10]

A second distinction between old and new realism is built on the first. Many of the biblical accounts are spare in detail. They suggest rather than express, as Auerbach puts it, exploring depth rather than surface.[11] Unlike the biblical writers, who are content to sketch in the social and historical background with a few strokes, concentrating instead on character and conflict, the realists of the last hundred years are concerned, even obsessed, with the enormous facticity of daily life.

This new "climate of sensibility" grew out of the social revolutions of the eighteenth and nineteenth centuries, the growth of cities and restless movement of peoples, the spread of factories and interlinking of people through bureaucracies, communications, and consumerism. "Such a development," says Auerbach,

> abrogates or renders powerless the entire social structure of orders and categories previous held valid; the tempo of the changes demands a perpetual and extremely difficult effort toward inner adaptation and produces intense concomitant crises. He who would account to himself for his real life and his place in human society is obliged to do so upon a far wider practical foundation and in a far larger context than before, and to be continually conscious that the social base upon which he lives is not constant for a moment but is perpetually changing through convulsions of the most various kinds.[12]

Gradually, says Auerbach, European novelists moved away from fiction that set up complex and rich resonances with the biblical tradition and toward a fiction that reconstructed in words the dense social life and ambiguous psychic life of English and Europeans. Where Dickens, Dostoevsky, Melville, and Tolstoy relied on knowledge of Christian tradition and a commitment to the reality, however benign or malignant, of the transcendent, Flaubert, Zola, and Dreiser make no such demands.

Alfred Kazin once observed that the central difference between European and American literary realism is that the Europeans shaped their movement in response to political and intellectual currents; American realism "grew out of the bewilderment, and thrived on the simple grimness, of a generation suddenly brought face to face with the pervasive materialism of industrial capitalism."[13] The antebellum novels of Hawthorne and Melville were realistic in this sense, in their engagement with issues of social change and reform, in their ambivalent treatment of "tradition," in their (particularly Melville's) concern with the "magnetic fields of attraction and repulsion between individual and community."[14] The postwar years, nonetheless, seemed at least quantitatively different: They were awash in new inventions, new sensations, new people, immensely more of everything for artists to encompass in their imaginative realms.

Where prewar writers like Hawthorne or Harriet Beecher Stowe could posit the existence of a common frame of reference, religious, historical, and moral, the postwar writers could make no such assumptions. Indeed, given the intense class antagonisms of the 1880s and 1890s, to say that the lives of working people have meaning only as intellectuals, philosophers, and theologians give them meaning in interpretive schemes seemed intolerably patronizing. Theodore Dreiser and Stephen Crane reject the symbolizing mode for precisely that reason. Unlike more established writers like William Dean Howells, Crane and Dreiser build up detail so that the reader may enter into the lives of characters and their circumstances rather than stand safely outside, imparting "meaning" but having no involvement. Howells, we might say, was concerned that his readers experience an increase in social compassion; Crane and Dreiser scorn compassion as charity, and demand recognition of the full humanity of the people about whom they write.

The subjects of Robert Coles's literary criticism find their place in the context we have just described. Williams, Agee, Elizabeth Bowen, George Eliot, Flannery O'Connor and Walker Percy were part of, or build on, the realist tradition. They reflect the struggle to free literature from the grip of sentimentalism and focus its energies on daily life expressed in ordinary language. Further, the realists Coles admires are often attracted to the marginal members of society. Like Crane and Dreiser, they are distrustful of large interpretive frameworks, whether secular or sacred, that insulate and shield readers from the intense life portrayed in the fiction.

As Coles reads him, William Carlos Williams well illustrates these general claims. Williams adheres to the realists' preference for the ordinary and overlooked person and situation. "Our cameras, our wordy spokesmen or propagandists, don't seek and celebrate an old man's pride, an old woman's faith, a housewife's ingenuity and intelligence. . . . Williams could not make up for the indifference of others, but he could approach 'the roar, the roar of the present,' and try to indicate who was making what noise, trying to get across what messages."15

Based on his experiences as a general practitioner in northern New Jersey, Williams's stories seem utterly discursive, close to journalism, without overt symbolic significance. Nonetheless, Coles argues, they serve as openings to dimensions of human life with which many readers may have little experience. "It is the genius of these stories that they are utterly concrete, yet lend themselves, without any help from the author in the form of discursive asides, to social comment or political analysis. Dr. Williams wants to carry his readers along . . . thereby capturing their imaginations, and not incidentally bringing them closer to a certain kind of 'life.'"16 Indeed, the doctor/writer is concerned primarily to render accurately the living reality of his subjects, not to convince us to like them, or even to like him. "In 'Jean Beicke' [one of *The Passaic Stories*], Williams seems to have in mind deliberate provocation of his readers' liberal, middle-class sensibility. When he praises the nurses, he does so at the expense, one could argue, of the children they are trying to help: 'You ought to see those nurses work. You'd think it was the brat of their best friend.'"17

Speaking of Williams, Coles concludes, "His patients may have been obscure, down and out, even illiterate . . . but they were, he had figured out early on, a splendidly vital people—full of important experiences to tell, memories to recall, ideas to try on their most respected of visitors, the busy doc."18 It is impossible to avoid applying these same words to Robert Coles and his encounters with hundreds of children and adults over a thirty-year period.

This effort to render the material of life honestly, without condescension or superiority, to respect the mixed motives and ambivalence of character, to leave oneself out as much as possible—these features that draw Coles to William Carlos Williams also attract him to James Agee. Agee was not seeking to illustrate psychological or sociological theory in *A Death in the Family,* says Coles. Rather, he gave us a series of vignettes drawn from a child's experience with his family in time of crisis. Perhaps, as one European reader complained, the book could have been condensed into one or two pages, but it is finally the detail that counts.

This same concern for specific detail, for intimate scene and gesture rather than for grand pattern, is evident in *Let Us Now Praise Famous Men.* The task of the artist, Agee argued there, is not to comment on the material; it is to reproduce the fullness of reality and thus to approach the beauty and perfection of nature. Neither an objective fact gatherer nor a propagandist, Agee confronts the complex reality of three Alabama tenant farm families with his own complex personal reality. In all this, Agee was concerned with establishing a "way of seeing" people who are utterly unlike the ones who might read his book. That approach involved the outrageous expedient of establishing genuine human relations with them. In short, says Agee, we should learn to love them.[19]

Coles praises writers like Williams and Agee who work sociologically, struggling to render faithfully the lives of working-class Americans. Theoretical sociologists meet with much less approval from Coles or from the writers he advances because of their tendency, as he sees it, toward reductionism. Speaking of Flannery O'Connor, Coles writes, "She resisted all conclusive sociological categorizations—efforts to subdue the complexity of human experience through words such as race, creed, religion, ethnicity, sex, age, occupation."[20] Like Coles, O'Connor wishes to convey the texture of life, in all its cross-grained, contradictory, and emotional features. In particular, Coles and O'Connor share an interest in the place of religion in the lives of individuals, and resist reductionist categories that seek to explain the phenomenon of religion. Speaking of Catholic novelists like herself, O'Connor once wrote, "I think he will feel a good deal more kinship with backwoods prophets and shouting fundamentalists than he will with those politer elements for whom the supernatural is an embarrassment and for whom religion has become a department of sociologist or culture or personality development."[21]

O'Connor strenuously resists prematurely symbolic readings of her stories. To her friend William Sessions she objected, "you see everything in terms of sex symbols, and in a way that would not enter my head— the lifted bough, the fork of the trees, the corkscrew. . . . It doesn't seem conceivable to you that such things merely have a natural place in the story, a natural use. . . . Your criticism sounds to me as if you have read too many critical books and are too smart in an artificial, destructive, and very limited way."[22]

In his studies of Williams, Agee, and O'Connor, as well as in his essays on English novelist George Eliot and Irish novelist Elizabeth Bowen and in the scores of essays written for various journals, Coles engages in practical criticism. He summarizes and describes; he gives "readings" of the works. Most of his book on Williams, for example, is taken up with a reading of the Stecher trilogy. Coles restates the action in his own words, commenting on and drawing out the implications of Williams's prose.

Coles's critical method is consonant both with the works he chooses to analyze and with his own social psychiatric work. He resists treating the texts as do many contemporary literary critics, as suspect material, hiding or distorting their intentions and assumptions. He resists seeing literature as artifact, existing only within the mind of the writer and reader. Some of the writers he chooses to comment on would insist that their work is not "symbolic," but is rather closer to journalism. Others would insist that whatever meaning their work has must arise from the felt and described circumstances of life rather than from any imposed system of values or interpretation. The writers Coles admires insist that their work is not fantasy, not artifice, but the very stuff of human life arranged into art without losing any of its gritty authenticity. As Coles said of Williams, he "could only be introspective or abstract in response to a concrete human situation or predicament. He was, again, the opposite of a metaphysical poet. . . . If there was to be transcendence, and one keeps hoping and working for it, then it will take place here on earth, in the human mind: a new ordering or reality, a diferent vision of what is possible."[23] Agee and Williams, O'Connor and Orwell, Bowen and George Eliot—these writers reveal the beauty and terror of this world and its inhabitants in all their "thereness." They resist commentary, summary, and premature interpretation, and avoid nudging the reader toward symbolic readings.

Robert Coles's profiles in *Children of Crisis* are marked by a tension between his desire to be absent from the narration as much as possible, and his awareness that he is inevitably implicated as author, or "translator," as we have preferred to call him. It should not be surprising then if the same tension between presence and absence should also mark Coles's literary criticism.

Coles admires authors who efface themselves from the text, who see themselves as conduits for the characters and situations they have observed. Sometimes, as with Orwell or Agee, there is a progressive political or at least humanitarian dimension to their literary work. These writers intend to provide a voice for the voiceless, a channel for the lives of people otherwise missing from public discourse and awareness. Coles joins them and other writers whom he admires—Georges Bernanos, Simone Weil—in rejecting the notion that meaning in the world comes only through intellect, through systematic analysis. Living the truly good life does not require the tools of graduate education or even the particular gifts of writers or artists.

There is, however, another side, or at least another dimension, to Coles's literary criticism, another tradition he finds invigorating. Novelist and essayist Walker Percy represents that tradition, a combination of existentialism and pragmatism. In the introduction to his study of Percy, *Walker Percy: an American Search,* Coles makes clear his debt to the Southern writer:

> Much of the work I have been doing since the late 1950s, represented by the five volumes of *Children of Crisis,* has been devoted to the evocation for others of the introspective thoughts, philosophical speculations, and ethical concerns I have heard a number of different American children express during various conversations. I have relied upon Dr. Percy's ideas constantly in the course of that work—to the point that I can scarcely imagine how I would have thought about either my own life or the lives of the children, parents, teachers I have met, were he to have decided, long ago, to keep his important and instructive thoughts to himself, deny them the access to others that essays offer in one way, the novel offers in another.

Indeed, Percy has influenced Coles not only in this general inspirational way, but also by way of method. Again referring to his book on Percy's fiction and essays, Coles writes, "Much is written in my profession about 'methodology.' Perhaps these pages furnish evidence of the kind of 'research' I have attempted over the years—*search* may be the better word."[24]

Coles's book on Walker Percy is his longest and most sustained piece of literary criticism to date, more fully developed than his essays in *Irony in the Mind's Life* or his books on Williams and O'Connor. In the opening chapter, "Philosophical Roots," Coles observes that the same writers and thinkers influential upon him also shaped Walker Percy's outlook. In particular, both are indebted to the work and example of Søren Kierkegaard. In 1952, Coles reminds us, W. H. Auden wrote an essay on Kierkegaard in which he stressed the example of the life over the philosophical contribution of the nineteenth-century Dane. Kierkegaard's whole effort, says Auden, was to oppose the separation of systems of thought from lived human experience, beginning with his own life. The life then becomes the fountainhead of thought, and thought reflects back upon the felt experience, an extension of the life.[25]

Historian of philosophy William Barrett echoes Auden's shift away from categories of thought to the intersection of life and reflection. Kierkegaard was concerned, says Barrett, with the meaning of the Christian life in daily, specific terms. As he pursued this question, his fellow Danes' public profession of their Christianity seemed to him increasingly false, hypocritical, and nauseating. He concluded that he was living in a society that had wholly institutionalized and thus neutered the original radical and transformative faith of Jesus. Out of his desire to live an authentic and uncompromising life, Kierkegaard gave up his engagement to be married, and the promise of an uneventful but happy life, and lived out his days in Copenhagen, a figure of public ridicule.[26]

This decision, to forswear a place in society, was accompanied by Kierkegaard's insistence that the pursuit of truth by attainment of objective knowledge was barren. All genuine truth is subjective, he argued, an engagement of knower and subject in relationship.

> When the question of truth is raised in an objective manner, reflection is directed objectively to the truth, as an object to which the knower is related. Reflection is not focused on the relationship, however. . . . If only the object to which he is related is the truth, the subject is accounted to be in the truth. When the question of the truth is raised subjectively, reflection is directed subjectively to the nature of the individual's relationship.[27]

Pursuit of the ethical life, which society promotes, involves the search for what we are pleased to call universal truths, while the religious life, which can only be personal and particular, usually involves violating the community's code of acceptable behavior.

Sitting in the park at the center of Copenhagen, his favorite haunt, Kierkegaard reflected on the successes of so many of his generation in making life materially more comfortable and philosophically more understandable. "It occurred to him then," writes William Barrett, "that since everyone was engaged everywhere in making things easy, perhaps someone might be needed to make things hard again; that life might become so easy that people would want the difficult back again; and that this might be a career and destiny for him."[28]

Kierkegaard was engaged here in what Walker Percy calls a "rotation," a deliberate stepping out of the ordinary, a breaking of the spell of everydayness. Much of Percy's work, both the philosophical essays and his novels, consists of describing rotations and their consequences. As Percy's commentator, Coles pays particular attention to rotation and to a variant of rotation, "repetition." In this mode, the subject deliberately reenters a familiar place or situation in order to reexperience it with heightened consciousness.

Coles sees in Percy a fascination with new angles on ordinary life, achieved through rotation and repetition. In "The Man on the Train," for example, Percy describes New York commuters as alienated, trapped selves. Imagine a situation, he says, in which a commuter could be taken off the train, could see in more detail and with more immediacy the life he had only glimpsed flying by his window. This stepping out, or "zone crossing," represents the initial break with an alienated situation. In movie-watching, says Percy, a lifelong film fan, the viewers are engaged in zone crossings, stepping out of their ordinary experiences into something strange, then returning to life. In Percy's first novel, *The Moviegoer,* Binx Bolling is in search of that rotation, that zone crossing that will break the grip of his alienated ordinary life and lift him into a fuller and richer existence.

Percy develops the notions of alienation, rotation, zone crossing, and repetition more fully in "The Loss of the Creature." Here Percy notes how difficult it is to see anything on one's own, because perception is so clouded by prior experiences and by cultural frames of reference. Seeing the Grand Canyon, for example, is supremely difficult because viewers have distinct preconceptions about how it is "supposed" to look. How can we break through these assumptions and see authentically, freshly, with our own eyes? Various strategies are possible: One might seek an unused path to gain a different angle of vision. But since taking an unused path might itself easily become a predictable response, one might "deliberately seek out the most beaten track of all, the most commonplace tour imaginable." All these strategies, Coles says, represent attempts to recover our own "sovereignty," our own authentic being.

As with "The Loss of the Creature," Coles is moved and exhilarated by Percy's essay "The Message in the Bottle." Here Percy imagines the self as a castaway on a strange island who has settled down, married one of the inhabitants, and made a life for himself. Walking the beach, the castaway comes upon bottles with messages stuck in them. What distinguishes these messages? Some, Percy explains, are pieces of information that are true everywhere and to all people. Others are what he calls "news," the truth of which depends on the specific situation and receptivity of the hearer. The distinction between information and news echoes Kierkegaard's distinction between objective and subjective knowledge, between truth out there and truth in here. For Percy, the Christian gospel is an example of such "news from across the sea." Unlike a piece of information, the gospel requires receptivity from the hearer for it to be meaningful; it also demands a response. The message in that particular bottle is true only if one chooses to make it true.

In many of his essays, Percy seeks to work out the existentialist insight that twentieth-century people are trapped in banal, repetitious, meaningless lives and rarely recognize that this is so. Freedom requires acknowledgment of one's condition, an effort to break the grip of the ordinary. Notions like alienation, rotation, and repetition suggest a struggle between culture and the individual, in which the self wrestles to burst free of conventions and experience life intensely and authentically. But there is another side to Percy's philosophical reflections and another theme in his novels. Like Coles and Williams, he is a doctor, though nonpracticing. He is impressed not only with the solitary splendor and freedom of the self, but also with the collective dimension of life. In several essays on language and symbol, Percy addresses the theme of intersubjectivity.

Walker Percy is decidedly unsympathetic with any system of thought that seems to him reductionist or determinist. For example, Percy asks, how does one explain language itself? In "The Delta Factor," he constructs several answers. The physiologist might describe neural episodes along synaptic pathways that link the sensing agents with various sectors of the brain. The psychologist may focus on the repetition of external stimuli and may map responses to the environment. The linguist may describe the structure of language. But what *is* language? What goes on when we speak and listen, write and read? Percy claims that no single explanation is sufficient. Language, particularly symbolic language, is fundamentally an attribute of humanity: The ability to communicate symbolically is a central defining mark of being human.

In so treating language as symbol and as distinctly human, Percy is in company with several other thinkers—Gabriel Marcel, George Herbert Mead, Harry Stack Sullivan. They all propose, in varying ways, that human consciousness cannot be fully achieved or realized in isolation from others. To be human, despite Kierkegaard's witness to the contrary, requires communion with others.

Here then is the dialogue, or tension, in Percy's work, the twin themes that wind through his esays and novels. Escape from alienation requires rotation, a seizing of freedom often at the expense of norms and expectations. Zone crossing is done one person at a time. On the other hand, full humanity requires language, which is collective and shared, a joint production of the entire species.

Robert Coles is drawn equally to both sides of Walker Percy. The incident on the Biloxi beach was a "rotation" for Coles, a moment in which he was lifted out of the ordinary and propelled, however unwillingly, into a new awareness and subsequently a new career. Bored, restless, uncertain about his future, Coles was, in short, alienated. His witness of the "swim-in" was bitter and painful, but it was a genuine rotation, the first of his many "zone crossings."

Partly through Percy's inspiration, partly through his own growing sensitivity to finding spiritual insight in unexpected places, Coles finds himself listening for moments of rotation in the lives of his subjects. A young migrant woman, slowly dying of congestive heart disease, tells him,

> My lungs are bad, and I can't catch the air very good. Suddenly, I'll see my youngest child, and she'll be coming to me, and I'll be different. It's not a second breath of air. I'm still struggling for the first breath! It's God, giving me His strength. It's me becoming a different me; I'm free of my old weary self. . . . I'm a new person. For a few minutes I'm almost a stranger to myself, that's what, because I feel like this new person.[29]

But however private these moments are, they require language for communication. And language, as the recent French critics have reminded us, is abstractive and linear, its use involving a fundamental separation from the original experience it seeks to convey.

What attracts Robert Coles to Walker Percy is the Southerner's struggle to maintain a creative tension between the opposing claims of empirical truth and intuitive truth. This is, I think, what Coles means in the introduction to his study of Percy when he calls him an "American and Christian" existentialist: American, in Percy's respect for pragmatism and empiricism, in his interest in concrete particulars; Christian, in the Kierkegaardian sense of accepting the truth-claim of the Gospel rather than constructing elaborate systems to "prove" its truth; existentialist, in his preoccupation with alienation and in his emphasis on the need for rotation and repetition to break the grip of the ordinary.

Coles's preference for certain writers parallels the issues that concern him as a social psychiatrist. He has worked to immerse himself in the lives of ordinary people in times of crisis, in order to reveal the interplay between individual lives and the social and cultural context. He has insisted on his role as a conduit, a pipeline for the voices and views of others. In his literary criticism, he admires writers who also sought to immerse themselves in the lives of others. Whatever larger meanings or symbolic significance may arise from that literature, Coles concludes, is already there in the stories and lives of Williams's and Agee's and O'Connor's and Orwell's hard-pressed people, the artist only providing the words to set it free.

On the other hand, Coles acknowledges that *Children of Crisis* is a composed work, not simply a transcription. These volumes comprise the patient weaving together of many testimonies and interviews taken over time; the words, says Coles, belong to the subjects, but the order is his own. Thus, *Children of Crisis* is the product of an artist who, however deeply sympathetic he is to his material, must also stand at some distance from it. This side of Coles, the artist, the person who stands apart, is drawn to the work of Walker Percy. Percy himself stands apart—a doctor who does not practice medicine, a novelist who writes articles for philosophical journals, a philosopher who scorned the positivism of the 1950s and chose to write novels instead. Rooted in the work of Kierkegaard, Heidegger, Marcel, rotation and repetition are after all the insights of intellectuals, people like Percy and Coles.

What do the works of Agee and Williams and that of Percy have to say to one another? How do the opposing tendencies of observer and friend, of dispassionate interviewer and creative artist, of intellect and character—how might these find their place in one self? Perhaps these two stances can be synthesized after all. Moments of existential insight, Coles realizes with Percy's help, are not limited to intellectuals, artists, the well-educated and well-fed. That such rotations may happen to anyone is powerful proof that no systematic explanation of behavior will suffice, no cultural or psychological or biological theory can fully account for such moments of illumination. They are, simply, mysteries.

All people, Coles concludes, regardless of class or education, may have flashes of intuition, may regain their sovereignty. Further, all people seek to express themselves in language, for that is a mark of their humanity. If artists have a particular gift of expression, that does not mean that they alone have had great moments of insight; it simply means that they have found the words, or the audience, or the opportunity for expression. By looking at Coles's literary criticism in its entirely, we can see that it is possible to be faithful to the existential view embraced by Kierkegaard and interpreted by Percy. It is also possible to be faithful to the vision of William Carlos Williams and James Agee, who wished to take their readers into the life experience of others without patronizing or distorting that experience.

I have offered a rather schematic view of Coles's literary affinities, with Williams and Percy representing distinct and opposing polarities. But like many schemas, this one offers analytic simplicity but sacrifices depth and complexity. We need to look again at the impressive range of writers Coles has written on and currently teaches in several courses at Harvard University. Coles engages in a form of moral criticism as he comments on these various authors and texts, echoing in his criticism the moral vision he discerns in his literary subjects.

"You teach through lives," Robert Coles once remarked; "you teach through stories, through autobiography, through poetry." To a visitor who remarked on the way certain writers recur in Coles's written work and in his teaching, he replied, "That reading list is really my personal reading list. I get reconnected with Agee, with *Paterson,* with Orwell. . . . They're 'art,' in the nonpejorative sense of the word, and I'm afraid that's where I am too; I love Silone, Orwell, Agee, Percy, O'Connor."[30]

What exactly attracts Coles to this disparate array of American, English, and European writers? "What they have in common," he once responded to an interviewer, "is that they've struggled with moral and religious issues. They have had their literary sides . . . and . . . there is the issue of service, the 'haunting question,' 'what does one owe?'"[31] In very different ways, then, the writers to whom Coles has been drawn seek to combine fidelity to their literary craft with a passion for the world. As commentator, Coles highlights not so much their craft, their wit, subtlety, wordplay, and allusion, as their moral vision, their imaginative appropriation of a real world of struggle, suffering, and redemption.

It is a vast understatement to say that moral criticism is in the eclipse at the present moment. Feminist criticism partakes of a distinctly moral vision and set of commitments, but even this criticism (and one does it an injustice by implying that there is a singular entity called "feminist criticism") is much entangled with the currently fashionable approach of poststructuralism.

In the broadest sense, much contemporary literary theory derives from the great nineteenth and early-twentieth century "masters of suspicion," Marx, Nietszche, and Freud. Marx has taught us to suspect claims to universality as fronts for class-based political and economic privilege. Nietszche exposed claims for sentiment and good taste as hypocritical *ressentiment*. And Freud showed that rational behavior is rooted in unconscious drives and desires, stemming in large part from repressed childhood traumas.[32]

It is the spirit of Friedrich Nietszche that has most infused current critical practice. Jacques Derrida and Michel Foucault, to name the two most influential critics, have used Nietszche's insights to uncover the metaphysical claims in literary texts and reveal them to be politically and culturally provincial rather than universal. In exposing these claims, critics engage in a kind of power struggle with the author and text. Having come belatedly to the text, critics desire to be not subservient and deferential, but aggressive and domineering, and find in the act of exposure of the text's metaphysical claims a way of gaining leverage over the text. Nonetheless, the reading of any particular critic is soon supplanted by that of another, so textual engagement is a series of never-ending layers of reading over reading over reading.[33]

This radical approach assumes that there is no correct reading of a literary text, that changing culture and changing arrangements of power alter one's reading, and therefore alter the text itself. One is typically over against the text, suspicious of its claims, eager to discover its contingencies rather than its universalities. The reader is left with an ingenious arrangement of words that assumes radically different meanings to different generations of readers. As Giles Gunn puts it, "All cultural forms are viewed as more or less arbitrary constructions which bear little or no intrinsic relation to the things to which they refer, thus making of culture itself, and all talk about it, a web of artificial and largely self-serving constructs."[34]

In contrast to this sophisticated set of theories and methods, moral criticism seems not merely hopelessly quaint, but also dangerous, a relic of an age of intellectual imperialism and narrow-mindedness. Tolstoy's emphasis on the communicatory function of art—"a means of union among men, joining them together in the same feelings and indispensable for the life and progress toward well-being of individuals and of humanity"[35]—would seem ludicrous to those who see art as historically and culturally determined. More recently, in *On Moral Fiction*, John Gardner put forward an argument similar to Tolstoy's. The task of the artist, Gardner proposes, is to work out in narrative the timeless truths about fidelity and courage and self-sacrifice that humanity, or at any rate Western civilization, has traditionally upheld. Unlike some contemporary literary critics like Geoffrey Hartman, who see criticism as a kind of equally matched competitor to art, Gardner sharply distinguishes between the two activities:

> The critic's proper business is explanation and evaluation, which means he must make use of his analytic powers to translate the concrete to the abstract. . . . To understand a critic, one needs a clear head and a sensitive heart, but not great powers of imagination. To understand a complex work of art, one must be something of an artist oneself. Thus criticism and art, like theology and religion, are basically companions but not always friends. At times they may be enemies."[36]

In his championing of fiction that is traditionally narrative, densely plotted and thematic, even philosophical, Gardner put himself strenuously at odds with much postmodernist fiction. In reply, *his* critics charged him with being fussy, cranky, ad hominem in his attacks, and simply nostalgic for an imagined time of secure beliefs.[37]

In Tolstoy's insistence that the greatest art is ultimately Christian art, and in Gardner's rejection of contemporary fiction as unplotted and therefore immoral, we find examples of what Giles Gunn has called the tradition of critical moralism. Together with other practitioners over several generations like Paul Elmer More, Irving Babbitt, Ivor Winters, Randall Stewart, and T. S. Eliot, these critics have sought to measure art against a "secure moral standard" derived from tradition and/or religion.

Gunn has identified another kind of moral criticism, however, one that avoids the moralism and bitterness of Tolstoy and Gardner, and one which, I suggest, Robert Coles practices. "To writers like [Edmund] Wilson, [Lionel] Trilling, Kenneth Burke, and others, literature does not criticize life overtly . . . but covertly, as Dewey suggested, by disclosing to the imagination specific possibilities that contrast with the actual conditions."[38]

In linking together such a wide variety of critics, and adding to their number such writers as Alfred Kazin, R. W. B. Lewis, and Barbara Herrnstein Smith, Gunn sees the common element in their work as fidelity to experience. Indebted to the American pragmatism of William James and John Dewey, these moral critics seek to identify and hold up texts in which moral claims are worked out in specific, concrete circumstances. Even more, they claim, texts in all their specificity and historicism engage us, the reader. In their "otherness" they present a mode of being different from the one we are accustomed to, and thus expand our sense of the possible. The critics Gunn prefers engage in a kind of dialogical criticism, in which text and reader confront each other in their differentness, and yet in which the reader learns how to enlarge his/her world in response to that confrontation.

The best literature, then, presents us with experience; experience we had not known or imagined, or had known but not in that particular shape. Literature is not philosophy or criticism, but experience heightened and shaped so as to tease out its essence. Such literature, especially in our own time, is achieved through a process of "decreation," as Simone Weil calls it, a return to authentic experience beneath the cultural accretions, fantasies, and illusions, "Ivan Ilych's discovery of the suffocating darkness of death that can sometimes inexplicably provide a tentative opening to the light."[39]

This return is of course precisely what poststructuralist critics deny. To them, there is no center to text or experience; no core to descend to. Each interpretation is provisional, each determination of meaning contingent on historical and cultural qualifiers. But other writers share Weil's plea for a decreative plunge back to authentic experience and Gunn's appreciation of critics who find in the act of reading such an experience. Josephine Donovan, in an echo of Tolstoy, argues that all great art is sustained by the integrity of a moral vision. "The aesthetic dimension of literature and of film cannot be divorced from the moral dimension, as we have facilely come to assume under the influence of technique-oriented critical methodologies." All art assumes a moral order larger than itself. As a feminist critic, Donovan attacks works that deny moral efficacy and consciousness to women, a list that is long indeed.[40]

As Donovan constructs her argument that aesthetic elements must be integrated with moral vision, she relies on the work of Iris Murdoch. In "On 'God' and 'Good,'" Murdoch points out the realism of Freud's description of human behavior:

> Freud takes a thoroughly pessimistic view of human nature. He sees the psyche as an egocentric system of quasi-mechanical energy, largely determined by its own individual history, whose natural attachments are sexual, ambiguous, and hard for the subject to understand or control. Introspection reveals only the deep tissue of ambivalent motive, and fantasy is a stronger force than reason. Objectivity and unselfishness are not natural to human beings."[41]

In this analysis, Murdoch's central term is fantasy, by which she means the human's propensity for self-aggrandizement, for indulgence in illusion and falsity. Such propensity is quite natural, she says, given humanity's psychic makeup. Fantasy for Murdoch is similar to Simone Weil's "gravity," mechanical and ordinary responses, filling the void of our lives with imaginings that give a false sense of significance.

For Donovan, Murdoch, and Weil, as indeed for William James and John Dewey as Giles Gunn understands them, true human liberation is found in cutting through fantasy, loosening the grip of gravity, getting out from "under the net," to use the title of one of Murdoch's novels. "The greatest art is impersonal, because it shows us the world, our world and not another one, with a clarity that startles and delights us simply because we are not used to looking at the real world at all."[42] Ultimately, says Murdoch, and the others would agree, it is *love* that motivates such liberating vision, for love demands an awareness of realities beyond the self, a notion similar to Simone Weil's concept of "attention." The sense of *otherness* conveyed in literature, Giles Gunn affirms, reminds us of the world beyond the self, and encourages a "conversation" in which the text is brought to life and the reader actively involved and quite possibly changed.

Moral criticism, the kind Gunn prefers and which Murdoch and Donovan, among many others, practice, focuses not on theory so much as on story. This is not to say that moral critics are not theoretically sophisticated; Murdoch's essays, like Trilling's or Gunn's, put that suspicion to rest. Rather, these critics insist that literature is not the same as its paraphrasable content. The emphasis of criticism should be refocused on literature's narrative elements. Stories are the author's shaping of life's messy facticity into coherence and order. Stories are inherently moral, says Nathan A. Scott, Jr., because they lead us to ask: What happened? To whom? Why? Then what? Is the future open or closed?[43] As R. W. B. Lewis pointed out some time ago, whatever moral vision there is in literature needs to be teased out of the unique and particular features of its narrative or lyric or dramatic life.[44] Whatever ideas literature contains are embodied ideas, ideas brought to life in specific situations. Hence all these people in one way or another can be called "pragmatists," according to William James's description, for they turn "away from abstraction and insufficiency, from verbal solutions, from bad *a priori* reasons, from fixed principles, closed systems, and pretended absolutes and origins." They turn "toward concreteness and adequacy, toward facts, towards action and towards power. . . . [Pragmatism] means the open air and possibilities of nature, as against dogma, artificiality, and the pretence of finality in truth."[45] For James as for the others, "ideas (which themselves are but parts of our experience) become true just in so far as they help us get into satisfactory relation with other parts of our experience."[46]

For Robert Coles, the writers in his "reading list" possess just such "love" or "attention" as Iris Murdoch or Simone Weil hails as prerequisite to great art. James Agee, Elizabeth Bowen, and George Eliot, the subjects of *Irony in the Mind's Life*, are all master storytellers. In their novels "there most certainly are points of view to be found. These are, however, tied to concrete situations summoned and fashioned by the novelist's imagination."[47] The same rootedness and love of the particular draws him to Flannery O'Connor. Like other American regionalists, O'Connor probes large human issues by looking hard at one particular region, and refusing to separate moral concerns, which she obviously possesses, from the lives of people she observes and fictionalizes. Robert Fitzgerald's observation of another "regionalist," William Carlos Williams, equally applies to Flannery O'Connor and indeed to many of Coles's favorite authors: "The good thing about the intelligent anti-intellectual is that he scents with appropriate alarm the dangers of committing himself to abstract attitudes that a later or rougher or rounder experience would show up; he distrusts not only 'those large words that make people unhappy,' but all the apparatus of ideas that can get in between us and the things we do or witness."[48] That is, the authors on Coles's reading list work to decreate, to plunge beneath convention and self-preoccupation and narcissism, to recover authentic experience, sometimes their own (as in Agee's autobiographical novel *A Death in the Family*), more often that of the world they so keenly observe, as in Eliot's *Middlemarch* or Dickens's *Bleak House* or *Great Expectations*.

Still, to recur to the tension we earlier observed in Coles, between reporting and creating, these writers do not simply record. William James did not recommend seeking truth in experience if he did not believe there was a truth there to be found; R. W. B. Lewis did not believe that moral vision would emerge from narrative complexity if he did not think it was there in the first place, or that people were incapable of discerning it. As Josephine Donovan said, aesthetics imply ethics.

As they listen and observe and write, the authors Coles admires do indeed discern echoes, intimations, of a moral vision, and for most of them it can justly be called a biblical vision. Calling it "biblical" returns us, belatedly, to the "figural" interpretation of reality Erich Auerbach offered of the biblical narratives: characters and situations fully themselves, concrete, earthy, conflicted, yet redolent of larger mysteries and incarnational truth. The sense of human potential and failure, the omnipresence of sin and the promise of redemption, the ironic and mixed nature of life, all this may be found in O'Connor and Shirley Anne Grau, in Percy and George Eliot, in Tolstoy and Dostoevsky, in Orwell and Agee. Even in Freud and Williams, who were hostile to religion, one finds a secular equivalent to biblical realism. This sense of the mixed nature of life, to repeat, is not simply presented and discussed; it is shown working itself out in particular life situations. Of George Eliot's *Middlemarch,* Coles notes, "Certainly Dorothea is at all times a genuinely decent person. . . . Her suitor, then husband, Casaubon, is so obviously pretentious and humorless. She is the woman desirous of doing good. . . . He is the dried-up pedant whose appetites are larger than his capacities." And yet Dorothea exhibits a distinct and damaging sense of pride in her desire to "save" him, to reclaim him for the human community.[49] George Eliot is remarkably our contemporary, Coles observed elsewhere, in her desire to fathom the inner life, the mix of emotions, the combination of instinct and desire. Hers is a mind at ease with irony, unafraid of uncertainty, ambiguity, and complexity.[50]

Clearly this synthesis of experience with moral, particularly biblical, vision is exactly what Coles intends for his own writing. He steadily refuses to moralize and summarize, insisting that the stories of his many "subjects" are his main concern. Whatever larger truth or significance there is, in the lives of Appalachian miners and farmers, in the reflections of the old ones in New Mexico, in the angry outbursts of black ghetto youth, must arise from their words, their stories. As Coles once heard William Carlos Williams say, "The stories develop their own energy; they take over—leaving me behind. . . . If I've managed to get rid of myself as an annoyance to the reader, but still give the best of myself and what I've experienced to that reader—then the effort has been worth it, and is a success."[51] Coles wants very much to cultivate a certain detachment, an irony, that he found most attractive among Indian, Chicano, and Eskimo children: "a tendency toward ironic self-effacement, as a counter to the very real danger of over-sentimentalizing."[52] In any event, while Coles does much commenting, shaping, narrating, the center of his work, he would insist, is these stories, stories, stories of ordinary people. Indeed, in the popular two-volume *Women of Crisis* there is no commentary at all, except brief introductions to each volume; it is simply one story after another of desperate and courageous women.

We have tried to widen our sense of Robert Coles as reader of literature, seeing him operate in a tradition of moral criticism, attracted to books that are rich in human experience and sensitive to moral issues. No analytic or descriptive category, however, can quite explain the long fascination that Georges Bernanos's *The Diary of a Country Priest* has held for Coles. "I have read it and reread it, and I keep it in front of me on my desk." The 1937 novel possesses an almost scriptural status for him: "Something particularly provocative or troubling has taken place, in my own life or in the larger world that we all share, and I am drawn to 'The Diary,' drawn to a number of well-marked passages." Coles had read the novel first while in college, and then again while in psychiatric residency in Boston after hearing Paul Tillich refer to it in a lecture. Now, as he says, it is his constant companion.[53]

The novel takes as its fictional device the diary of a young curé in a remote French village. Very little happens to the young man, who is already ill when the novel opens and dies at its end. He conducts catechisms, says weekly masses, visits an older priest who tries repeatedly to rouse him out of his agonized self-doubt and introspection. He has various dealings with the local gentry, a decaying noble family— philandering husband, rebellious daughter, grieving mother. In the most memorable passage of the book, the young priest confronts the countess with the way she has been carefully cultivating grief for her dead son as a way of insulating herself from the possibility of comfort and solace, proudly blaming God, as it were, for her own continuing isolation. As background to these small but intense human dramas is the dull village and landscape, where it seems always to be raining steadily on the mass of dispirited, poor citizens.

It is hard at first to see exactly what in this story appeals to Coles. The novel is slow, wordy, sometimes pretentious. While the device of the diary allows us both to see and to judge the character of the curé, it allows us to know only as much of the other characters as the priest himself understands. Consequently, the others, including the countess, seem wooden and lifeless.

Perhaps its very elliptical quality, its gnomic, scriptural aspect, is what Coles finds appealing. In several commentaries on the novel, he tells us more. For all his self-doubt, naïveté, awkwardness, the priest is also "honest, strong, and clear."[54] He is, in short, just that combination of "self-doubt, genuine humility and blindness" that Coles so admires in fictional characters and in real life. The curé is after all a man trained, in those pre-Vatican II days, to have the answers, to channel the grace which makes for eternal salvation. Yet he is tormented with his own inadequacies and with the failure of the Church; he finds himself and his institution lacking both pastoral skill and prophetic insight.

Most of all, Bernanos depicts his hero as a child, and for Coles the figure of the child is an enormously suggestive and attractive one. Like Agee in *A Death in the Family* and Freud in *Three Lectures on Infantile Sexuality,* Bernanos rejects both the Lockean and the Romantic views of the child. Neither *tabula rasa* nor uncannily insightful and winningly innocent, the priest-as-child is disarming, direct, even wise. He is also thoughtless, even cruel at times. As Freud knew, the child demonstrates the same mixed, ambivalent, unpredictable traits that the adult does, but often without the guile and easy smoothness of adults. And, says Coles, Bernanos, like Freud, sees the child as a continuing reality in the adult life long after puberty.[55]

I suppose it is correct to say that *The Diary of a Country Priest* presents a nearly pure form of introspection. The plot, what plot there is, is skeletal, the other characters simply foils for the hero. The setting is monochromatic; the focus is nearly all interior. The curé struggles with himself, with his calling, his background, his adequacy, his doubts, his insights. He is, after all, a marginal man, appalled by the apathy of his parishioners, by the venality of the Church and the corruption of the State. He does his duty, angers the powerful and well-connected count, alienates his flock, struggles against the despair that rains down like the steady downpours that drench the village. It is a book to appeal to the introspect, the Calvinist, the Augustinian, yes, the Puritan. And it is Robert Coles's favorite book.

·4·

Psychology, Psychiatry, and Children

*F*or all his antipathy to orthodox psychoanalysis, Robert Coles does in fact share a good deal in common with its founder. Despite his early medical training, Sigmund Freud moved steadily away from physiological explanations and toward psychological readings of much human behavior. Resisting the reigning materialist bias of the late nineteenth century, Freud adopted what we might call an "interdisciplinary" approach to mental and emotional disorders, searching for an understanding of "human concerns."

Freud argued that neurosis was not an external, invasive threat; rather, it was part of character. Thus, illness is woven into the very fabric of being. Its cure, he believed, required not diagnosis and cure, in which the pathogen might be isolated and removed, but renarrative and recovery. Patient and therapist rehearse the historical record of the individual, bringing to the surface buried elements that help explain current behavior. In all this, illness, like every other element, becomes a language of the self. And each self speaks a unique language. The work of therapy, at least as Freud saw it, was not predictive; rather, it was individual and historical.

In his masterful creation of an archeological method by which to grasp the hidden, buried life of the self, with all its powerful influence on behavior both personal and social, Freud made full use of his remarkable erudition and enormous range of reading. As Bruno Bettelheim has pointed out, Freud's German is richly allusive and poetic, relying on verbal echoes and puns to flesh out his sharp analytic insights. In his use of the Oedipus myth, says Bettelheim, Freud assumed an audience familiar with this story and its implications. But in translation, Freud's humanistic German becomes a coolly and rigidly "scientific" English prose, the deliberately ambiguous use of words now codified into fixed terminology.[1]

Another kind of translation, this one across the Atlantic in the late

1930s and the 1940s, also resulted in a substantial alteration of Freud's original vision. In the 1920s, psychoanalysis in Europe was linked with various radical movements, with Marxism and feminism, and with its Jewish theoreticians and practitioners. In the hands of such figures as Otto Fenichel, Kate Friedlander, and Annie Reich, Freudianism was becoming an influential means to criticize repressive social institutions. These "political Freudians," as Russell Jacoby calls them, linked psychic difficulties with political structures. But with the advent of National Socialism, such analysis was severely criticized and increasingly dangerous, and political Freudians joined the great diaspora of European intellectuals to England and the United States.[2]

During the 1930s, American students of psychiatry tended to be cautious and conformist, lacking the humanist or political convictions of an earlier generation. Interested primarily in personal therapy for wealthy clients, American psychiatrists looked with alarm at the landing of European therapists and theorists.

One issue in particular divided Europeans and Americans: the medicalization of psychiatry. In the 1920s, the majority of psychiatrists and psychotherapists were lay people, without a medical degree; among their numbers were Anna Freud and Erik Erikson. By the 1940s, the medical establishment had emerged victorious in their struggle to require that certified psychiatrists have an M.D. degree. This shift toward the medical dominance of psychiatry was indicative of the entire postwar direction of the profession, according to several critical observers.[3]

When Robert Coles entered his psychiatric residency in 1955, the prestige of orthodox psychoanalysis was at its height. There were, to be sure, other approaches: Ego psychologists like Erik Erikson and Anna Freud and neo-Freudians like Erich Fromm and Karen Horney all claimed lineage from Sigmund Freud. But the professionals at the New York Psychiatric Institute and the Boston Psychoanalytic Institute, and somewhat less so the New Orleans Psychoanalytic Institute were the genuine "true believers," the protectors of a sacred faith, an orthodoxy. A medically trained practitioner confronts a patient manifesting certain symptoms. A case history is recorded, clinical observations are made, a complex and technical language is employed to describe the symptoms and probable cause. Variables are reduced or ignored—social, cultural, historical dimensions are bracketed away as too fluid for scientific treatment. A judgment is given: The patient suffers from some form of neurosis or, even worse, a psychosis. A course of treatment is prescribed, usually more therapy. The central thrust of such analysis is the redefinition of the patient's situation, away from the language he or she employs, full of irrelevancies, vague, wandering, repetitious, and toward a sharp, well-defined, theoretically defensible and clinically useful language.[4]

This was, in any event, the intellectual system that Coles was absorbing in the mid-1950s. Powerfully analytical, it was also powerfully reductionist. His mother was among the first to point out to him the arrogance of behavior, in which the search for the *real* motive had become virtually second nature, even a kind of parlor game. After observing a group of psychiatric residents practicing on one another, his mother chided Coles, "What is the point to all that self-consciousness? Why do you all *behave* that way? It is so silly; and so boring, I have to add."[5]

Her words hit the target. Coles was already feeling restless and unhappy as he neared the end of his residency. He would soon be a certified psychiatrist, with a practice of his own. But he had such doubts: "why do some people become 'sick' while others from equally troublesome backgrounds stay reasonably well? What about the millions of people on this planet who have never heard of psychiatry, or would never think of seeing a psychiatrist, or never be able to afford one? Do they know things about survival, endurance, courage, growth, strength that make people like me seem arrogant and narrow-minded [?]"[6]

Coles's patients had the odd effect of corroborating his growing doubts about his chosen profession. He volunteered to work in an outpatient clinic for alcoholics, and in another clinic that offered "medical and psychiatric assistance to delinquent youths."[7] He found the men and women of skid row stunning in their honesty, in the power of their "outrageous and often refreshing questions." And the juvenile delinquents, labeled "borderline," socio- or psychopathic, he found "bright, warm, affectionate, witty, in their own way honorable . . . intensely loyal."[8]

One young man in particular he recalls, a car thief and armed robber. Coles's work, his supervisor insisted, was to discern the oedipal mother-son relationship, in which the stolen car represented forbidden sexuality. But was it not important, Coles wondered, though only briefly, that this boy was black, that his family had recently come North, that they lived in poverty, in the ghetto?[9]

Another young patient memorably penetrated the mask of objectivity that young psychiatric residents labor to perfect and assume during therapy. It was in fact his very first patient, a twelve-year-old boy who suffered from a variety of intense fears. Carefully, the young psychiatrist allowed the boy to talk around the subject, but gradually Coles grew frustrated at their lack of progress.

One day, the boy announced that he knew the doctor wouldn't be able to "budge him," to break through his silences and evasions. Even more, he was convinced the doctor was "hiding something." It turned out that upon another visit to the hospital, the boy had seen Coles wearing an Adlai Stevenson campaign button (this was during the 1956 election year), but that during their sessions he had carefully removed it, to maintain professional objectivity. The boy went on to observe that college professors admired Stevenson, but that Eisenhower was clearly the superior leader, since he "beat the Nazis."

"I'd never before even thought of politics as a likely or appropriate subject for psychotherapy with adults," much less with children. He had been taught that political opinions were often masks for private attitudes, that the therapist was obliged to penetrate this subterfuge and determine what the client was "really" saying.[10]

Coles tells this story in the Introduction to *The Political Life of Children* to indicate his growing awareness of the place of politics in the shaping of character. But the story may equally stand for his emerging sense that human reality is far more complex and fascinating than psychoanalytic orthodoxy could admit. His residency, which was designed, like other professional programs, to produce the next generation of the keepers of the flame, had produced a misfit. Coles had learned the language, but refused to use it; he knew the interpretive framework, but saw it as profoundly inadequate.

He was glad, finally, to leave his residency, even though he had been called up for military service and assigned to, of all places, Mississippi, rather than Europe or Japan or some other interesting place. Even so, he was still pleased to begin his work as a psychiatrist even in such an unpromising setting. "There I could practice on my own and learn the value of my profession by seeing its tenets (the best of them, learned at great sacrifice and cost by Freud) come alive in concrete situations—which I was under no forced and arbitrary constraint to formulate."[11] He would be free to read those theorists who learned from Freud, but were not slavishly imitative of him:

> Erik Erikson, Anna Freud, Frieda Fromm-Reichmann, Allen Wheelis, Harold Stearns, Charles Rycroft, D. W. Winnicott—men and women who think clearly, who know how to write a straight sentence, who admit to honest uncertainty and bewilderment, who admit to and respect and even take comfort from life's ironies, and

finally men and women who don't drown their doubts and worries in a muddied, turbid river of jargon."[12]

So, by the time Coles headed for the South, he was already "righting his balance." He would, right to the present moment, work as a psychiatrist (although, he once observed, he has no stationery and sends no bills) and as a medical doctor. But the rich and subtle combination of visionary mother and practical father, of the example of Perry Miller and William Carlos Williams, had kept him from fully absorbing the orthodoxy he had fully expected to learn and then practice.

Nonetheless, Robert Coles was not yet done with classic psychoanalysis. The real "end of the affair" came not with his assignment to the air force hospital in Biloxi. It came during his own psychoanalysis. Now an air force captain and the owner of a white sports car, he would drive into New Orleans daily to attend classes at the New Orleans Psychoanalytic Institute and to continue the analysis he had begun in Boston. The officer in charge of the hospital wondered if he were not simply looking for a reason to visit the city. No, Coles responded; he seemed to be suffering from "low spirits, down in the dumps, moodiness that won't go away."[13]

Actually, Coles's escape from his continuing sense of malaise took the form of obsessive movie-going: *Purple Noon, Sunset Boulevard, East of Eden, Rebel Without a Cause.* When his own patients questioned him, confided in him, Coles would recall scenes from films he had seen repeatedly.

Then, in the fall of 1961, he happened to come upon Walker Percy's first novel, *The Moviegoer.* Coles was astounded. Here was a novelist writing about *him*, or rather, about his obsession. He read the novel all afternoon and evening. Coles was further amazed to discover that he had, after all, read Walker Percy before: That essay Paul Tillich had torn from the pages of *Partisan Review* was Percy's, and there were others, too, equally brilliant and original. At first unimpressed, his analyst finally acknowledged, "You seem to be shadowing Binx [Bolling, the novel's hero]." Years later, Coles elaborated on his analyst's insight: "I had, long ago it now seems, 'shadowed Binx,' as many of us have—lucky and comfortable heirs of Western civilization who nevertheless are quizzical, at loose ends often enough, not sure what really matters, even as we go about our appointed rounds, accumulating certifications and cash and nods and having our 'relationships.'"[14]

So here is one more irony in the life of Robert Coles: In the midst of analysis, the patient-therapist centerpiece of Freud's "talking cure,"

Coles discovers a book that uncannily mirrors his own life, a book written by an author he had in fact previously read, an author whose recording of the ambiguity of life was (yet another irony) probably closer to the spirit of Freud's "archeological" method than was the scientism of his devoted followers. That is, literature, not psychoanalytic orthodoxy, is Freud's true companion.

> The texture of any life is, in the end, a mystery—or if that word scares or embarrasses the twentieth-century reader then at the least he or she has to settle for an astonishing degree of complexity, the result of irony and contingency and paradox and inconsistency and chance or luck (good and bad) all doing their exceedingly intricate work, so that one's fate, so often regarded as linear by us in the convenience (and ambition) of retrospect, has in actuality been a matter of personal circumstances gradually emerging. . . . History both public and private has been an intensely shaping force on the development of personality, character, talent.[15]

Clearly in his work as a social psychiatrist, Robert Coles has been profoundly influenced by texts and personal example—Dorothy Day, Simone Weil, James Agee, Walker Percy, William Carlos Williams, and many others. He has been moved and instructed by stories, fictional and real, that reveal unexpected moral depth, courage, and insight, lives that cannot be reduced to formula or cliché.

Nonetheless, as we noted earlier, Coles is not unacquainted with the founders and shapers of the psychiatric and psychoanalytical movements. Coles's often conversational, even folksy, prose, generously fleshed out with quotations from his subjects, might give the impression that he is unfamiliar with the psychiatric literature. A brief perusal of the footnotes in *Children of Crisis, The Moral Life of Children,* or *The Political Life of Children* quickly dispels that suspicion. Like other maverick and original thinkers, Robert Coles picks and chooses the figures to admire. Many of these, as we have seen, are writers and artists, activists and contemplatives, restless and unconventional people. Like these mentor-figures in other areas, the psychiatrists he admires are odd, quirky, marginal, visionary.

Scattered through his books and essays are various references to Sigmund Freud. The Freud Coles most admires is the clinician, the historian of the personality. In his study of Leonardo Da Vinci, for example, Freud traces the adult's massive artistic achievement to recurring patterns and themes already apparent in childhood. How might we uncover, Freud asked in effect, the "evidence that explains some of the contradictions and ambiguities of his life?"[16]

Much as Coles admires this historical and archeological side to Freud, so he admires Freud the self-reliant pioneer. In the early years of the century, Coles reminds us, Freud was an outcast, ignored or ridiculed by the medical establishment; this treatment was made even more pointed by the kind of patient Freud chose to treat. "Anxious and fearful men and women," suffering from hysteria, sexual maladies, unexplained depressions, these Viennese were, in Coles's estimation, "unquestionably members of an oppressed minority."[17]

In listening to their stories, and in working out a method whereby the surface accounts might be mined for the buried truth, Freud became increasingly convinced of the correctness of that method, confident that eventually he would be vindicated. Nonetheless, in those early years he sought consolation and corroboration in a small circle of disciples who would later, ironically, transform his flexible humanistic method into rigid scientism. Freud thought of himself as a kind of prophet, discerning a truth the world would subsequently find illuminating.

I do not suggest that Coles thinks of himself as a latter-day Freud. It does seem evident, however, that the words he uses to describe Freud are applicable to Coles as well: outsider, removed from the dominant majority; misunderstood, "social rejection [and] constant economic insecurity over a significant stretch of his life."[18] Like Freud, Coles has chosen to work among people whom conventional practice has ignored: children, members of minority groups, the poor. In a 1964 review of the Yale study, *Social Class and Mental Illness,* Coles indicts his profession for avoiding the poor, who can ill afford psychiatric care, despite the fact that mental illness is powerfully present in the lives of the poor. The problem, of course, is that mental disturbance is usually linked with conditions of social disorganization, poverty, and injustice, with which American psychiatrists have little to do. "What do they do, these millions of our poor? What happens to their neuroses and psychoses? They live with them and die with them or of them. In cities, violence, vagrancy, alcoholism, addiction, apathy, high suicide rates, high murder rates, high delinquency rates bespeak the hopelessness which becomes depression. . . . In rural areas, on farms or reservations, the same human scene can be found: retarded children, epileptic children kept, and their limitations accepted, not as possible challenges to be overcome, but as grim reminders of an all too-familiar fate."[19]

There is another side to Freud, however, that Coles finds much less appealing. Freud once described himself as a conquistador, a world-explorer and conqueror.[20] Here, in contrast to the humanist and clinician-historian, the poet of the German language, this Freud is the determined searcher after scientific law, predictability, regularity. In his study of Leonardo, to which Coles devotes much attention in his essay "On Psychohistory," Freud combines attention to the particularities of the artist's life with grander and more sweeping interpretations. From a treatment of why Leonardo was interested in flight, Freud observes that the human desire to fly is linked to concerns about sexual performance. Leonardo's artistic triumphs derived from rebellion against his father. His mother's tenderness determined his destiny. These powerful, law-like statements derive from Freud's vision of himself as a kind of "messianic explorer," seeking patterns of behavior as yet uncharted, even unacknowledged.[21]

In "On Psychohistory," Coles charts the consequences of Freud's search for the hidden key to behavior: *This* means *that, this* childhood event/relationship/trauma determines *that* adult behavior. He reserves his greatest anger for psychobiographies of recent political figures: Bruce Mazlish's *In Search of Nixon: A Psychohistorical Inquiry* and Nancy Clinch's *The Kennedy Neurosis: A Psychological Portrait of an American Dynasty*. In the former, a complex public person is reduced to three traits: "role identification," "ambivalence," and "denial." In the latter, a book that particularly enraged Coles, judging from the uncharacteristically fierce prose, Clinch wished to cut through the Kennedy legend to expose "neurotic conflict." Parental demands led to self-destructive traits in the children. John Kennedy's fear and distrust of women led him to surround himself with males, who collaborated with him in the design of a disastrous foreign policy in Vietnam. Robert Kennedy's passion for the poor in the last years of his life is dismissed as compensation for his "underdog position in the family and the emotional insecurity he never lost."[22]

Despite his nineteenth-century mechanistic psychology, in which single causes produce identifiable results, Freud was equally aware that human personality and behavior are complex, unpredictable, even mysterious. He acknowledged in the Leonardo study that everyone experiences childhood trauma and mental/emotional disquiet as adults. The line that separates neurosis from normality is difficult to discern. "Leonardo was indeed 'obsessional,' but so are millions of other people. The real question, of course, is what Leonardo did with his life; not just with his neurosis, but with his remarkable energy."[23] Commenting on his own work, Coles writes, "increasingly these past years psychiatrists and psychoanalysts (some of them, at least), have learned to look upon people as citizens of a nation, as members of a given society, and *particular* members at that, not merely as members of an Oedipal family. . . . The exchanges we once had with our parents, or continue to have with ourselves in the form of fantasies or nightmares, are not the only things that upset the mind or drive it to distraction."[24]

When pressed by his Swiss colleague and friend Ludwig Binswanger as to why some patients break through into deeper levels of self-understanding and are able to live less compulsively and neurotically, while others do not, Freud responded in a surprising fashion. Binswanger, Coles notes in his book in Walker Percy, expected the Viennese to argue that such patients for whom analysis is simply not working require even more years of analysis. Instead, Freud answered, "Geist ist alles," spirit is all. He was simply trying to uncover some of the biological and psychological phenomena of certain lives; this was not to be confused with the totality of human nature. What goes on in the psychiatrist's office, in the best and healthiest relationship between analyst and patient, is a joint project, a creation of a plausible interpretation of life. This creation is the work of spirit just as much as of the application of certain technical terms and therapeutic insights.[25]

Coles once imaginatively paraphrased the mentor-student relationship between Freud and Erik Erikson; The words might as suitably describe Coles's stance toward Freud. He imagines Erikson saying to Freud:

> I am not here to "change" or "revise" your suggestive and hard-won theories—which I know you yourself respected enough to change constantly; nor am I here to quibble and haggle with your words, to draw implications from them that you never intended, or to put meanings into them that succeed in making you narrow, boring, or cruel. I want your ideas as companions, to whom I can turn for advice and help while I walk my own way—in a direction you seemed to have set for yourself toward the end of your life, when you turned your attention to historical figures, religious problems and social events as subjects for psychoanalytic inquiry. I will go about my work in your manner, because psychoanalysis in the most profound sense of the word is *style*—of looking at the world and of ordering various facts and feelings. On the other hand, I will pay you the respect of working hard to bring whatever ferment I can to your ideas. You once called yourself a "conquistador." If we are to emulate you, we will have to be more than slaves or literal-minded acolytes of yours.[26]

In 1955, as Robert Coles was finishing his medical school training at Columbia, Anna Freud came to lecture on child psychiatry. Coles was deeply impressed with her, read her essays and books, and eventually established a relationship of correspondence and interviews. In 1966 he published a long essay in the *Massachusetts Review*, "The Achievement of Anna Freud," mentions her contributions repeatedly through *Children of Crisis*, and weaves her commentary throughout his recent study of Simone Weil.

For Coles, the single most important term in Anna Freud's glossary is "direct observation."[27] Clearly, this is what Coles has employed over the years, in spending hours and days with his subjects, talking, observing, simply being with them. This "method" (he would say the process hardly deserves such an academically impressive word) was Anna Freud's, and equally was the "method" of James Agee, George Orwell, George Eliot, Dorothea Lange, and William Carlos Williams. From her first publication, *Introduction to the Technique of Child Analysis*, to her last, *Normality and Pathology in Childhood*, Anna Freud was concerned to weave together theoretical insights with reports of clinical and field observations. During World War II, she helped organize and administer nurseries for English children. Her most influential work during the war dealt with the emotional responses of children during air raids and evacuations.

In all this work, Anna Freud stressed that behavior was the pathway to understanding the unconscious.

> For a long time psychoanalysts were quite naturally suspicious of what they saw, of the "surface" manifestations of the mind's life. They saw that after weeks and months of listening to a patient they found hidden truths about his feelings that nothing "observable" . . . could reveal. As a consequence, any conscious expression, any kind of behavior that might simply be watched and noticed, seemed at worst an irrelevant distraction or disguise, and at best a mere pathway to a truth that is always hidden and deviously expressed.[28]

Though an elegant expositor of theory, Anna Freud is perhaps best remembered for her patient and detailed observation of children, of their developing selves and developing relationships. Coles would be drawn to her "theoretical reluctance," her unwillingness to label certain behavior as evidence of certain pathologies, her suspicion of the messianic uses to which psychoanalysis has been put in our century. The history of child psychiatry as a sure guide to child-rearing is a sorry one, she writes in a passage from *Normality and Pathology* that Coles names "a cultural document of this century":

When psychoanalysis laid great emphasis on the seductive influence of sharing the parents' bed and the traumatic consequences of witnessing parental intercourse, parents were warned against bodily intimacy with their children and against performing the sexual act in the presence of even their youngest infants. When it was proved in the analyses of adults that the withholding of sexual knowledge was responsible for many intellectual inhibitions, full sexual enlightenment at an early age was advocated. . . . When anxiety was recognized as playing a central part in symptom formation, every effort was made to lessen the children's fear of parental authority. When guilt was shown to correspond to the tension between the inner agencies, this was followed by a ban on all educational measures likely to provide a severe superego. . . . Finally, in our time, when analytic investigations have turned to earliest events in the first year of life and highlighted their importance, these specific insights are being translated into new and in some respects revolutionary techniques of infant care.[29]

Thus, each new analytic discovery is touted as providing the best avenue for raising the perfect, anxiety-less, neurosis-free child. In contrast, Anna Freud argues, and Coles agrees, that conflict is an intrinsic and inescapable part of life. Even more, the future of individuals is shaped by a multitude of factors, not only by their childhood experiences. While observers and theorists like Anna Freud can discern "general *patterns* of growth," individual development is thoroughly individual, quirky, even mysterious. While some patients present classic symptoms, obviously requiring therapy, in others, "the analyst is faced by nothing but enigmas, with no certainty about the therapeutic possibilities."[30]

In 1966, after nearly ten years in the South, pursuing the interviews that would become *A Study in Courage and Fear* and *Migrants, Sharecroppers, Mountaineers,* Robert and Jane Coles returned north. The South had changed dramatically in that decade, reluctantly coming to terms with integration. The civil rights movement also had changed, and the Coleses, along with other young whites, no longer felt welcomed or needed in the increasingly black-identified movement. They considered returning to their native region, but the question of employment pressed upon them. Jane Coles applied for high school English teaching positions all around the Boston area and was finally accepted at Concord High. (Robert Coles once said that his Harvard colleagues kidded him about living in Concord, in light of his fondness for the Concord circle of American writers; in fact, he said, it all had to do with the fortuitous offer of a teaching job to Jane Coles.)[31]

Now thirty-seven, Robert Coles had few of the conventional marks of success. He had published articles and many reviews, but as yet no books. He had no extensive psychiatric practice, though he and Jane Coles had collected hours of tapes and hundreds of pages of interview transcripts. He had no regular academic position and no steady income.

In autumn 1966 he became a "section man" for Erik Erikson's undergraduate course at Harvard College, a position usually reserved for graduate students in their early twenties. He loved the teaching, nonetheless, and relished the interaction with students and fellow section leaders, among whom were graduate students Kenneth Kenniston and Carol Gilligan.[32]

Coles's acquaintance with Erikson long preceded this co-teaching, however. He had read *Young Man Luther* and *Childhood and Society* when they came out in the late 1950s, and was impressed with their linking of personality development with historical and cultural context. In the early 1960s, he recalls, he visited three black SNCC activists imprisoned in Alabama, and noticed that they had been reading *Childhood and Society*. He saw that book several more times in Southern freedom houses, in dormitory rooms and sharecropper shacks where black and white young people trained and labored to undo decades of racism and segregation.[33] Erikson's book was one of a number of influential works that seemed to shape the consciousness of that generation of civil rights activists in the early Sixties, texts and artworks that richly interacted with the social struggle, danger, and death that were part of daily life: "I heard the folk songs. I heard the poems, the selections from John Donne and Shakespeare and Dostoevsky and Thoreau and Tolstoy and W. H. Auden. I heard the phonographs play Beethoven and Brahms and Berlioz. . . . I was astonished at the sight of those books: *The Plague, Crime and Punishment, Light in August, The Mind of the South, All the King's Men,* the poems of Wallace Stevens or W. C. Williams or W. H. Auden."[34]

Erikson would prove influential not just on those black and white activists, but on Robert Coles as well. In August 1964, toward the end of Mississippi Freedom Summer, Coles heard a black youth observe that if they survived that dangerous time, "We ought to go read someone, someone who lights up our thinking, and we ought to stop and ask ourselves—we'll each of us do it differently—what this life is all about, and what we should do next with our energy."[35] Together with Anna Freud, Erikson has been that thinker and writer for Coles. "I decided that if I was going to write one book after another about the various 'children of crisis' I would meet and come to know, I had better well look at the particular viewpoint I was using in the course of my work, using to look at others and understand them, to fathom their purposes, to comprehend their weaknesses and problems—and hopefully, their strengths."36 Coles had already contributed an essay ("Serpents and Doves: Non-violent Youth in the South") to Erikson's collection *Youth: Change and Challenge* and had reviewed *Insight and Responsibility* for *The New Republic* in October 1964. In 1964 and 1965 Coles began to read Erikson more systematically, and in 1966, while he taught with Erikson, began to take notes toward the study that would appear first as a profile in the *New Yorker* and then as a separate volume in 1970.

Like virtually all Coles's books, *Erik H. Erikson; The Growth of His Work* is a "reading," an engagement of a body of experience and insight by a sensitive and discerning observer. If one had to classify it, the book would serve as an intellectual biography "of sorts," the latter term added because, as Coles says, "I find the term 'intellectual biography' rather pompous."37 Coles warns the reader what not to expect from this book: It is not a conventional biography; it is not an attempt to fit Erikson's work into the larger body of psychoanalytic theory; it is not an assessment of Erikson's impact on other disciplines. Most of all, writes Coles, it is not an exposé, "an analytic 'explanation' of the heroic and charismatic 'personality.'" Clearly for Coles, Erikson is an engaging and admirable figure, and he has no intention of stripping him of his "warmth, his humor, his liveliness, his infectious charm, the grace he has as a particular human being, and the grace to be found in his books."38

We can approach Coles's study of Erikson by looking first at his review of *Insight and Responsibility*. Written after that emotionally draining and physically dangerous summer of 1964, Coles's essay identifies those traits and insights in Erikson that he had found helpful, stimulating, corroborative.

Erikson's volume, a collection of essays and addresses, takes up a variety of topics: an account of the origins of psychoanalysis, a treatment of the growth of conscience and ethical accountability, the nature of clinical evidence. Judging by the intensity of Coles's prose, the essay that made the deepest impression on him was "Human Strength and the Cycle of Generations." There Erikson discusses the ways in which such "old" virtues as Hope, Will, Purpose, Competence, Fidelity, Love, Care, and Wisdom are transmitted from one generation to the next. Coles clearly admires Erikson's use of these terms, anticipating and rejecting the criticism that they are "the hackneyed soporifics of sermons." In all these pieces, says Coles, Erikson demonstrates "richness of thinking" and "considerable beauty of style," a blending of Anglo-Saxon simplicity with Germanic profundity. The style mirrors the intellect at work: the combination of artistic sensibility and scientific clarity. For younger psychiatrists like Coles himself, weary of what they consider social scientific jargon and vacuity, Erikson's humanism comes as a powerful and instructive alternative.[39]

It is not my intention to summarize Coles's book on Erikson. To do that would be to engage in a kind of infinite regress: Erikson "reading" Freud, Coles reading Erikson reading Freud, this writer reading Coles reading Erikson reading Freud, the reader . . . Rather, I wish to trace those characteristics in Erikson's life and work that seem to impress themselves forcibly on Robert Coles, instructing him, moving him, corroborating him in his own insights.

The place to begin is with Erikson's own emphasis on the auto-biographical dimension of his work. In response to a letter from Coles inquiring about his family and personal background, Erikson remarked on some of his "marginalities": He was born to Danish parents; Erikson's parents separated soon after his birth and his mother married the family pediatrician, who was Jewish. The family relocated to Karlsruhe in Germany. At first identifying strongly with German nationalism, Erikson was repelled by the growth of anti-Semitism in the 1920s. Much like Coles himself, part of Erikson's background is that of assimilated Jews: "In Denmark baptism and intermarriage are old customs, so one of my ancestors . . . was chief rabbi of Stockholm and another a church historian and pastor in H. C. Andersen's home town. I have kept my stepfather's name as my middle name [Homburger] out of gratitude (there is a pediatrician in me, too) but also to avoid the semblance of evasion."[40]

The young Erikson became a kind of wandering artist, making a living as a sign painter. Invited to teach at a private school in Vienna organized by Dorothy Burlingham and Anna Freud, Erikson absorbed the insights of the psychoanalytic movement through the work of these two gifted women, one a wealthy American, liberal, reformist, the other the immensely talented and original daughter of Sigmund Freud. Particularly from Anna Freud, Erikson adopted the clinical, observational, individual side of psychoanalysis, less the theoretical and speculative.

In his major works of the 1950s and 1960s—*Childhood and Society, Identity: Youth and Crisis, Young Man Luther, Gandhi's Truth*—Erikson worked to combine the insights of artist and scientist. In his concern for data, his careful formulation of theory, he is grounded in the work of Freud, Heinz Hartmann, Ernst Kris, and in the writings of an-

PSYCHOLOGY, PSYCHIATRY, AND CHILDREN | 97

thropologists and biologists like Margaret Mead, Gregory Bateson, Ruth Benedict, Henry Murray, and Kurt Lewin. Equally, in his biographical studies of Gandhi, Hitler, Gorky, Luther, Erikson displays a gifted artistic sense, a flair for phrasing, a profound insight into the recesses of character that is often associated with novelists like George Eliot or Dostoevsky. As Don Browning puts it, "Erikson's work as a therapist and as a student of human development is really the work of an *artist*. Therapist as artist, or better, scientist as artist—this is the way to understand Erikson's contributions."41 Indeed, once Hannah Arendt confided in Coles that Erikson's studies of Luther and Gandhi were two of the best novels she had ever read. By this she intended a compliment, said Coles, although she allowed she would never put it that way to Erikson.

In 1933, at the urging of Hans Sachs, Erikson and his wife, Joan Serson Erikson, left Austria and settled in Boston, where Erikson became the city's first child analyst. He accepted positions at Harvard Medical School and Massachusetts General Hospital. Although these appointments put him in contact with some of America's foremost intellectuals, Erikson also wished to spend time with poor, delinquent children, and with those whose culture normally did not encourage the pursuit of psychoanalysis. "At Harvard his research allowed him to see students who had no problems at all, at least none that prompted them to seek help. For the rest of his life he would follow a similar course, one that balanced clinical work with research, and one that kept him in touch with people who are not usually seen by analysts or for that matter many doctors—Sioux and Yurok Indian children and poor children treated in big-city pediatric clinics."42

In 1936 the Eriksons moved to New Haven, where Erikson had accepted positions at the Institute of Human Relations and Yale Medical School. Two years later, Erikson traveled out to South Dakota to observe Sioux Indian children on the Pine Ridge Reservation. From that encounter came "Observations on Sioux Education," published in 1939. In this essay, Erikson tries to link individual psychological circumstances with the historical fate of being Sioux. One finds in this essay equal concern given to pathology, to social and individual maladjustment, and to normality. Erikson attends to the daily round of life, particularly to the interaction of parents and children. Unlike some anthropologists, he is unwilling to treat the Sioux as cultural freaks, a primitive group clinging to their quaint ways in the face of dominant white culture. Rather, he treats them with both respect and honesty. Throughout this essay, says Coles, Erikson employs a strong, vigorous, simple prose, balancing clinical observation with "the perspectives of social and economic history."[43]

From 1939 to 1950 the Eriksons lived in Berkeley. During this decade Erikson carved out his distinctive point of view. Throughout his work, Erikson has been careful never to repudiate Freud. Following the lead of Anna Freud, Erikson extends Freud's insights in the direction of ego and personality integration. In his writing from early in the twentieth century, Freud stressed the powerful and buried compulsions that drive behavior. Gradually, however, in the 1920s and later, he began to explore the role of the ego, which Freud saw as possessing considerable "executive strength" as mediator among the self's conflicting psychological forces. But it was in fact his daughter and Heinz Hartmann who focused the analytic community's attention on the creative role of the ego. "Without in the least forsaking Freud's view of an unconscious powerfully grounded in biological 'needs' and 'drives,' Miss Freud and Dr. Hartmann showed how we develop the energy, readiness and will to turn the child's insistent and impertinent urges into the grown-up person's reasonably sane and sensible state of mind."[44]

It is this emphasis on the successes of the ego, the usual ability of the normal person to achieve reasonable competence and mastery, that contributes to Erikson's famous concept of identity. There is a somatic, biological dimension, to be sure: The individual, as infant and child, develops through several stages, is focused on different physical needs and drives. But with this genetic scheme Erikson interweaves a psychological one: It is true that the infant is focused on satisfying its very basic needs, and expresses its outrage when it is denied. But what is the meaning of this physical/biological datum? From his scientist's observation and his artist's leap of insight, Erikson frames this possibility. The meaning of these experiences lies in the tension between a basic sense of trust and a basic sense of mistrust. And so through the physical development of the self; each stage Erikson matches with a corresponding stage of ego development, thus shaping his notion of the life cycle: trust versus mistrust, autonomy versus shame and doubt, initiative versus guilt, industry versus inferiority, identity versus confusion, intimacy versus isolation, generativity versus self-absorption, integrity versus despair.

In all this, Erikson is impressed with the ability of selves to proceed from one stage to the next, the success of the average person to construct and integrate a reasonably successful life. This is not to say, of course, that people are not sometimes overwhelmed by social or personal difficulties, struggle, and collapse, or become distorted, sick, and malignant. The essays on the Sioux, on Hitler, on the Yurok, all demonstrate Erikson's profound awareness of widespread social and individual pathology. Nonetheless, success, adjustment, coping, transforming difficult circumstances—these are truly Erikson's lifelong themes.

From his earliest encounters with Anna Freud at the Hort School in Vienna, Erikson was committed to a psychiatry that was observational and interactive. He went to his patients and, since so many of them were children, played with them. Like the late Freud, Erikson was convinced that personality was individual and unique, but that it was historical as well, shaped by the larger circumstances and forces surrounding it. Thus in his biographical studies—of George Bernard Shaw, Hitler, Gorky, Luther, Gandhi—Erikson worked to place the characters amid the dense, rich circumstances that preceded and surrounded them.

Erikson's great insight, his concept of identity as a psychosocial process, was to combine these two themes, the epigenetic and the historical. Each person moves from one stage to another prompted both by biological changes (and their relational complements) within and by changing social circumstances without. Thus personal identity, as Don Browning understands Erikson, is a successful variant of cultural possibilities, in accord with the self's unique materials at hand.[45] As the self transits from one stage to another, it undergoes an identity crisis. These are, Erikson stresses, normal struggles in the self's successful motion toward maturity. Nonetheless, he is drawn to those figures—Luther, Gandhi—whose personal struggles are representative of the struggles of their larger society, whose particularly powerful identity crises at some developmental juncture mirror the crisis of their culture. For example, in Erikson's treatment, Martin Luther's agonized struggle with his own sinfulness and his search for a new ground on which to experience God's redemptive love led to a bold public gesture of criticizing the Church for its abuses. This gesture ignited an immense wave of popular support among a great variety of people, all restless, unhappy, chafing under new circumstances and changed conditions—the poor and dispossessed, small businessmen, princes, intellectuals, knights. But in all those works, Erikson labors to retain a vision of the unique personality, the distinctiveness of the individual synthesis of inner and outer.

As we consider the influence of Erikson on Robert Coles, we need lastly to treat the place of ethics. Paul Roazen notes that Erikson was trained in the Freudian tradition of analytic neutrality. But in its concern with childhood as the first of many scenes of "human exploitability," psychoanalysis reveals a profound moral commitment. Erikson follows in this "implicit utopianism," as does Robert Coles.[46]

In his emphasis on *relationship,* on the movement from one stage to another as prompted by inner change, by significant others, and by the larger culture, Erikson stresses what Browning calls a "psychology of recognition." The ego takes the materials of psyche and soma, of inner life and outer world, and shapes them into the unique self of that stage. Thus for Erikson, the ego is the agency for wholeness, centeredness, synthesis, the agency for coordinating the fragments of experience into a meaningful whole.[47] "Virtue" is the ego's capacity for making a positive synthesis out of life's several developmental crises, and in Erikson's view, more people than not make such a successful synthesis.

Nonetheless, Erikson's vision of humanity as successfully negotiating, within the limits of cultural variation, the various stages of human development, may be seriously in danger in our own time and place, says Don Browning. For Browning, the key to understanding Erikson's psychosocial ethics is the word "generativity," the ability, based on one's own successful development, to nurture the next generation as it progresses through the stages of development. Erikson is convinced that the terms of the identity crises—identity versus identity confusion, intimacy versus isolation, and so on—are universals, although presented and handled differently in different cultures and historical times. In our own time, says Browning, so shaped by social and economic forces leading to individualism and alienation, it is increasingly difficult to identify universals. We are cut off from the past, uprooted, lacking in rituals that help us move from one stage to another. Our privatism has profound effects both in psychological life and in our shared cultural life. Browning's insights, derived from Erikson, are remarkably similar to the cultural criticism that Coles has voiced recently. Like Christopher Lasch, Coles believes that dominant Western culture fosters a way of life that is private and irresponsible. Lacking a public ethic that is communally responsible and spiritually informed, modern Western society has no sense of its own future.[48]

It does not take a very astute reader to see the remarkable parallels in the lives and careers of Erik Erikson and Robert Coles. Both came from partly Jewish backgrounds, both consider themselves "marginal" men. Both have sought to combine scientific training with artistic sensibilities. Both are indebted to Anna Freud's emphasis on "direct observation," and to her insistence on the remarkable ability of the ego to master and synthesize the unconscious drives and social requirements. Both have been committed to research and writing among people not usually treated by psychiatrists. Even the details are disconcerting: Both men are married to women who read every word of their prose and are their most severe editors and constant advisors.

But I have no wish to find in Erik Erikson a father figure for Robert Coles, nor do I wish to match every characteristic of Coles's life and work with a precursor from Erikson's. We can recognize in Erikson a powerful influence, a mentor and role model for Robert Coles, without detracting from Coles's own synthesis of Erikson and the many other influences in his life.

Here then are some of those powerful influences, in summary. Erikson has sought to combine an artistic gift with scientific rigor. This corroborates Coles's own interest in literature and literary criticism, balanced against his fidelity to empirical research. Erikson has stressed the ability of the ego to guide the self through the various stages of development, and the remarkable ability of the self to integrate the inner and outer elements that make a unique person. Likewise, Coles is struck by the astonishing psychic health of many people who live in the midst of immense social and cultural crisis. Despite his certainty that he would find children and adults, living in the midst of the New Orleans and Atlanta desegregation crises, suffering from all sorts of emotional disorders, Coles found them to be strikingly "together." Erikson wishes to see personal identity as a phenomenon existing simultaneously at the core of the self and at the core of the culture, and has been committed to seeing people in their particular historical circumstances. Robert Coles too has worked to embed his subjects in their distinctive settings, whether in the Appalachians, Alaska, a wealthy New Orleans suburb, or the favelas of Rio de Janeiro. Erikson has shaped an ethical dimension to psychiatry, seeing health and wholeness in the successful growth of the self through each stage of development, in the achievement of generativity. For his part, Robert Coles reveals an ethical dimension in this work, an effort to honor the dignity and survival of ordinary people, a critique of modern Western culture as materialist and secular, insufficiently aware of religious values and of the value of tradition.

Finally, both Erikson and Coles acknowledge the interplay of public voice and private life. Coles is more tormented at the thought that his own concerns and obsessions may somehow distort his observations, or be of more interest to the reader than the lives of his subjects. But both men realize that even a profession like psychiatry (or shall we say, *particularly* a profession like psychiatry) that values objectivity and neutrality is practiced by living human beings who bring to their work distinctive life histories. These stories are by no means incidental to the daily work such professionals perform. As Erikson once observed, "in order to approach this whole matter psychoanalytically, it may well be necessary for the individual psychoanalyst to ask himself what particular configuration of drives, defenses, capabilities, and opportunities led him into the choice of this ever-expanding field."[49]

As an heir of the intellectual estate of Sigmund Freud, Robert Coles has necessarily spent much time thinking about children. After all, Freud claimed that our early life experiences predispose much of what follows; we spend our adult years working out the implications of those first, ghostly, elliptical moments. Coles has, to be sure, swerved from the master's example; it is one thing to follow Freud's way of patient and careful listening, his sharp observations and keen storytelling ability. It is quite another to worship him as a cultural demigod.[50] Like Anna Freud and Erik Erikson, Coles has chosen to spend time with children themselves, rather than talking with adults about their recollections of childhood. Further, Coles has emphasized the action, behavior, the lives, of children rather than their thoughts, noting that Piaget and other child psychologists have studied such matters exhaustively.[51]

Coles's concern with and for children stems in part, then, from his profession. It also derives from the accidents and coincidences of his life: his brief encounter with pediatrics, his decision to go into psychiatry, his further specialization in child psychiatry, his work with polio victims in Boston in the late 1950s, his unfocused interest in how certain black children were coping with desegregation in New Orleans and Atlanta. But it is also the case that the concern with the child is not simply Coles's alone; it is a large-scale Western fascination at least three centuries old, having its most powerful articulation in the Romantic writers of the late eighteenth and early nineteenth centuries. Coles has had an intricate relationship with that Romantic tradition of childhood, echoing its celebration of the child's spiritual intuition and moral sensitivity, rejecting its claims for childhood purity and innocence.

For many American Romantics of the 1830s, 1840s, and 1850s, the most central and influential text was Wordsworth's "Ode: Intimations of Immortality from Recollections of Early Childhood" (1803–1806).[52] In that powerful and moving poem, Wordsworth presents the rhythmic movement between engagement in adult life and recollection of an earlier time when things seemed lovelier, more radiantly celestial. The adult poet celebrates the delicate beauty of a May morning: "And the Children are culling/On every side,/In a thousand valleys far and wide,/

Fresh flowers; while the sun shines warm,/And the Babe leaps up in his Mother's arm:—/I hear, I hear, with joy I hear!" But even amid such rejoicing, the poet is aware "of something that is gone." "Whither is fled the visionary gleam?/ Where is it now, the glory and the dream?"

In an echo of Plato's dialogue "Phaedrus," Wordsworth composes a myth of preexistence in order to explain the sense he has that young children are in touch with a world of intuition and immediacy that adults have lost.53

While the poet regrets the loss of that special vision of the child (whom he calls "Mighty Prophet! Seer blest!"), he offers this consolation: that the child's creativity and insight linger on in the adult as a continuing gift, however altered, and as a promise of immortality. Most particularly, the child's penetrating wisdom remains as the adult's refusal to live in a totally material world. He is grateful, the poet writes, "for those obstinate questionings/Of sense and outward things (lines 142–43)."

There is compensation to be gained from the very process of maturity. Having lived and suffered, the poet is able to say, "I love the Brooks which down their channels fret,/ Even more than when I tripped lightly as they (lines 193–94)." Nature's beauty and human companionship are more to be prized now, in adulthood, when the poet is aware of mortality, than they were in childhood, when one's life seemed eternal.

One hundred fifty years after Wordsworth's influential poem, the child psychologist Edith Cobb corroborated the poet's insight. The essential genius of childhood is plasticity of response to the environment, a power that remains throughout life, producing "the pressure to perceive creatively and inventively." What children want to do most of all, says Cobb in a memorable phrase, is "to make a world in which to find a place to discover a self." This engagement with the world in order to create a self is a whole-person activity: "The child, like the poet, is his own instrument. His whole body, erotized and highly sensitized . . . is the tool of his mind, and serves with a passionate enjoyment in a creative engagement with the forces of nature." So, for Cobb, this "unmediated vision" of children is possibly the source and certainly the primary example of the imaginative, creative impulse in humans. Seeing wholeness, discerning relationships, creating worlds—these are the gifts of childhood and of children to their adult counterparts.54

Several influential American literary romantics in the middle third of the nineteenth century would not have accepted such a conclusion that stressed the importance of memory and the consolations of adulthood.

For Ralph Waldo Emerson, at least before 1842, the adult world of experience and all it involves—history, community, relationship—unacceptably compromises the life of self-absorbed creativity and oneness with the divine. Emerson called for a self who is reborn out of the world of common human relationships into a "saved" condition of child-likeness. Real little children become constant reminders of the possibility of a return to conditions of spontaneity, openness, and wonder. Thoreau, Bronson Alcott, Jones Very, Hawthorne, in stories like "The Gentle Boy" and "Little Annie's Ramble" all share Emerson's sense that children symbolize radical openness and intimacy with the divine.

Many of the men and women who associated with Emerson in the 1830s and 1840s were essentially religious thinkers who used literary forms to express their insights. What would happen, however, when the Emersonian sense of the child—preternaturally wise and guileless, in contrast to the corrupt and fallen adult—is dramatized, put into action in a social setting? Such children, insightful but powerless, are nearly all doomed. Hawthorne's "Gentle Boy" is a Quaker child stoned and beaten to death by Puritan children, and of course Harriet Beecher Stowe's Eva in *Uncle Tom's Cabin* has her eyes fixed firmly on heaven, where she eventually is allowed to go.

In more complex treatments, children's keenness of vision and sharpness of moral insight derive in large part from their very condition of powerlessness, their dependency on untrustworthy adults. Here Henry James provides the primary examples, in such stories as *What Maisie Knew* and *The Turn of the Screw*. In both these tales, the children try to balance what they know to be true with what they sense the adults want to hear, and this interplay creates the dramatic tension.

In all the cases noted, the reader understands that the authors have something else in mind other than a minute recording of the accurate details of child life. In the cases of Emerson and his circle, we have some claims about human nature. Transcendentalists tended to celebrate the divine child, from whose lofty state all the rest of life is loss and regret. For Stowe (and other novelists like Sylvester Judd), perfect, innocent children become means of social criticism: The world of slavery or religious warfare is no place for children. In his fictions of childhood, Henry James sets up his famous experiment, duplicated in other works like *The American* and *The Portrait of a Lady:* Take an innocent self, all keen senses, clever intellect, and open heart, and put him or her into a situation of moral ambiguity and dense social relationships, and see what happens.

In the late nineteenth century, sprawling cities, industrial complexes, millions of immigrants, and bureaucratic systems assailed Americans with the immense facticity of life. While middle-class families sought to shelter their children from the dangers of the city, many more hard-pressed parents could not do so, and children were swept into factory labor, peddling, street-sweeping, and prostitution. Children lived, as did adults, in squalid tenements, suffered from abusive grown-ups who were themselves overwhelmed by poverty, suffered from malnutrition and disease, died of industrial accidents and often preventable illness. The Progressive reform movement of the turn of the twentieth century paid particular attention to the conditions of child life, and several notable writers chronicled those conditions. Jane Addams, Jacob Riis, John Spargo, and Stephen Crane (in *Maggie, Girl of the Streets* and in his journalism) all sought to awaken their middle-class readers to the stunted lives being produced in America's tenements and sweatshops.

Robert Coles has worked in the space between these two approaches, in the territory between the Romantic and the sociological visions. Like Jacob Riis and other Progressive reformers, Coles attends to the actual, dense life circumstances of children and adults: What does the environment look like? What do people eat? What photographs are on the walls? What is it like to work in a mine, or be a migrant laborer, or a fireman, or a secretary? What does it feel like to walk to school, as did Ruby Bridges in New Orleans in 1960, between crowds of angry white adults, screaming obscenities and threats at you? Details, the stuff of life—Coles patiently gathers and presents all this to us because people live in the details.

Still, as we have already seen, Coles refuses to be yet another chronicler of the outward circumstances of life. He continually presses for the signs of the inner life, for the word, the look, the gesture, that suggests moral consciousness, spiritual awareness. Like the photojournalists he admires—Walker Evans, Dorothea Lange—Coles presses on the surface of life until it gives off its inner meaning.[55] As he seeks to synthesize both outer circumstances and inner luminousness, Coles is in company with several other American writers whose work, like his, is difficult to classify but impossible to forget: Twain's *The Adventures of Huckleberry Finn*, Henry Roth's *Call It Sleep*, Agee's *A Death in the Family*.

Rather than beaten down, cowed, inarticulate, the children from "disadvantaged" or hard-pressed backgrounds reveal an astonishing awareness, awareness of moral and spiritual issues, awareness of the political and economic forces that keep them members of America's proletariat. Again and again the insight forces itself upon the doctor who in 1960 went looking for signs of maladjustment, psychic breakdown, mental and emotional disturbance: "Circumstances prompt inquiry, and desperate circumstances may prompt the most taut and intense and enormously urgent kind of inquiry . . . such as Christ made; whereas a padded, self-centered, luxurious set of circumstances can prompt idle reverie, self-infatuation, indolence, and a lack of any kind of inquiry."[56]

Coles once questioned a migrant girl about her thoughts of the future.

> "Well, I'll tell you," the girl says gravely in answer to the question. Then she doesn't say anything for a long time and the observer and listener gets nervous and starts rummaging for another question. . . . Yet, once in a while there does come an answer . . . and a question, too. . . . "Well, I'll tell you, I don't know how it'll be ahead for me, but do you think my people, all of us here, will ever be able to stop and live like they do, the rest of the people? . . . No, I don't think so. I think a lot of people, they don't want us to be with them, and all they want is for us to do their work, and then good-bye, they say, and don't come back until the next time, when there's more work and then we'll have you around to do it, and then good-bye again."[57]

This child has learned some profound lessons about class privilege and dispensable people; she also has, Coles would want us to note, considerable dignity and self-possession as she speaks honestly about her marginal status in a rich nation.

Over and again the stories of children flow through Coles's pen and out to the reader. Eduardo lives in a favela, a slum, on the hills above Rio de Janiero. Daily he cruises the wealthy section of the city, the Copacabana, "now selling shoelaces, now suggesting to passersby that they stop at this vendor's, purchase one of his fancy Italian ices, now asking to wash a car, now offering a well-off resident help with a package, a beach chair, while crossing the street." Coles listens intently to Eduardo, to his observations about wealth and poverty, about the military and politics, about whose side the Church takes in social struggle. And Coles discerns something more in this keenly observant, street-wise boy: "He has not lost what I suppose can be called moral pride, a kind of self-respect."[58] That such qualities exist in children, especially in hard-pressed children, is a miracle, a mystery. "Why don't such 'qualities' dissolve in favor of an utterly rapacious 'animality,' or in favor of apathetic despair, a last-ditch self-centeredness?"[59]

All too often, the qualities Coles prizes in children—decency, conscience, moral sensitivity, love and generosity—*do* warp and shrink under the insistent pressures of poverty and oppression. Migrant children suffer from "hunger and chronic malnutrition . . . diseases that go undiagnosed and untreated, diseases of the skin and the muscles and the bones and the vital organs, vitamin- and mineral-deficiency diseases and untreated congenital diseases and infectious diseases and parasitic diseases and in the words of one migrant mother, 'all the sicknesses that ever was.'"[60] By the age of nine or ten or eleven, migrant children have stopped their "formal" education, indeed ended their childhoods and are "getting ready to go out on dates and love and become parents and follow their parents' footsteps."[61] They begin to accept their fate as America's underclass, an analytical term to most readers, a description of life itself for these "uprooted children."

> It is bad enough that thousands of us, thousands of American children, still go hungry and sick and are ignored and spurned— every day and constantly and just about from birth to death. It is quite another thing, a lower order of human degradation, that we also have thousands of boys and girls who live utterly uprooted lives, who wander the American earth, who even as children enable us to eat by harvesting our crops but who never, never can think of any place as home, of themselves as anything but homeless. There are moments, and I believe this is one of them, when, however we are, observers or no, we have to throw up our hands in heaviness of heart and dismay and disgust and say, in desperation, God save them, those children, and for allowing such a state of affairs to continue, God save us too.[62]

But migrant children are not the only young sufferers. In May 1967, together with five other doctors, Coles investigated rural poverty in Mississippi and reported to a U.S. Senate subcommittee in July:

> Almost every child we saw was in a state of negative nitrogen balance; that is, a marked inadequacy of diet has led the body to consume its own protein tissue. . . . We found in child after child the need for surgery: hernias, poorly healed fractures . . . evidence of gastrointestinal bleeding or partial obstruction. . . . The teeth of practically every child we saw—and of their parents, too—were in awful repair—eaten up by cavities and often poorly developed. Their gums showed how severely anemic these children were; and the gums were also infected and foul-smelling. . . . Many of these children were suffering from degenerative joint diseases. . . . The children were plagued with colds and fevers—in Mississippi in late May—and with sore throats. . . . What particularly saddened and appalled us were the developmental anomalies and diseases that we

know once were easily correctable, but now are hopelessly consolidated. Bones, eyes, vital organs that should long ago have been evaluated and treated are now all beyond medical assistance. . . . In sum, children living under unsanitary conditions without proper food, and with a limited intake of improper food, without access to doctors or dentists, under crowded conditions in flimsy shacks pay the price in a plethora of symptoms, diseases, aches, and pain. No wonder that in Mississippi (whose Negroes comprise 42 percent of the state's population) the infant mortality rate among Negroes is over twice that of whites; and while the white infant mortality rate is dropping, the rate for Negroes is rising.[63]

I quote this long passage (which is even longer in the original) in order to make sure the reader understands this crucial point. Robert Coles is not a romantic or a sentimentalist with regard to children. He is fascinated, moved, and instructed by the way children, and adults, in difficult circumstances cannot be understood with reference only to sociological or political or economic categories. They resist stereotypes. Most particularly, they have remarkable insights into "the way things are" which Coles perceives as moral and spiritual in nature. But in none of that is Coles in any sense recommending the hard-pressed life for its moral strenuousness, or glossing over the physical difficulties and political injustices that millions contend with daily. "It is no small thing," he writes of migrant life, "a disaster almost beyond repair, when children grow up adrift the land, when they learn as a birthright the disorder and early sorrow that goes with peonage, with an unsettled, vagabond's life. We are describing millions of psychological catastrophes, the nature of which has been spelled out to me by both migrant parents and migrant children."[64] Of the rural poor, both those bonded to the land and those wandering on the land, Coles says,

> However the early lives of sharecropper and migrant children differ, one from the other, by the time the children . . . become eleven or twelve a common fate awaits them, a fate that distinctly overshadows all the differences I have taken such pains to describe. I am talking about the swift decline of childhood, the abrupt beginning of a working and loving life—all in a matter of months. . . . At twelve or thirteen the light and tender moments begin to wane, the world begins to shrink and toughen. Then the wisdom and humor gets curbed. . . . Suddenly they were no longer children and all too much the burdened, troubled grown-ups their parents had always been.[65]

So once again, as so often in his life and work, Coles confronts a tension, this one between the remarkable insights of poor and dis-possessed people, particularly children, and the material conditions of their lives that drive them into despair and apathy and their parents into alcoholism, domestic violence, suicide. But what of more privileged children? If the heavy weight of hunger and deprivation were removed, would inwardness and moral sensitivity flourish unimpeded?

If Coles refuses to romanticize the poor or elevate children into moral miracles, he is equally reluctant to begin such an investigation with a bias against children whose accidents of birth bring them wealth and privilege. "One is not per se virtuous because one is born poor; I am not saying, either, that one is per se wicked for being born well-to-do or rich."[66] Certainly children at risk and children in comfort ask questions about their life situations, "and once people start asking why about their lives, fates, and destinies, they're entering religious inquiry."[67]

Coles is deeply moved by children from privileged backgrounds who do ask troubling, troubled questions. "Many wealthy children go through a stage of questioning," Coles once observed. "They hear words at church that cause them to think of justice and injustice. In their innocence, they ask what Christ would be like if he came back. Would he identify with the rich or with the poor and humble?"[68] An eight-year-old girl from a wealthy New Orleans family began to spend hours staring at the old cemetery across from their mansion. "She wondered about who 'those people' were, the departed. . . . She would, in her own way, meditate about life's meaning." Her parents were annoyed, then determined to stop her aberrant behavior. Filling the child's life with activities, they managed after several months to "cure" her. She had "recovered." But the family's black maid had another perspective.

> These people here, they've got all that money, and all this big house, and another one out in the country, and they still won't let that little girl just be herself. She's eight or nine, and she's got an independent spirit in her, but they're determined to get rid of it, and they will, let me tell you, and soon. That girl asks me a lot of questions. That's good. She looks out on that cemetery, and she starts to wondering about things. That's good. She wonders about life, and what it's about, and what the end of things will be. That's good. But she's stopping now. That's what they want; no looking, no staring, no peeking at life. No questions; they don't want questions.[69]

A Florida boy, the son of a wealthy planter, began to question the economic order of things, stimulated by his understanding of the message of Jesus. Like the parents of the New Orleans girl, this boy's parents were upset and put the boy into psychotherapy. Eventually he lost his Christian preoccupations, wrote Coles, and became another American entrepreneur.

While there is the occasional child who tries to break through the parental expectations, privileged children "forget their ethical questions about life. It's far easier for them just to go along with the prevailing narcissism of our times." Indeed, Coles believes that such children's preoccupations with their "entitlements" simply mirror the larger society's pervasive materialism. Consider these children from the pages of *The Privileged Ones:* James, who despite, or perhaps because of, enormous social privilege and abundant opportunity, thought of himself as besieged in his New Orleans home, playing with his toy soldiers, fighting and refighting the defense against "them"; or Richard, whose rigid patriotism clearly reflected his parents', and who even at the time of the interviews was in the process of crushing his own questions and authentic responses; or Sally, living privately on a huge estate in the northeast, obsessed with manners, how the privileged have them and the poor, like their family's maid, do not.

The title of the last volume of *Children of Crisis, The Privileged Ones,* is ironic, Coles once pointed out. In what sense are these children privileged? Materially they are blessed; their futures in this money-obsessed society are assured. But ease of life may lead, as with the children in that last volume, to a deadening of the moral sensibility, a narrow preoccupation with self, a stifling of compassion.

> There is a worldview which says that anxiety, pain, and fear are part of what life is meant to be, that God himself assumed such a life, that he lived under continual anxiety, pain, and fear, and ended up as a common criminal strung up on a cross and killed. Now, if you take that kind of existence as a very important one and as a model of sorts, then you're going to have a difficult time becoming as "successful" as you may have been told you ought to be if you come from a middle-class family. You have a moral dilemma.[70]

· 5 ·

Politics and Culture

*I*n August 1974 Robert Coles traveled to the University of Cape Town to deliver the fifteenth annual T. B. Davie Memorial Lecture. His address, "Children and Political Authority," appeared as an essay in *The Mind's Fate* and as the opening chapter (called "Political Authority and the Young") of *The Political Life of Children*. Coles begins by referring to Simone Weil's 1939 essay "The Great Beast," in which the French writer and political activist traces the new fascist totalitarianism back to its roots in the Roman imperium. Barbarians, said Weil, are intermittently cruel, their violence interspersed with loyalty and generosity. In contrast, the Romans were the first, in her analysis, to develop a myth of mastery, a self-understanding that was acted out in unremitting, unrelenting subjugation and repression. Those born to rule were given early instruction in cruelty and violence by the gladiatorial games, by the omnipresence of slavery, by the whole weight of empire.[1]

Thus the belief in the legitimacy of the political system was promptly and early inculcated in Roman children, and, Robert Coles observes, in other children born into similar situations of privilege. Indeed, children in a great variety of circumstances, whether privileged or oppressed or somewhere in between, are keenly sensitive to messages about the political order. In innumerable subtle and not-so-subtle ways, children quickly come to understand the world of power and powerlessness, the world of rules and mastery, the intricate ways in which people are sorted out in societies.

In "Children and Political Authority," Coles acknowledges the insights of Australian social scientist Robert Connell. Connell has observed that children do give voice to "standardized responses" in answer to questions about politics, but that over long periods of time, and given encouragement, they will respond in freer, more authentic speech. Connell calls this "intuitive political thinking," in which children demonstrate not just the expected political socialization, the answers one would expect from certain children from certain racial, social, economic backgrounds, but also "outspoken, idiosyncratic, blunt and imaginative political opinions."[2] For his part, Coles is once again struck by the way particular children combine the materials from the outside world with their own unique sensibilities. No abstraction or general statement can quite capture the distinctive way individual children make sense of the political world; one needs to listen to them patiently and over a period of time. Coles excerpts from Connell's *The Child's Construction of Politics* a passage that mirrors Coles's own viewpoint:

> We have built up a collective portrait of the groups of children and the developments to be seen among them. To do this it has been necessary to summarize and to use short extracts from here and there, but to do *that* is to violate the concrete whole of the interview, to tear statements from their contexts and to present them, in a way, as disembodied types of forms rather than real episodes. To overcome this drift into abstraction it is necessary to see the statement in the context of the full interview—itself a distorted projection of the life and thought of the child onto the plan of interrogation, but the nearest we can come, with these methods, to the actuality of which we wish to speak.[3]

Like Connell, Coles wants to hold out for an area of human freedom and possibility, a sense that people, children, cannot be understood fully by resort to theory. Coles in particular has always upheld the mystery, the unexpected breaking through despite all pressures to the contrary.

Still, like Simone Weil, Coles is intensely aware of "political socialization," of the way in which life's circumstances, often mediated quite intimately through parents and schoolmates, shape the child's political (not to mention social and moral) awareness. On a larger scale, children and their parents live according to rules other people have made—people in business, government, the military—but these rules and decisions become personalized in daily life, become part of the self's own self-understanding. The stories that Coles narrates reveal again and again that dynamic interplay between areas of freedom and areas of constraint, an interplay made all the more intricate as people articulate the opinions of their class, region, race, nationality, as if they were their own original opinions and observations. Still, Coles refuses to predict or label people and their political views. Gloomily hopeful, he looks for, and often finds, those moments when people do justice to their own experience, their own moral intuitions, rather than parrot the prevailing political propaganda. With Iris Murdoch, he looks for the moments when people slip out of fantasy, out from under the net.

"I come from a fairly conservative, conventional background," Robert Coles once said. He was "not one of these Kenniston [Kenneth Kenniston, author of *Young Radicals*] kids. My father was a Republican; he was an engineer, came from England. My mother came from Iowa . . . from a middle-class farm family. . . . I had no great interest in politics."[4] Harvard in the late 1940s, despite the presence of Socialists like F. O. Matthiessen on the faculty, presented no great political challenges to the young Coles. It was, rather, a great bastion of Republicanism and bipartisan Cold War politics.

As a resident in psychiatry, Coles was taught to see politics as a screen, a kind of rhetoric masking deeper, unconscious needs and drives. He became briefly interested in politics when his young patient accused him of taking off his Stevenson button before their sessions. But even after he became engaged in the decades-long interviewing that resulted in *Children of Crisis,* Coles was, by his own admission, not fully sensitive to the political insights of his subjects. "Instead, we emphasized the racial aspects of thinking that came across in what the children said or pictured for us. Next we spotted the social and economic forces at work in their lives."[5] It was not until Coles and his wife began their work among the native Americans of New Mexico and Arizona, in the early 1970s, that they began to listen more carefully to the political implications of what people were saying.

After his address in South Africa in 1975, Coles began reflecting back on those hundreds of interviews conducted over the previous fifteen years. Jane Coles pointed out that in that material one could discern political awareness, political consciousness, perhaps less striking than among the South African children Robert Coles had talked with in 1975, but still there, still present. "My wife's contention was that I had been shifting many political observations by children in the United States to other rubrics, so to speak—to racial awareness, to regional loyalty, to social class, economic conflict, historical consciousness, cultural struggles, traditional sentiments of the neighborhood."[6] All these concerns are political, of course. But as dependents, children have a keen sense of power and power relationships, and power ultimately is what politics is all about. So Coles embarked on a research project, returning to South Africa, visiting other countries, reacquainting himself with children and families he and Jane Coles had interviewed a decade earlier, shaping a "'cross-cultural' study of 'political socialization'"[7] that resulted in *The Political Life of Children.*

We will return a bit later to the insights and conclusions that Coles records in that book. It is Coles's own political development that is our concern here. Even after his "conversion experience" on the Biloxi beach in 1958, Coles's political awareness was slow in growing. He found himself reading stories of the integration struggle, listening to people talking about race relations. But his background had not at all prepared him for the Byzantine entanglement of Southern politics, folkways, customs, and personal relationships. Once, he recalls, he invited a group of his air force co-workers, including a black nurse, to his apartment; needless to say, the nurse did not attend, and it took Coles the longest time to figure out why.

As he began his interviews with the children and high schoolers in New Orleans and Atlanta, he also began reading about the South: Lillian Smith's *Killers of the Dream,* Wilbur Cash's *The Mind of the South,* C. Vann Woodward's *The Strange Career of Jim Crow,* and Southern novelists like Welty, O'Connor, Faulkner, Shirley Ann Grau, and James Agee. So when he first encountered people intent on changing the entire Southern political system, Coles had not just his psychiatrist's training and doctor's credentials, but a growing sense of "the mind of the South," a feel for its customs, climate, and history; indeed, he once observed, "Where would I be without the South?"[8]

In 1961 Coles was interviewing the ten Atlanta blacks chosen to integrate that city's high schools. One of them mentioned attending a meeting of SNCC, the Student Nonviolent Coordinating Committee, at its downtown headquarters, and Coles asked to accompany him. At first, Coles recalls, he was treated coolly, even suspiciously. After the lunch-counter sit-ins and freedom rides of 1960 and 1961, SNCC was attracting more media attention, which threatened to distract from the main work at hand, even sabotage it. As "Snicker" Bob Zellner told Coles, "If you want to talk with us, you should work with us. It's the only kind of arrangement we can have!"[9] Coles followed this advice, and began doing office work, licking stamps and running errands. After several months, "They decided that others could stamp envelopes. I would be their physician and psychiatrist. . . . I heard their medical and emotional complaints. . . . At the request of attorneys I visited them in jails, to appraise their survival under often unjust and wretched conditions."[10] By 1963 Coles had also begun working for the Congress of Racial Equality and the Southern Christian Leadership Conference as well. This latter group was headed by Martin Luther King, Jr., whom Coles first met in Montgomery, Alabama, in 1958.[11]

In summer 1964 Coles worked with SNCC leader Bob Moses preparing hundreds of young blacks and whites for the Mississippi Freedom Summer project, an uncertain, even dangerous effort to register black voters and conduct "freedom schools." Coles's task was to determine the psychological fitness of these young recruits who were gathering for a two-week orientation at the campus of Western College for Women in Oxford, Ohio. "Even before Oxford I had noted that the students interested in the project seemed consistently serious, dedicated and well aware of the serious implications of the kind of work they were asking to do. Every effort was made to acquaint them with the hard facts of life facing the Negro citizens of that state, and the firm conviction of its leading white citizens that no change could occur."[12] A few went home, unable to face the dangers described.

But the entire mood of the gathering changed when news came of the disappearance of three civil rights workers who had recently left Oxford for Mississippi. Coles recalls that announcement with particular clarity: "I was supposed to go with them," but "Bob Moses, whose central, visionary dream was the so-called Summer Project of 1964 . . . asked me at the last minute to turn back. . . . I remember when they left in that Volkswagen of Mickey Schwerner's; I said goodbye to them. And they joked with me, they said I should come along [be]cause Mickey Schwerner was a social worker and Andy Goodman was the son of a psychologist, so they said we'll have a team there. . . . I remember when we got word they'd disappeared." "They're dead, they're absolutely dead," Stokely Carmichael told Coles, with whom he shared responsibility for a seminar on "methods and techniques of nonviolence."[13] Were it not for Bob Moses, Robert Coles, who had already faced a Mississippi sheriff's gun and been in a dynamited Freedom House, "would now be buried deep in that soil of Neshoba County, Mississippi, alongside those . . . three youths with whom I'd planned to travel South and work."[14]

The project's organizers watched the mood of the group anxiously, as the lesson of the disappearance began to sink in: "Going to Mississippi meant the concrete, explicit risk of death."[15] Guilt and anxiety, fear and uncertainty combined with their undeniable idealism and passion for justice to create, in the next few days, a volatile psychological climate. A few more decided, or were encouraged, to resign from the project. Many more sought medical consultations, as if "doubtful of their strength of body and mind to face their own possible Philadelphias [the Mississippi town near the murder site]. There was an increase in those openly anxious, fearful or unable to sleep."[16]

Then, Coles writes, "something quite surprising and wonderful and . . . awesome happened. Suddenly hundreds of young Americans became charged with new energy and determination. Suddenly I saw fear turn into toughness, vacillation into quiet conviction. . . . I saw several hundred young men and women—black and white, rich and poor, Northern and Southern—form themselves into a huge circle, hands held together or arms locked into one another."[17] On another occasion, Coles recalled the entire group "in a big circle singing 'We Shall Overcome.'"[18] The essays in which Coles recounts the two weeks at Oxford are among several devoted to the youthful civil rights workers of the early 1960s. In retrospect, Coles sees that he "bent over backward to salute them. . . . To my mind they were not only themselves doing important and valuable and commendable work; they were a sign of something else in our country: a new kind of youth, more idealistic and self-sacrificing and sensitive and thoughtful and compassionate."[19] Although the civil rights movement shifted its ground in the mid-1960s, becoming an increasingly black-identified movement, Coles has had no inclination to qualify or retract his praise for those youthful soldiers of the movement, only to regret that their successors in other liberation struggles seemed obliged to resort to vilification, violence, and social polarization to gain their ends.

Certain portraits in Coles's books and essays radiate, at least for this reader, a luminousness that captures the essence of the scene or individual. The descriptions of Ruby Bridges are one; Sally the mountaineer is another; Hendrick the Afrikaner yet another. For me the collective portraits of young civil rights workers seem absolutely correct, not just in their details, but in their depth. Coles has caught, in interview after interview, the fragile balance of idealism and practicality, of raw fear and immense courage. To reread these accounts, and recall those days, is a deeply moving experience.

For a young man in his mid-thirties, reared and educated in an apolitical atmosphere, the willingness of these young people to sacrifice education and careers, to risk their lives in some cases, was both a moral and a political phenomenon. In "Serpents and Doves: Nonviolent Youth in the South," Coles allowed himself this much generalization:

> There are in America today young men and women, black and white, who are going to jail for the freedom of their fellow men. They are doing radical things in novel and challenging ways; and they are doing them in every man's sight . . . wherever they are and wherever they go, they test and defy. Here, certainly for the first time in my life, I have seen American students behave toward their society with the "ideological" concern said to possess young people in Europe or Asia. . . . They are concerned with their own country, and they want to become her true citizens. They very definitely want to change

social and political customs, but they want to change them peacefully and in their time. They are not lost or confused; they know exactly what they want, and they are ready to give their lives for that goal. I went to study them and I came to respect them; and so I will tell their story so as to let them come to word, and through them, their tasks and their fate.[20]

And so their stories are told: The young white Southern woman, a college student, always frightened of black people, but ultimately convinced that change was necessary: "After a while I decided I'd actually *do* something about all of this, and so I started speaking up whenever the subject came up, and you'd be surprised at how many people are just waiting for others to take the lead."[21]—The black college sophomore: "Every time I feel afraid I just remind myself that we've got nothing to lose. I think of all the things I've had to put up with in my life. . . . I tell you, I can get so angry that they could have atom bombs on their clubs and police dogs and I'd keep on walking or sitting. We've got our rights as human beings to gain, and absolutely nothing to lose, not a thing."[22]—The black activist to whom Coles devotes an entire essay: "You can't do this kind of work and not ask yourself all kinds of questions. What is life all about? What is a person supposed to do—challenge the status quo or submit to it? How much can you take—of fear and danger and the threats we get every day? I ask myself questions all the time now. . . . I can't come up with any answers at all some of the time. I'm mixed up—not in my mind, but about life. Maybe you shouldn't think too much. Maybe it's dangerous."[23]—Or the not-so-young community organizer, taking a break in a comfortable Atlanta hotel and reflecting on his life:

> There, in Atlanta, I decided I wasn't a nut, not really. I remembered all our struggles, all our losses—but our victories, too. We've become an important part of that county. People listen to us—and I mean poor black people, never mind the rich white ones! I love the people I work with; I think they're fond of me. . . . My mother is the one wrote me a letter a year ago and told me she was praying for me, in church, that I "find myself," and that I "get a regular job." I wonder what Jesus said, listening to her prayers! I felt like writing her back and asking her if Jesus ever held "a regular job"—or ever "found himself." Jesus, the migrant preacher, who became so unpopular and disturbing to everyone big and important that He got crucified![24]

To be sure, Coles writes, these youth suffer from emotional stress, depressions, various forms of neurosis. But consider the circumstances under which they are living and working.

> Those students who leave school for some months and venture into these troublesome sections, live different lives once there. If you know the cramped, desolate, dreary quality to the Negro sections of Southern towns, if you've heard the spirituals and seen the funerals, diagnosed the tuberculosis and vitamin deficiencies, smelled the cheap, bad booze which blots out poverty, persecution, the whim of the alien white lords, then you will know how some of these students live.[25]

They face arrest on trumped-up charges, brutality and foul language in the jail house, farcical trials, sentences, records, the loathing and contempt of fellow whites, distrust and fear of fellow blacks. So if civil rights workers do suffer from "nerves," become jittery, irrational, have disturbing dreams, become depressed, irritable, unable to go on, it is because they are engaged in a war: "It's almost like going into an army," says one activist who had been arrested eighteen times. "Well, a better example is the Crusades, where men went off for their religious convictions, almost voluntarily."[26]

As Coles observed, interviewed, and worked with the young activists of the early 1960s, he came to distrust the way psychiatric categories were being used against them. "In 1963 I heard a decidedly sensitive and well-educated Southern judge send a youthful black civil rights worker to a state hospital, where he was to be 'observed,' where his 'mental status' was to be evaluated, where possible 'delinquent' and 'sociopathic' trends would be ascertained and studied—and where, perhaps, the young man would begin to get some 'treatment.'" Did the worker have difficulties with adjustment? he was asked. Did he have a problem with authority? The young man saw through this approach— "We protest our inability to vote, to go into a movie or restaurant everyone else uses, and they call us crazy, and send us away to be looked over by psychiatrists and psychologists and social workers"—and Coles saw through it, too. "Those who protest are not psychotic, retarded, delinquent." These youth do not fit categories of "the crazed, lawless or mentally inadequate." Rather they are, given the particular stresses they labor under, very much like "that vast body of mankind which is alike and unalike: sometimes sad, sometimes joyful; gifted, and tiresome."[27]

What does it mean, Coles asks, prompted by the example of these activists, to be "normal"? "Were slaveholders 'normal'? Did Nat Turner have 'a problem with authority'?" If influential men—doctors, lawyers, judges, businessmen—wished to use psychological categories to explain and dismiss civil rights activists as "immature," not in touch with reality, "paranoid," "psychotic," acting out deep-seated problems, then why should such categories not be applied also to pilots who drop napalm, agents of the CIA, indifferent politicians?[28] Ultimately, Coles believed, it was the students' *message,* not their emotional health, that was the issue: "Perhaps these students challenge our assumptions, our concepts, our language, our present ability to answer many problems; they make us aware of some of our limitations."[29]

These youthful activists of the early 1960s meant so much to Coles not only because of their idealism, their blend of mysticism and practicality, their use of literature and art and music for nourishment in hard times. Even more, these workers demonstrated to Coles the way in which people break out of their categories, do the unexpected. Many came from privileged, sheltered backgrounds, were confident of prosperity and meaningful work in adult life, and yet they left their homes and campuses to live and work in desperate and dangerous circumstances. What accounts for this behavior? Like Ruby Bridges and the other "children of crisis," these workers provided Coles with powerful illustrations of the radical mystery of human behavior. In reflecting on these matters in the pages of *The Moral Life of Children,* Coles asks, "Why do some youths persist with their idealistic preoccupations or affiliations for long stretches of time, whereas others shun idealism altogether" or are limited in their commitments? "If the ego has 'mechanisms of defense,' it also has properties that may be described as perceptual energy or a capacity to think and not only to use language, but respond to its power and suggestiveness. . . . As with all of life's many ironies, some of the more unpromising childhoods on this planet . . . may well be the surprising preludes for a later earnestness if not tenacity of good will."[30] If some of the "privileged ones" remain locked in their fortresses of fear and possessions, others, quite unaccountably, break out and engage the real world.

Like many other "liberal," Northern professionals, Robert Coles took the side of the Southern blacks and their youthful allies in the civil rights struggle. What distinguished Coles from some of his Northern peers was his persistence. "He wasn't a day-tripper," recalls Pat Watters; "he was there month after month." Even more, Coles was interested in "the other side." He wanted to understand Southern segregationists, not as sources of sociological data, but as human beings. Julian Bond remembers this trait: "We had one fellow demonstrating against us who'd been accused and acquitted of bombing a synagogue; a real hater, this guy.

Coles just patiently drew him out and the guy burst out in tears one day and sobbed to Bob that his mother always hated him and somehow he was getting back at her. I know it sounds theatrical, but he had this special way with people."[31]

In 1964 Robert Coles wrote "Social Struggle and Weariness," an effort to explain exactly what emotional difficulties were plaguing the activists who were putting themselves on the line. He intended to explain, as we have seen, why some do indeed experience depression and fatigue and nervous disorders. They were, after all, "abandon[ing] an old identity, achiev[ing] a new one, and fight[ing] for it."[32] In the course of his work (intensively with twenty-three student activists), one told Coles, "I'm tired, but so is the whole Movement. We're busy worrying about our position or our finances, so we don't do anything anymore. . . . We're becoming lifeless, just like all revolutions when they lose their first momentum and become more interested in preserving what they've won than going on to new challenges."[33]

In fact, this young person was prescient; soon after Mississippi Freedom Summer, the civil rights movement began to fragment, its fragile alliance of white and black crumbling. Coles recalls one such divisive meeting in 1965, out of which would come Stokely Carmichael's cry for "black power": "Even now, I cringe as I recall what I saw and heard. Old friends, comrades in a common struggle, self-declared soul mates, turned on each other sadly, bitterly, sometimes viciously." Jane Coles tried to explain to her husband that the movement had always had its ideological, politically radical side; the activists had never been quite as "innocent and wide-eyed and uncalculating and purely idealistic as I had at times persuaded myself" they were. Still both Coleses were "dismayed, jolted and badly troubled by what we'd heard—the insults, denunciations, even threats: brother and sister against brother and sister, so to speak, not to mention the sweeping assaults on the United States, a nation I thought we wanted to improve, not denounce unreservedly or dismiss outright." Throughout 1965 Coles was stunned to hear a new kind of rhetoric, militant, class-conscious, deliberately polarizing. Finally and ironically, the Coleses, like other white activists and supporters, "heeded the taunts of the segregationists: *Go home!*" and returned to New England in 1966.[34]

Robert Coles had seen that "systems" could be moved, even changed by people who acted with remarkable, unlooked-for courage. He had had his first encounter with politics, despite the bitterness of its ending. But the civil rights movement was not his only political mentor in the 1960s. In 1967 Coles and several other doctors traveled through the

Mississippi Delta, and reported their findings to a U.S. Senate subcommittee. In 1968 Coles was part of a similar investigation in South Carolina, where he visited, among others, a family in the congressional district of Mendel Rivers, then a powerful member of the House Appropriations Committee: "There is no running water, no central heating, no electricity, not even an outdoor privy. Water is toted from afar, and it is bad water, pumped from a well that does not go deep enough, and is contaminated. The fields nearby take human waste, and flies and mosquitos are everywhere. The house has no screens." According to Dr. Donald Gatch, a local doctor, the children of Mendel Rivers's district suffer from rickets, scurvy, beriberi and pellagra, diseases "medical students are taught no longer exist in America."[35]

Coles also testified about conditions in Appalachia, and because of his words and that of many other experts and local people, Congress voted larger appropriations for food aid in Southern states, for food stamps and a migrant health program.

Valuable, indeed priceless, as these contributions were to what should be called the "political process," it may well be that the most powerful political influence on Robert Coles from 1965 to 1968 was the junior senator from New York, Robert Kennedy.

"I didn't like the Robert Kennedy of the 1950s," Coles once said, referring to Kennedy's all too-conservative political record of the 1950s.[36] But after President Kennedy's death, the younger brother seemed to come into his own. Coles first met him in 1965, testifying before a Senate committee looking into Northern ghetto conditions.

> He relentlessly questioned us witnesses about those problems, and so doing, we seemed to be getting away from the usual facts-and-figures approach. The Senator was wondering about how people who are extremely vulnerable regard not only themselves and their neighbors, but this life—its purposes, its ethical underpinnings, if any. Later, he took us to lunch, and as we talked I could again feel the moral intensity of the man, a certain thirst and hunger in him as he probed and probed, those blue eyes always staring directly at one's face, and the ears never missing a single word, and for that matter, hearing the silences, too.[37]

In 1967 and early 1968, Coles accompanied Kennedy on tours of the Mississippi Delta and Appalachia, regions Coles knew well. Indeed, Coles is indebted to Kennedy for prompting him to extend the *Children of Crisis* work to other hard-pressed and minority young people:

One day in early 1968, as we talked about the impoverished, hungry, and often enough sick young people we both had seen in the delta of Mississippi and in various hollows of Appalachia, he suddenly turned to me (he could concentrate upon one the most relentless, unflinching, penetrating of stares) and asked me: "What about the Chicano children, and Indian and Eskimo children of this country? How do we make things better for them?" . . . With no faith that I could do a thousandth of what he could do, I told Robert Kennedy that I would extend my work to the children he had mentioned, try hard to comprehend the nature of their lives, and evoke for others what I had witnessed and felt to be important.[38]

There was even talk, in early 1968, of moving to Washington, taking up a post in a new Kennedy administration, Coles recalled. But he was uninterested in politics, he insists. No, Kennedy's appeal was on a wholly different level. Like Coles himself, Robert Kennedy was a man on the boundaries: an intellectual in politics, a cool, enormously reserved young man plunged into the political circus where every twitch is scrutinized; a man of immense independent wealth daily growing in compassion for America's dispossessed. In Coles's view, Kennedy was the last American populist, a political leader who appealed to both white and black working-class people. It is no accident that many people who voted for Robert Kennedy in the spring primaries voted for George Wallace in the November 1968 general election.

In that year of assassinations and police riots, Coles, like so many other Americans, was pessimistic about the future of American politics. Nonviolent civil disobedience had produced only a handful of victories. "It's damned hard to change the rules and values in the society, I am telling you. I sat through this in Atlanta. I saw New Orleans, with everything going for them there, how many years it took, how many lives had to be lost, how many truncheons had to be wielded, how many guns had to be shot out, and how many churches had to be burned down before we could even get a voting bill."[39]

In the first volume of *Children of Crisis* published in 1967 but written earlier, Coles writes of youthful black protestors: "Southern Negro children, eager for sit-ins and marches, are not willing to accept the prevailing values of a segregated society. They are committed to action, dedicated to affirming new values. It is their actions that make them guileless and powerfully innocent, and in tune with our time; and it is this very time that enables them to strike out and claim successfully once forbidden territory."[40] But by 1968 that vision of broad social change had faded. "There's a difference between that [social activism] and being active with the expectation that this will transform the society in some fundamental utopian or large-scale way. This I just don't see happening."41

No political movement since the early phase of the civil rights struggle (if indeed one can call it political, with its fierce individualism, disdain of "traditional" politics and distrust of "working within the system") has so captured Robert Coles's enthusiasm and no political leader since Robert Kennedy has attracted his loyalty. When the Coleses returned to the Boston area in 1966, they came to a city then just beginning a bitter and prolonged school integration program, with busing as its most controversial element. While walking in Cambridge one day, Coles recalled, he came across a group of children boarding a bus. He got on with them, asked if he could ride with them. At first they were suspicious, but when he assured them he was not a policeman, but a doctor, the children allowed him to stay. He met their black parents, who had initiated the then-voluntary busing. Suddenly he found himself, he reported to his wife, doing his same old work again, finding people on hunches, talking with them, listening to their stories. These are recorded in *The South Goes North* and *The Image Is You,* among other places.42

But as in Atlanta or New Orleans, so in Boston: There were other sides to the story, and in the late 1960s and early 1970s Coles began to visit the homes of white working-class men and women. He heard their stories, their fears and hopes, their concerns about their city and their nation. To *Time* he said,

> We categorize people, call them names like "culturally disadvantaged" or "white racists," names that say something all right but not enough—because those declared "culturally disadvantaged" so often are at the same time shrewd, sensitive, and in possession of their own culture, just as those called "white racists" have other sides to themselves, can be generous and decent, can take note of and be responsive to the black man's situation.

So Robert Coles, liberal doctor, priest in the modern cult of psychiatry, friend of Bob Moses and Andrew Young and Martin Luther King, Jr., Harvard graduate, began spending time with firemen and policemen, machinists, gas-station owners, typists, bank tellers, and their families, people who make up working-class America, people his Harvard friends called "awful, vulgar, reactionary."43

When he began the work that would result in *The Middle Americans* and parts of *The South Goes North,* Coles had already spent ten years working to disabuse himself and others of stereotypes. Southern blacks and Appalachian whites, despite poverty and oppression, were not necessarily cowed, apathetic, beaten people. Their children did not collapse under the pressure of white crowds resisting desegregation. The South was not simply divided into racists and victims, but contained whites who supported integration and blacks who were dubious about it. Civil rights activists were not working out buried psychic hostilities, nor did they suffer from martyr complexes. The same complexity, Coles insisted, must be recognized in the lives of "middle Americans." These people are not simply "ethnics," "hard hats," "Archie Bunkers"; they are people with complicated, often ambivalent feelings and responses. There is "blindness distortions, racism" among them, to be sure, Coles admits. But they require a special sympathy, for "it is they who must bear the brunt of change in American society."[44]

Joe and Doris, for example, struggle to make sense out of American life. Joe is enraged by student demonstrators he sees on television, calls them vulgar, wild, crazy, insulting, obscene. But people with power and authority are equally suspect.

> There are times when I wonder who really runs this country. It's not people like us, that I know. We vote, we do what we're supposed to do and we go right in the wars. . . . There are some big people in Washington, I guess, and they make all the decisions; and then it's left for us to go and send our boys to fight, and try to pay the high prices that the politicians have caused us to have. Don't ask me more. I don't know who the big people are.

Joe's sister summarized her feelings this way:

> There's something wrong, that's what I say, and it all started with this civil rights business, the demonstrations, and then the college radicals and on and on. It used to be that you could go to church and pray for your family and country. Now they're worried about colored people and you even get the feeling they care more about the enemy, the people killing our boys in Vietnam, than our own soldiers. . . . It's pretty bad for you these days if you're just a law-abiding, loyal American and you believe in your country, and in people being happy with their own kind, and doing their best to keep us first in the world."[45]

Cut off from the full human complexity of the speakers, such views can easily sound racist, chauvinist, uncaring of the struggles of others for justice, equality, dignity. And complexity is what Coles hears in John, a factory worker:

> I guess you have to have changes. You can't stay still. The colored people need more changes than anyone, though I hear the Indians have it real bad, too. It's always tough for poor people when they're trying to get their share of the pie. . . . I think the colored man is in trouble; he's not getting a fair shake from the country. I believe that's true. Don't ask me what should be done, though. I don't know. One minute I'll say we ought to give them a break, the colored, and the next minute I'll be fed up with them. . . . Who can agree with himself all the time? Not me! We'll be talking at the plant, and we catch ourselves contradicting what we just said, and we laugh. It's crazy, the world; that's what I believe. You can't make sense of people. They're too mixed-up.[46]

"People like him," Coles comments, "possess a richness and complexity of thinking that often enough social observers (writers or university-based scholars) simply fail to notice."

It is, in fact, "university-based" people that these Boston-area whites scorn, fear, and distrust the most. For them, education is a prized achievement, and students who ignore their studies to demonstrate against racism or the war in Vietnam seem to be ignoring or discarding a precious resource. Most of all, the middle Americans Coles interviewed bitterly resent the labels they feel such privileged members of society place on them—racist, reactionary, hard hat—and link these "snobbish" attitudes with the political powerlessness they feel. The father of a young man killed in Vietnam put it this way:

> I'm bitter. You bet your goddamn dollar I'm bitter. It's people like us who give up our sons for the country. The business people, they run the country and make money from it. The college types, the professors, they go to Washington and tell the government what to do. Do this, they say: do that. But their sons, they don't end up in the swamps over there, in Vietnam. No sir. . . . I hate those peace demonstrators. Why don't they go to Vietnam and demonstrate in front of the North Vietnamese? . . . To hell with them! Let them get out, leave, if they don't like it here! My son didn't die so that they can look filthy and talk filthy and insult everything we believe in and everyone in the country—me and my wife and people here on the street, and the next street, and all over.[47]

To this the boy's mother added, "I think my husband and I can't help but thinking that our son gave his life for nothing, nothing at all."[48]

Smart talkers, big thinkers, students, protestors, demonstrators—these are the special enemies of middle Americans, or ordinary working people. They resent the easy categorizing, the labeling, the verbal manipulations that often precede or accompany political and social manipulation.

The same Robert Coles who sat on front porches or in living rooms or kitchens, talked, became "a regular guest," even "a friend," also had an office in Harvard Yard, a ringside seat on student protest of the late 1960s.

> I remember watching the marches through the Yard, viewing the assault on University Hall, hearing the slogans at a succession of impromptu or well-advertised rallies. . . . "Hell no, we won't go." Nor did they; the ones who went were the poor (literally), the "brainwashed," and "one-dimensional" members of the "proletariat." To my office came upper-middle-class, politically alert and activist Harvard students, anxious for a letter to help them get deferred from the draft.[49]

To be sure, there were many students whose antiwar feelings echoed the "decency, the idealism, the thoughtfulness, the compassion we saw in Mississippi," people whose care for the "weak and humiliated and badly exploited" forced them to examine and protest against an unjust war in Asia.

Still, the facile use of "pig" and "fascist" and "bourgeois" disturbed Coles. He was, after all, spending a good deal of time talking with those Cambridge city and Harvard University "pigs" and their families. Were these people, hard-pressed by economic circumstances, their sons prime targets for the draft, really the enemy? Were Harvard undergraduates and their faculty supporters really so much wiser and more insightful than these people? Were university people never troubled, anxious, conflicted themselves? Were they always confident of their political judgments, correct in their cultural analyses?

Returning from a situation, in the South, where ideology was employed to heap contempt on white activists, now living and teaching in a situation where class analysis seemed to reduce complex people to categories, Robert Coles had all the more reason to see the university as one more flawed institution. Despite their professed sympathy with hard-pressed people, university people, thought Coles, were all too often simply "Privileged Ones" after all.

Still, Coles recognized in the late 1960s that there *was* racism, militarism, chauvinism, classism in America, and that these inequities were intolerable. While he disliked the wholesale assault on America that marked much protest at the end of the decade, Coles knew the problems: "I think if we all know how close we are to disaster, if we can all know what we might do that is wonderful, if we would all know therefore that we're walking on the edge, on the border . . . and not be paralyzed by it, we will have made some contribution to their solutions," he said to an interviewer in 1968. He ended that conversation with guarded optimism, but its central theme was how American society was "close to disaster."[50]

Like other people of progressive sensibility, Robert Coles had, in a sense, come to the end of politics by the end of the 1960s. He had joined a movement of social protest, had testified on behalf of social legislation, had seen the possibility of systems change through charismatic leaders like Robert Kennedy. But he had also seen it come unglued. He was frankly uncomfortable with Marxist analysis, with the call for black separatism and nationalism. He was suspicious of the gender-based analysis of the feminist movement then gaining in strength and influence. In all these systems, he thought, the rich, stubborn, densely textured lives of ordinary people vanish in a stream of abstract language and categories.

In 1970, Robert Coles met Daniel Berrigan; we have already told the story of their encounter. The book that grew out of their conversations, *The Geography of Faith,* reveals in its intensity and power the myriad ways in which Berrigan influenced Coles, encouraged him in his response to the public life. For Coles, in despair about politics and social change, Berrigan exemplified a completely different orientation, a new *cultural* criticism. If the liberalism of the civil rights movement had failed to undo American racism, and if a Marxist critique seemed alien to Coles, then Berrigan offered him a positive alternative, that of Christian radicalism.

Robert Coles acknowledged in the introduction that *Geography,* like *Children of Crisis,* is a "shaped" conversation. He has edited, rearranged, organized thematically the material accumulated over two weeks of conversation. Coles worried whether the book seemed to fix the two speakers too firmly into opposing positions, radical priest and moderate doctor. So the "geography" of the book may be Coles's doing rather than the way the conversation unfolded. Nonetheless, we have in these pages a movement, a development on the part of each conversationalist. Berrigan moves inward, progressively revealing his contemplative side. Coles moves outward, seeing (not for the first time) the links between psychoanalysis and the larger culture.

In the first two chapters, Coles is the cautious, warning voice, presenting the other side, voicing skepticism about Berrigan's radical critique of American society. Berrigan's criticism of the nuclear family opens the volume. For him, the duties of family life—rearing of children, caring for a home—tie people to "the service of the war-making state, the service of the consumer society."[51] Bold and willing to take risks when single, too many people, including "Movement" activists, become cautious when married, fearful of future consequences for themselves, their spouses, their children. The family is the "structure in our society [which] seems to offer the greatest resistance to change."[52] Coles phrases Berrigan's criticism this way: "You claim it is because I am a husband and a father that I am cautious. In another sense of the word I 'husband' my resources and remain loyal to the system, the social system, the economic system, out of fear, out of trembling for my children."[53]

Not all families need operate in this "suffocating and totalizing" way,[54] but most Americans see nothing wrong with the family, or indeed with "the system" as it is presently constituted, Coles points out. "I think we are basically a very conservative country. I think that by and large the people in this country . . . do not want radical change of any kind. . . . Not that they don't want changes here and there; but in the main they feel satisfied with the life they have, and unwilling to have you or me or any other smart-aleck intellectual come along with our brainy ideas."[55]

Reflecting the feelings of the "middle Americans" he was then interviewing, Coles asks Berrigan about pride and violence. The property damage committed by the Weathermen (especially in their "Days of Rage" in Chicago in 1969) seemed to Berrigan, while not defensible, at least understandable. "Their violent rhythm was induced by the violence of the society itself—and only after they struggled for a long time to be nonviolent. . . . And I can excuse the violence of those people as a temporary thing. I don't see a hardened, long-term ideological violence operating, as in the case of the Klansmen."[56] Coles dislikes this line of reasoning very much; Berrigan seems to be approaching the "revolutionary violence" position of Herbert Marcuse: "You feel *you* have the right to judge what is a long-term ideological trend, and what isn't, and you also are judging one form of violence as temporary and perhaps cathartic and useful or certainly understandable . . . whereas another form of violence you rule out as automatically ideological. It isn't too long a step from that to a kind of elitism."[57]

Whether Robert Coles intended to or not in the shaping of this narrative, the reply Berrigan gives seems to mark a shift in the conversation. Surely on some other points the two will differ, but gradually, from this point in the midst of the second chapter to the end, the two begin to work together, to share insights, to build on each other's comments. Berrigan's reply to Coles's charge of radical elitism is simply this:

> It seems to me that we, that *you,* are looking at the society as a kind of platonic entity which is self-justifying on principle and is functioning on behalf of individuals and for human life with a kind of structured compassion and justice and decency—and it is exactly those suppositions I take issue with. That is to say, the society itself is under judgment; I refer to its values, its deeds, its relationship to the international community, especially to the Third World.[58]

Coles's experiences in the deep South and in Appalachia had already provided him abundant evidence of social violence, institutional injustice, evidence to support Berrigan's radical critique. Even at Harvard, he pointed out, no one asks (or asked in 1970) who owns certain buildings, who sets rent, salaries; these questions expose the gap between rhetoric and reality. And his own skepticism about the profession of psychiatry makes him responsive to the question Berrigan poses at the opening of Chapter 5, "Professional Life": "What issues [do] you believe your profession ought to be struggling with in times like these[?]"[59] Psychiatrists are taught to treat individual disorders, not press for the social reasons as to why people behave in peculiar ways. Such questioning is likely to get one into trouble: "When young psychiatrists in training start to question their teachers too strenuously or speak too critically of theories sometimes handed down to them like laws or articles of religious faith, they can be called 'troubled,' be told that they need 'more analysis,' be asked what their 'problem' is that prompts such radical doubt."[60] Even those who want to press more deeply are sometimes seduced by their own theories "and ignore all kinds of things, while emphasizing what it suits their purpose to emphasize as citizens of a particular nation and as men or women alive at a certain moment in history."[61]

Indeed, Coles comes around, in this chapter, to seeing how one might understand, if again not condone, revolutionary violence. Coles contrasts his own situation with that of Stokely Carmichael, with whom he conducted a training session for civil rights workers in 1964. Carmichael had moved rapidly toward a strenuous and uncompromising "black power" position, while Coles continued his work as interviewer, writer, child psychiatrist. Is it not too easy, and too self-congratulatory, to criticize Carmichael for his turn toward armed self-defense, and to praise the white doctor for his "maturity" and "good sense," for his contributions to his profession? Are not these possibly "signs of my death"? "I am fatally compromised; . . . my way of looking both at Stokely's political position and his psychological development, as well as at the economic and social realities of the world around me, reflects my willingness to live as I do . . . as the beneficiary of a colonial world power."[62]

Gradually, as Berrigan and Coles work through issues like the future of the priesthood, the promise of the university, the witness of Georges Bernanos and Simone Weil, the notion of living "on the edge," a genuine ease and rapport emerge between them. They both speak eloquently of the calling to "live a life," not simply to espouse positions. It is never possible, Berrigan says, to quantify the number of people who are moving to a more radical critique, or to measure the impact of heroic lives. One simply (but far from easily) lives out the consequences of one's own beliefs, becomes, in the very nature of the life, a witness to an alternative vision. Here is Berrigan on being underground:

> I have tried to enter each home as a quiet member of a growing discussion—one my presence naturally triggers, because it is a moral decision for a family to accept me, a man sought by the FBI. So, in every family that I've stayed with, a discussion naturally grows as to who we are and where we are going. . . . And as a stranger, but not as a zero, I can bring a certain good news to the scene, out of my own experience.[63]

Though not sought by the FBI, Robert Coles too has entered homes, has prompted reflection and discussion, has simply been a presence there.

The question always is: How is one to live? Berrigan phrases his role this way: "I believe from my own experience and from what I have seen happen to others that a new kind of life, a new way for people to live with one another, is quite possible."[64] And in order to test out the possibilities of that new life, one needs to taste "some of the powerlessness which is the alternative to the wrong use of power today." For Berrigan, for others in the "Movement," that meant living "on the edge."

> I remain convinced that in view of what goes on in the world, we must each of us explore and prod the world, and enter into *some* kind

of jeopardy. . . . I could not remain at peace at the center, so the issue
continues to be spatial—an issue of one's geography, one's place,
one's decision to stand here, not there, and for this rather than for
that. . . . The issue is geographic.[65]

And in all this, one seeks out, Berrigan says, certain models, certain
witnesses for support and encouragement. For him and other Christians, it is the life and death of the young rabbi in an obscure corner of
the Roman Empire:

I suppose at the time many people thought Him and His followers
quite "provincial," but from the point of view of the spirit a floodgate
was opened and the result is still felt by us. Thus does a life pass into
history, thereby to nourish the living at every point in which their
lives are threatened and in danger of suffocation.[66]

Robert Coles too has pondered the question of living "on the edge," of
being, in some sense, "in jeopardy." Beginning with his selection of
William Carlos Williams as the subject for his Harvard thesis, Coles has
consistently been attracted to "marginal" people, in part no doubt
because of his own feeling of marginality. Even more, these are attractive people because their refusal to be categorized suggests that they are
not captive to institutional life or "normal" thinking. Dorothy Day,
Simone Weil, James Agee, Daniel Berrigan—these are genuinely coun-
tercultural figures. They challenge not simply particular injustices, but
entire ways of thinking and feeling. They organize no political movements, hire no lobbyists, have no legislative agenda. Rather they employ
the witness of their lives to stand against the entire direction of the
culture they find themselves in.

While Coles had long been drawn to these figures (and other like
Edith Stein, Georges Bernanos, George Orwell, and Ignatio Silone),
they seemed to have increasing significance for him after 1970 and his
encounter with Daniel Berrigan. Like Berrigan, who is critical of the
excesses of the Nicaraguan Sandinistas and deplores abortion, Coles
eschews the standard liberal progressive political line. He has, as he put
it, "grave doubts about abortion considered as a casual right," concerns
about the women's movement, reservations about gay rights as a public
movement.[67]

His disenchantment with the direction of American culture in the
1970s is evident in his review of Christopher Lasch's *The Culture of
Narcissism*.[68] Coles's reading of Lasch reveals his own concerns—the
interplay of self and society, the pervasiveness of irony, the abuses of

psychology. Lasch "links his psychological title to a sociological subtitle: 'American Life in an Age of Diminishing Expectations.' He is a strong-minded cultural theorist, eager to reveal us to ourselves—an ironic effort," for the revelation of narcissism becomes simply one more interesting diversion in the bored and satiated lives of American narcissists.

Like Coles, Lasch is critical of "the evil of psychologizing," a phrase Coles has no difficulty explaining. "All those psychological explanations, not only naive and sometimes absurd but ephemeral as well—replaced by new guides or contradictory ones: psychology as an instance of consumerism." This rush to embrace psychology "is a measure of how uncomfortable we have learned to be with an open acknowledgment of any moral—never mind spiritual—concerns we may yet have, despite the age and its culture." Lack of parental self-restraint can lead to a child whose behavior oscillates between "wanton, senseless cruelty" and "self-abasement" to religious cults or worship of superstars.

Liberation movements, Lasch argues and Coles agrees, that take place in capitalist, consumer societies have the unhappy effect of producing people who simply want more than they had before. Clearly for Americans suffering from inadequate nutrition, housing, medical care, pensions, this is not an unreasonable demand. But the youth revolt, the women's movement, the gay rights movement—these in Lasch's (and Coles's) estimation run the risk of confusing self-indulgence, self-gratification, with genuine liberation.

Two years later, Coles had more to say about the way contemporary culture interprets liberation as self-gratification, and about the role of English psychiatrist R. D. Laing in that interpretation. In 1967, Coles had praised Laing's *The Politics of Experience,* which disputes the easy use of psychiatric categories to label and dismiss patients. Then, Laing's understanding of schizophrenia as a "special strategy that a person invents in order to live in an unlivable situation," of madness as "potentially liberation and renewal" seemed plausible to the young American psychiatrist who had seen psychiatric categories employed to restrain and suppress social protest. In 1967, Coles believed Laing was not glorifying or romanticizing madness, but rather was engaged in serious and courageous criticism of his profession and the larger society.[69]

But in 1981 Coles offered a different reading of Laing.

> It is something of an irony . . . that psychoanalysis has been spuriously and romantically used (by [R. D.] Laing and others) to discredit hardworking, law-abiding men and women on the one hand and to proclaim as prophets, savants, the "liberated," those who

experience hallucinations and delusions, those who have made (for one reason or another) a mental break with the concrete realities of psychological life, as experienced by millions and millions of others. . . . The issue . . . is celebration, and a constant, caustic assault on social constraint as the enemy, as the true madness.

Freud's insight, that repression, for all its psychic costs, is the bedrock of civilization, is preferable to Laing's advocacy of schizophrenia. Then Coles makes his most impassioned point:

Have we witnessed in these recent years—after all the widely proclaimed changes in the sexual customs of some of us, in the educational techniques of some schools, in the interpersonal lives of some men and women—a number of New Jerusalems? Have our communes, our Esalens, our open classrooms, our Laingian halfway houses, our endless proliferation of encounter groups, with the dreary jargon-riddled self-consciousness they have foisted on us, spared us the risks and hazards of our humanity? Have they eased the ironies, ambiguities, inconsistencies, and contradictions of nature and desire and motive to which each of us is heir: the vulnerability and susceptibility to fate, to circumstance, to luck, to accidents, to countless unpredictable incidents—in short, to this life's puzzling character, to the sometimes good and sometimes bad times, personal as well as social and economic, we all experience?[70]

In the early 1980s, Coles began writing a regular column, "Harvard Diary," for the *New Oxford Review*. Reaching a largely Catholic clientele, the journal, under the leadership of Dale Vree, has tried to remain respectful of Catholic tradition yet critical of its abuses. Always intellectually rigorous, the journal solicits contributors from the *National Review*, but also embraces the social activist tradition of Dorothy Day's Catholic Worker movement. It has tried to avoid standard American political affiliations, although frequently its positions on politically controversial issues resemble that of neoconservatives. Like Christopher Lasch, the *New Oxford* people see contemporary "liberal" society as morally bankrupt, possessing no larger vision to lift it beyond gratification of physical needs or indulgence of pleasure. And like Robert Coles, they see in religion (for them, specifically Catholic Christianity) an alternative to the secular materialism that they would claim is truly our national faith.

In his column for October 1983 Coles took up the issue of abortion. Sixteen years earlier, in the pages of *The New Republic*, he had praised the liberalized abortion laws of Colorado and North Carolina, and had observed that the poor always suffer from unavailable or incompetent medical treatment. But even then, he noted the irony in one young mother's comment: "One of the few times I feel good is when I'm pregnant, and I can feel I'm getting somewhere, at least then I am—because I'm making something grow, and not seeing everything die around me."[71] Now in the eighties Coles finds himself still struggling with the issue of abortion, still in flux, torn up by careless pregnancies, by a world full of unwanted, neglected children. Still, "I believe with no special or surprising insight, that an abortion willfully terminates a life. . . . [It is] not only an utter tragedy but an affront to the Lord." Abortion is part of our global death wish, Coles believes, and if we need to make exceptions and perform abortions regularly, "then we have to do so with aching agony, with reverent reflection, in an awareness of our constant temptation to the sin of pride . . . and not least with sustained prayer."[72] Where once he worried primarily about the physical conditions of abortion clinics, the suffering of the poor, the consequences of carrying a pregnancy to term, now he sees the young mother's comment as profoundly wise. Many women, particularly (and ironically, given the likely fate of their children) poor and rural women, see pregnancy as a gift from God, a promise of new life and new possibilities.[73]

The women's movement likewise prompts very mixed feelings. Coles acknowledges and deplores discrimination against women and applauds the efforts to correct these injustices. But the women's movement, arising as it does in a culture fixated on "entitlements," inevitably focuses on women's rights and fulfillments. What about the relationships women find themselves in, particularly mother-child relationships? Must these suffer in order that women be liberated, Coles asks? Coles's sense is that the "traditional" nuclear family, often identified and attacked as the power center of patriarchy, has become an endangered social form in an age of epidemic divorce and surrogate childcare.

> I know no other way to put it: I believe that children need mothers and fathers both; that mothers are not fathers, and fathers are not mothers, nor ought the two be blurred into one—as in the dreary neuter word "parenting"; that it is wonderful for two individuals to complement one another, add to each other's store of possibilities—as inheritance for their children; and that the significance of the biological distinctions between men and women, amplified by centuries of religiously and culturally encouraged and sanctioned differences, are not to be altogether scorned, even as some of those

differences must be gladly discarded, and even as individuals sort themselves out according to both their aspirations and responsibilities—and our world becomes a more equitable place for all of us.[74]

In a similar way, Coles feels deep ambivalence about the issue of homosexuality. As with the women's movement, he sees clearly the great injustice done to gay people in the United States and elsewhere and unequivocally condemns it. But for him, sex and sexuality are essentially private matters, and they do not define an entire way of life. He dislikes the way in which various gay rights groups have made their sexual orientation a public (and in his mind intrusive) issue. Coles prefers "tact, discretion, the right of individuality," the value of privacy. "I dislike the politicization of a personal matter."[75]

"I am not a neoconservative," Robert Coles once said firmly. He thinks of himself as a populist in politics and a conservative on social and family issues. In April 1976 in the pages of the journal *Current,* he wished that the next president of the United States would be a Christian populist. Coles advocated worker ownership or voice in decision-making; rural co-ops; guaranteed jobs or a minimum income; stricter enforcement of job safety. More recently, he has denounced Allen Bloom for his intellectual elitism, and has defended the current generation of college students for having a far keener social consciousness than students in the mid-1970s. Still, Coles clearly has "grave doubts" about the liberal/progressive social agenda, believing, with his colleagues from the *New Oxford Review,* that absence of tradition and restraint and maximum personal freedom do not comprise true liberation.

These columns from NOR are tense, sometimes unhappy pieces. If Coles were writing about a woman suffering sexual harassment in an office, a gay man barred from employment, a ghetto mother pregnant for the fifth time, then most likely his compassion, his empathy, would be richly and warmly evident. But the post–civil rights progressive social movements have somehow not captured Coles's imagination. This in turn is because they—antiwar, feminism and abortion, gay rights—offer a structural analysis and critique of American culture. With years of patient conversation with "ordinary" people, "middle Americans," behind him, Coles is simply unwilling to accept an analysis that he believes identifies these people as dupes, brainwashed, or indeed the enemy.

Impatience with the "liberal establishment" is equally evident in Coles's recent involvement in the Mobile, Alabama, court case of evangelical parents opposed to the "secular humanism" of school texts. The school board's lawyers asked Coles to testify on behalf of the school's right to judge books on their educational merit, not their fidelity to a particular version of the truth. But, as Coles tells it, his deposition, taken before the case opened, was so equivocal that the lawyers chose not to use him as a witness. Having looked over the books in question, Coles found them full of psychological and sociological jargon. "Those textbooks are abominable. They're full of psychological, sociological junk. It isn't what I'd want my kids reading. The so-called intellectuals who leaped to oppose ought to take a look at those books. Let them get outraged about these books, which are crap."[76] This position put him in league with Pat Robertson and other fundamentalists, but Coles insists that his critique of contemporary secular culture is, like Christopher Lasch's, radical rather than reactionary.

Coles's reluctance to embrace *movements* for political change is readily apparent in his writing on the nuclear freeze movement of the early 1980s. In "Children and the Nuclear Bomb," the last chapter in *The Moral Life of Children,* Coles provides his view of the efforts of child psychologists and scientists to elicit from children their views about nuclear weapons. His dubiousness about these efforts is clear from the start. After summarizing the work of Drs. William Beardslee and John Mack, who solicited answers to questionnaires from elementary and secondary school students in Boston, Baltimore, and Los Angeles, Coles notes that "a group called Educators for Social Responsibility took upon itself, in October 1982, to distribute their version of a questionnaire all over the country, in conjunction with a so-called Day of Dialogue, an obvious effort to get more and more people talking about the dangers of the nuclear bomb."[77] The results of the Beardslee-Mack, the ESR, and several other surveys consistently reveal high percentages of children in the early eighties deeply concerned about their futures, fearful of nuclear weapons, even able to link the rise in drug use to anxiety about the Bomb.

But Coles is not convinced. Is it not quite possible that children thus surveyed told the adults what they wanted to hear? And can we really be sure that a child's fear of the future is solely linked to the danger of nuclear war? Again, with Anna Freud, Coles believes that "it is hard for us to know what to think about any particular moments of a child's life—unless we have the time to know the child over the months and years."

In his own nonstatistical but in-depth conversations with children, Coles found that awareness and concern about nuclear issues was very much linked to the class position of the children. Among children of Spanish ancestry in towns north of Santa Fe, teachers could not "detect a special concern . . . that our nuclear bombs will be used."[78] A teacher in a Boston-area school reported that a black student, bussed in daily, thought of the nuclear freeze movement as "head talk." When asked to explain, the girl said, "When I talk about racism, I know what I've gone through. It's not an idea. . . . These kids, it's like going to a class or something."

On the other hand, children from more secure economic situations and whose parents are thus minded, embrace the nuclear freeze movement with what Coles found was an unnerving seriousness. He interviewed Sue, a twelve-year-old Atlanta girl, who had a very clear and accurate sense of the consequences of nuclear war and drew Coles a picture of Atlanta in flames. She is, Coles thinks, preoccupied with images of devastation:

> Why is it that more people all over the world, don't push their governments to get rid of the bombs they have? They'd better do it fast, or there could be an accident, and that would be terrible. I heard a big explosion the other day, and I thought: it would sound like that, a nuclear bomb going off, only much, much worse. It would be like—as if God was coming down to judge us, and call us all bad for what we've done, for making these bombs.[79]

Is this child sick, obsessed, given to fantasies of violent death so grotesquely out of keeping with her pleasant and secure middle-class life? Coles is tempted to label her so, in part because her earnestness makes *him* feel uncomfortable. But, in the end, he recognizes that she is not "sick, or provocative, or a jejune moralist, or a smug dogmatist. I could finally let her be herself: a determined realist with an ethical worry or two."[80]

Nonetheless, Coles is sure that concern about nuclear weapons is not as widespread among children as the surveys indicate. He argues that each person has a limited capacity for "moral notice." For so many minority people, people of color, people hard-pressed economically, the nuclear issue—at least as it was articulated by freeze advocates—was simply too removed, too abstract. For others, "there is another life—one that offers the time, the ease, the personal and economic security, the social assurance that permits the mind to wander and wonder, to take up issues and causes, to take stands unconnected to a wage struggle, say, or a racial conflict."[81] For Coles, the pervasive issue is class, and then parental influence. Children concerned about nuclear issues have secure lives, by and large, and parents who voice their own concern about nuclear weapons. But in so many other families, the central parental concern is food, jobs, medical care, adequate housing.

So even in the nuclear freeze movement, Coles finds himself doubting, questioning, standing apart. In looking over Coles's attitudes and involvements in politics from the early sixties to the early eighties, are we to conclude that he, like others, has simply withdrawn from the political struggle? It certainly seems that Coles stands on the sidelines now, criticizing and cautioning, reluctant about the movements for change that have succeeded the early civil rights crusade. It also is apparent that Coles favors social change in the form of a populist political agenda, but cannot bring himself to embrace movements for change.

A reader of the *New Oxford Review* called Robert Coles a "New England Kierkegaardian individualist," a helpful description in grasping Coles's view of politics. What drew him to the civil rights movement with its moral dimension, its rather unorganized, unsystematic method, its cranky, idiosyncratic followers. What has repelled him from succeeding movements is their systematic analysis and what Coles believes is a rigid sense of certainty.

Like his nineteenth-century New England predecessors Emerson and William James, Coles believes in the irreducibility of the single self. He knows, of course, the power of class, of race, of region, in shaping the self. He often emphasizes those determinants in conversations with people he thinks overstress the solitary witness, as in his talks with Daniel Berrigan. He is aware of the burden of history as it presses down and molds acceptable selves. But for all that, he believes in the mysterious freedom of the self. To Daniel Berrigan Coles put it this way:

> At any given moment anyone *is* not only what he has *come to be*, but what he *might have been*. Each of us carries within himself (living in us even if not available or apparent) all kinds of resources and possibilities—and some of them may be hidden and known to no one, including the particular person in question. . . . I think that when St. Paul talked about the "new man" or the "twice born" he was trying to say that we don't have to be what we once were, and that we can be more than we presently are, and that every day (even every minute) of our lives offers us a chance to . . . realize for ourselves a certain coherence, a certain spirit of openness and concern.[82]

Coles's rejection of determinism—"What we *are* is a function of so many things: accidents, incidents, things that are unpredictable and yet have become the most important things in our lives"[83] echoes Emerson's belief in the possibility of continual rebirth.

> We are idolators of the old. We do not believe in the omnipotence of the Soul; we do not believe that there is any force in Today, to reveal or re-create that beautiful yesterday. . . . But the voice of the Almighty saith, Onward evermore! We cannot stay amid the ruins.[84]

Emerson was suspicious of the ways in which people tended to identify each other by virtue of their roles, by reference to their place in society, their obligations. These seemed to limit and stifle original insight:

> Man seems to me the one fact: the forms of the church and of society—the framework which he creates and casts aside day by day. The whole of duty seems to consist in purging off these accidents and obeying the aboriginal truth. . . . The true Fall of man is the disesteem of man; the true Redemption self-trust.[85]

Coles again would not go this far; he has a healthy respect for the influence of class, race, region, culture, on the self. We saw this, for example, in his reflections on the nuclear freeze movement.

There is, nonetheless, in Coles's life and work a strain of New England individualism, a belief in the irreducibility of the self. Like William James, Coles prefers to think of religion as essentially an individual's relation to the divine (although he knows how profoundly religion supports and encourages people in difficult circumstances). In *Varieties of Religious Experience* James wished

> to ignore the institutional branch entirely, to say nothing of the ecclesiastical organization, to consider as little as possible the systematic theology and the ideas about the gods themselves, and to confine myself as far as I can to personal religion pure and simple. . . . Religion . . . shall mean for us *the feelings, acts, and experiences of individual men in their solitude, so far as they apprehend themselves to stand in relation to whatever they may consider the divine.*

James's emphasis throughout the lectures that comprised *Varieties* was on "immediate personal experiences."[86]

Coles shows his affinity for these nineteenth-century forebears in his attitude toward political organization. As is well known, Emerson was deeply suspicious of political movements. Although his philosophy of self-reliance encouraged others to engage in social reform, he himself stood aloof. "Do not tell me," he wrote in "Self-Reliance,"

> as a good man did to-day, of my obligation to put all poor men in good situations. Are they *my* poor? I tell thee, thou foolish philanthropist, that I grudge the dollar, the dime, the cent I give to such men as do not belong to me and to whom I do not belong. . . . I confess with shame I sometimes succumb and give the dollar [to popular charities], it is a wicked dollar, which by and by I shall have the manhood to withhold.

Most of all, these three—Emerson, James, Coles—share a marginal status. Emerson was long distrusted by the Harvard establishment, informally banned from the college after delivering his notorious Divinity School address in 1838. Neither philosophy nor religious reflection nor literary criticism, Emerson's essays and addresses seem to be a new creation. They unfold organically, comment on themselves, double back. They are illogical, cranky, toplofty; they simultaneously invite and alienate. As for William James, his career is exemplary of marginality. Trained as an artist (although needing no gainful employment because of his inheritance from Henry James, Sr.), James also studied medicine and taught psychology at Harvard as well as writing his philosophical essays. Rejecting both idealism and materialism, James nonchalantly carved out a third possibility, pragmatism. And Coles's marginal status in his profession and in his own life seems abundantly clear. All this suggests that Coles, like his predecessors, is simply a loner, a man without disciples, without a movement, a man who eschews movements. When drawn into politics in the early mid-1960s, it was not for the sake of organizing or contributing to a movement, but for the sake of moral witness. This is what attracted him to Martin Luther King, Jr., to the early SNCC, to Mississippi Freedom Summer. As the civil rights movement shifted away from the notion of moral witness and into the arena of conflict, power politics, and ideological analysis, Coles became disenchanted.

It may be said that "moral witness" is a luxury which only the privileged, like Emerson, James, and Coles, white male professionals all, can afford. People hard-pressed by discrimination, poverty, unemployment, need to organize, need to make bold, even confrontational, demands. Ultimately, movements for social change require systematic analysis. Feminists and gay people have sought, for example, to understand the particular ways in which heterosexism is embodied, encouraged, and taught in all the various institutions of dominant American culture.

It would be reassuring, for people deeply engaged in such movements for change, to feel that men of such stature as Coles supported their efforts. But for Coles himself (as, I suspect, for Emerson and James), the lifelong tension between participation and observation, weighted in the area of politics toward observation, makes him unable and unwilling to be a true believer. Robert Coles will lead no crusades, political or otherwise. His admirers may regret that. Nonetheless, he is too skeptical of flawed human nature, too ironic, too given to seeing doubleness and complexity to be a political animal, to give himself to movements or causes. As he put it to Berrigan after a long evening of conversation, "I think that you and I have differed all along. You have hope because you believe a significant number of desirable things are happening. I have hope because I have seen a *few* desirable things happen, and I don't think that there is anything in man's nature or mind that necessarily prevents these things from happening. But I do not see widespread possibilities becoming actualities."[87]

·6·

The Religious Sensibility

In *Concluding Unscientific Postscript,* Søren Kierkegaard wrote:

> Christianity has declared itself to be the eternal essential truth which
> has come into being in time. It has proclaimed itself as the *Paradox,*
> and it has required of the individual the inwardness of faith in
> relation to that which is an offense to the Jews and a folly to the
> Greeks—and an absurdity to the understanding. It is impossible to
> express more strongly the fact that subjectivity is truth and that
> objectivity merely repels, even by virtue of the absurd. . . . It is
> impossible to express with more intense inwardness the principle that
> subjectivity is truth, than when subjectivity is in the first instance
> untruth, and yet subjectivity is the truth.[1]

For Robert Coles, of Jewish and Episcopal background, trained at
Harvard and Columbia, heir to the secular, atheist outlook of Sigmund
Freud and psychoanalysis, full of doubts, anxieties, uncertainties,
plagued with constant introspection, for this man, religion is subjective,
even absurd. Yet it is an inescapable, powerful, present force to be
accounted for in the lives of his subjects and in his own life. Unlike
many of his colleagues in academia and psychiatry, Coles refuses to treat
religion as a mask for other impulses, needs, evasions, or oppressions.
One cannot understand people's religious needs by invoking sociological or psychological categories, nor by dismissing religion as the
opiate of the people, or by approaching religion from an aesthetic point
of view. He has insisted, with increasing fervor, that spiritual matters
have an independent reality in people's lives.

Provocatively religious in a secular setting, Coles early experienced
the tension between spirituality and skepticism in his own family. His
mother, as we noted earlier, was a "warm, emotional and very religious
woman." She was "no fundamentalist," he said once, but had a lively
sense of the reality of the unseen world. His father, "a worldly scientist,
obviously found my mother's sly, opaque religious homilies rather
charming—when they were not terribly frustrating and maddening. . . .

"'I don't know about things like that,' he'd say when my mother would talk about 'grace' or a 'redemptive moment.'"[2] Kierkegaard and Pascal, Augustine and Simone Weil, the New Testament and the New England Puritans—these were Coles's subjects of study at Harvard College in the late 1940s, as he sat in classes and seminars conducted by Perry Miller, among others. Miller was, we recall, a man of intellect rather than a man of faith, but he insisted that students take religious studies with utmost seriousness. The Puritans, he stressed in *The New England Mind*, may have been compelled by various motives—economic, political, social—to criticize the Church of England, even to try to set up a more perfect "holy commonwealth" in the American wilderness. But they kept returning, in their public and private writing, to the spiritual motive, their desire for a more intense relationship with God, their desire to do more fully what they apprehended as God's will. So with the other writers and thinkers Miller assigned. We may not share the details of their vision, or even much of its core; but they—Weil and Pascal and the rest—were reflecting on matters of utmost, cosmic seriousness.

Religious questions, questions of meaning, kept intruding into Coles's life after graduation. At Columbia, repelled by the narrow and competitive professionalism, he formed a Bible study group with three other medical students. He sought out Reinhold Neibuhr's seminar at Union Theological Seminary. He rode the subway down to the Lower East Side and volunteered at the Catholic Workers' Saint Joseph House. Back in Boston, he audited Paul Tillich's course at Harvard Divinity and kept reading Simone Weil and Georges Bernanos. In Biloxi, Mississippi, he attended church regularly and met Martin Luther King, Jr. on a trip through Montgomery, Alabama.

But when he began his work among children and adults in situations of social and personal crisis, Robert Coles began to see religion not only as a series of provocative questions or reminders, reminders of realms of being that our social science orientation cannot answer. Now he began to see religion as a way of life, as intrinsically part of the daily routine, the hopes and anxieties of quite ordinary Americans.

He was not, Coles recalled, immediately prepared to recognize religion as a life-orientation. In interviewing Ruby Bridges in 1960, Coles looked for signs of psychic disturbance, eating disorders, behavior problems. He found instead a remarkable resiliency, courage, determination. He also found profound religious faith. One of Ruby's teachers told Coles, "I was standing in the classroom, looking out the window, and I saw Ruby coming down the street, with the federal marshals on both sides of her. The crowd was there, shouting, as usual. A woman spat at

Ruby but missed; Ruby smiled at her. A man shook his fist at her; Ruby smiled at him. Then she walked up the stairs, and she stopped and turned and smiled one more time! You know what she told one of the marshals? She told him she prays for those people, the ones in that mob, every night before she goes to sleep!"[3]

This behavior could be *understood,* Coles was sure in 1960 and 1961. Ruby lived in a religious environment; she was psycholigically imitative; she was doing what she was told to do; she was searching for security in an extremely hostile situation. Ruby's mother noticed how Coles kept looking for other reasons for her child's religious behavior. Why doesn't he ask her any questions about God? she wondered.[4] But this was not an appropriate scientific route of questioning, he was sure; Mrs. Bridges was being naive, even a bit simpleminded. Could she not see that Ruby's talk about God expressed her fear about the integration effort? If Ruby was preoccupied with God, the task of the research was to find the psychological, the sociocultural, reasons.[5]

It was, in fact, his wife who kept insisting that Coles take seriously the religious beliefs of his subjects.

> The more I tried to understand the emotional conflicts, the tensions and responses to tensions, the underlying motivations, and the projections and displacements; the more I emphasized the automatic or reflexive behavior of the children we knew, a consequence of their short lives, their lack of education, their limited cognitive development, their inability to handle all sorts of concepts and symbols; the more I read and commented on various developmental points of view, which emphasized stages and phases and periods—and, of course, consigned elementary school children such as Ruby Bridges to the lower rungs of this or that ladder—the more my wife kept pointing to the *acts* of these boys and girls, the *deeds* they managed.[6]

So, with Jane Coles's prompting, Coles found himself less and less interested in signs of "psychic disorder," more fascinated with "moral and political involvement." "I use the word 'involvement' because I was *not* primarily interested in what children *thought* about this or that moral principle or political idea. Piaget and others have been quite exhaustively helpful in that regard."[7] Rather, how do people of all ages live their lives? And how can we explain their often remarkable moral insight, their courageous ability to act, their refusal to countenance injustice without heeding their religious commitments? Where do people like Ruby Bridges or Martin Luther King get their courage? These questions, which led Coles from an early emphasis on "symptoms" to a study of people in the midst of social change to fascination with moral and political development in children, now impels him to his current research project. He is studying the spiritual life of children, interviewing youngsters attending religious classes in churches and synagogues. To add the Muslim dimension, one of his sons interviewed Pakistani children in London recently. For many college-age whites in the mid- and late 1950s, campus ministries and campus-affiliated YM and YWCAs introduced them to the possibility that racial segregation was at odds with the message of Christianity. The Methodist Student Movement's magazine, *motive*, challenged readers to embrace a faith that was prophetic and radical in its critique of injustice. Finly Eversole linked such a critique to what he called "Christian Existentialism": "the existential attitude is also one of passionate *concern* about one's world and oneself. . . . In choosing what he will be, man is free."8 For Southern blacks, the sources of a spiritual vision of human liberation were as close as the nearest black church. These two streams of influence, the "social gospel" concern of university-trained whites and the pervasiveness of black religion, may be seen in the highly charged religious, biblically cadenced language of the first SNCC statement of purpose: "We affirm the philosophical or religious ideal of nonviolence as the foundation of our purpose, the pre-supposition of our faith, and the manner of our action. Nonviolence as it grows from Judaic-Christian traditions seeks a social order of justice permeated by love. Integration of human endeavor represents the first step toward such a society."9

The spiritual intensity of many young civil rights activists was not difficult for sympathetic Northerners to comprehend. These protesters spoke of "redemptive suffering," of "transformed community," of putting their "bodies on the line," indeed of the Kingdom of God. Even if the specifically Christian language was not shared by all supporters, the reformist political goals were. But the religious worldview of Appalachian whites, of migrants, of sharecroppers black and white, was far more difficult to understand. "In my experience there is nothing about the life of rural people that is less understood by their city-bred sympathizers and advocates than the nature of so-called fundamentalist religious faith." The political situation, the economic conditions, the "life-style" and music—all these American liberals try diligently to understand and improve where needed.

But our forebearance wears thin at the church door. . . . What energy and imagination and combativeness is week by week drained away, carried off in a noisy, superstitious tide of prayers and hymns, all meant to make people compliant, slightly dazed, and ridiculously hopeful—in the face of the awful circumstances that characterize their "objective condition"![10]

The same charge could be laid at the door of the innumerable storefront, Pentecostal, charismatic, holy-roller black churches, even directed to the "main-stream" black churches in Boston and Chicago and Detroit.

It is exactly against this view that Coles struggles. Do rural people, do urban blacks, turn to religion because they have problems? We all have problems; perhaps a secular, material, or political means of addressing problems is no more or no less compelling than the religious response. Coles's effort, especially in the last chapters of *Migrants, Sharecroppers, Mountaineers* and of *The South Goes North,* has been to give a portrait of religion "without making caricatures of individuals who have been worked with, without turning them, people with sincere opinions and passionate beliefs, into opiated and deluded victims, or into philosophically duped and neurotically afflicted patients."[11]

As Coles traveled the back roads of Kentucky and West Virginia, as he sat in revival meetings in Georgia and Alabama and visited storefront churches in Boston and Chicago, as he talked with scores of people about their religious experience, one central theme began to emerge: The Chrisitan message was not meant as a Sunday-only package, neatly segregated from the rest of life. One black minister put it this way:

> The white man who lives in the suburbs, he goes to a beautiful church and he hears some sweetness and light for an hour. . . . His minister has learned to be as indirect and inoffensive as can be. Have you ever seen them coming out of those churches? . . . They all look as if they've had a nice little time for themselves—before lunch. Do they ever ask who Christ was and why he was hounded to death and what people like them, good and proper and well-off people, thought of Him?[12]

The Christian message that these often hard-pressed people hear, "relate to," is one of suffering and endurance, and one of hope that ultimately life is in God's hands. A white Southern woman observed,

> God's message is that we should try to be patient. Maybe He means for us to be patient with Him. . . . To me, church is where you meet God, where for a little while you find Him and keep Him, where He tells you that it's all right, and it's going to be all right, and no matter what, you'll come out on His side. . . . It's God, and how He does it, I don't know. I mean, I won't be so good on some of

these Sundays, and I'll go, but I'm not expecting much, and then I all of a sudden get the uplift.[13]

The God these rural folk worship knows, even shares, their suffering.

If we're never going to live an easy life, at least we can stop right still, come Sunday, and take ourselves to hear about Him and all they did to Him and how He never did have the big people, the rich people, the important people, out there helping Him, and they killed Him, that's what, and you know the sheriff and the growers would as soon do it to us, the same way, if they didn't need us to pull in all the crops.[14]

Many of the people Coles talked to appreciated the efforts made on their behalf by the Appalachian Volunteers and other advocacy groups, but had little inclination to put their trust in political solutions. They seemed to understand, intuitively, the forces arrayed against them, the power of corporations, the police, the courts, a largely indifferent consumer society. They understood their lot, did not like it, felt it was unjust, railed against it on occasion. But the message of the gospels, about a God who was likewise hounded and ridiculed and murdered, provides them a powerful reassurance, Coles believes. As he put it, "To 'them,' to the people who appear in this book, God's suffering requires no complicated explanation, nor does Christ's pain and humiliation, His harassment and exile. . . . The mystery of God and the world persists. . . . Muted protests continue to take place in those churches, but minds also become refreshed, relieved, newly at ease in those churches."[15]

This same theme of a suffering God who shares our suffering was voiced by some of Coles's Northern black subjects as well. One woman, recently departed from Georgia for Boston, understood God's sorrow this way:

God sees a lot of trouble up in the city. There's sorriness here, too much even for Him to keep His mind on all day long, and into the night. In Georgia you could always take your mind off yourself and everyone else. . . . Up here, though, you never can know what your child will be able to do . . . and that's because it's not God's world; it's all built by man, the city is.

I know my Bible, yes, sir, I do. To my way of thinking, God suffering, so we wouldn't be the only ones who suffered. Because He suffered, we can fall back on His example.[16]

For these people, theological terms like "sin," "grace," "redemption," are not abstractions, but lived realities. They know "existential despair," Coles believes; they are pressed down and surrounded by danger and death, as Jesus was, but still believe in a power larger than "principalities and powers."

> From childhood on, people like Mrs.Allen [a white woman from West Virginia] and Mrs. Williams [a black woman from Georgia] have understood how famished Christ must have felt those forty days, and known what he fed on. For them He very much lives as Jesus Christ, the Son of God, Who walked and wandered and knew the countryside and eventually knew the city, and was badgered and importuned and made light of and mocked; Who was judged suspect, dangerous, an outrageous dissenter, a threat to an empire's sense of law and order; Who was put to death; Who yet lives on in the mind and heart and soul of a Mrs. Williams or a Mrs. Allen; and Who thereby does indeed walk the streets of our American ghetto.[17]

How do we understand the religious sensibility of such hard-pressed people? Theologically, their fundamentalism is an offense to many fellow Christians, inexplicable to non-Christians. Their emphasis on suffering, on a God who is "with them" in their difficulties, seems self-delusion, the victim's justification of an economic and political system that keeps them in submission. Coles understands, even accepts in part, those criticisms: "I want to believe, and I want the reader to believe, that I am not evading either my mind's twentieth-century sensibility or my mind's responsibility to take a stand. I agree with the critics: it *is* easy to become misty and hazy and clouded and silly and make a million 'divine' excuses for what is in fact the product of a mean and heartless and unfair social and economic system."[18]

The rural and urban people of intense, emotional, even "fundamentalist" faith are occasionally inane, fatuous, gullible; they are noisy and superstitious; they are dogmatic and even bigoted.

Nonetheless, Coles insists, for so many of the people he has encountered, it is their religious outlook that causes them to keep going in the face of despair, that gives a sense of dignity, that provides a connection with larger purpose and meaning. We keep looking for reasons for their amazing endurance in everything else except the reason they offer, their faith.

As the reader makes her way through the last chapters of *Migrants, Sharecroppers, Mountaineers* and *The South Goes North* and compares the religious life described there with that of the "privileged ones" portrayed in the last volume of *Children of Crisis,* the powerful connection between suffering and spirituality becomes more evident. Coles's reviewers apparently found that connection inexplicable, or awkward. "I deliberately chose to end the books with those chapters, and in a way struggled harder with them than any others," but the reviewers studiously ignored them.[19] "People are all too willing to comment on my psychiatric conclusions. But they don't really care at all about what I'm reporting, what I have seen and heard about the religious life of the poor or . . . of poor children."[20]

Coles, however, found the poor remarkably able to employ their religious faith as a means to cope with, even to transcend, their situation. Far from being numbed or brutalized by conditions, Coles believes, hard-pressed people are often prompted into moral and religious reflection by those conditions. "The situation of poor and hard-pressed children is very much like the situation Christ himself experienced. It is a situation that prompts those important questions. Why do we live this way, what is justice, when will justice ultimately prevail, what is fair, what is decent, what is honorable?" Coles put his insight another way: "Circumstances prompt inquiry, and desperate circumstances may prompt the most taut and intense and enormously urgent kind of inquiry, again, such as Christ made."[21]

Except for those years in the early 1960s, living on family loans and the meager grant from the New World Foundation, Robert Coles and his family have not been poor. He has been in danger, it is true, during his time with SNCC. He faced a Mississippi sheriff's pistol, narrowly escaped injury from a dynamite blast, even more narrowly escaped the fate of Goodman, Chaney, and Schwerner in 1964. The risks were horrifyingly real, but the risks were nonetheless chosen, willed, voluntary. As a male, a white, a Harvard and Columbia graduate, a doctor, Robert Coles is a member of a privileged minority. And throughout the years as his reputation has grown and his books have multiplied, his economic situation has become ever more secure. He does not, to put it simply, inhabit "desperate circumstances."

This situation of privilege has troubled Coles a good deal, in large part because he sees the ways privilege undermines and weakens moral and religious sensitivity. He puts the danger this way:

> The problem for someone like me who desires that his children lead successful, competent lives, do well in school, get ahead in society, is knowing that the cost of this may at times be insensitivity to others, that in urging them to do well I may well be urging them to be

inconsiderate or lacking in thoughtfulness about others. In other words, the Christian values of community and equality are not the easiest standards to hold up when you're also interested in perpetuating your privileged situation in society through your children and your own behavior.[22]

In his conversations with Daniel Berrigan, Coles acknowledged the constraints that privilege imposes. He had become a family man, a professional, a teacher; he was unwilling to adopt Berrigan's more radical political critique. He was unwilling to go to jail for his opposition to the Vietnam War, as Berrigan soon would do. Was he not "fatally compromised," was he not in danger of a "death of the heart," in the words of his favorite Elizabeth Bowen novel?[23] And even if he were sufficiently morally sensitive, were not his children in danger of too easy a life?

My children have never suffered the way that Ruby [Bridges] has, and they're not sure what the Bible means as far as their lives are concerned. . . . As I try to make inroads in that kind of sensibility in them and, I might add, in myself too, I find myself in a kind of moral anguish that I've never known Ruby to be in, nor her parents, who are extremely poor, hardworking people. So over and over again I am forced to make this sort of existential analysis of the poor as against the well-to-do in American capitalist life.[24]

Coles has sought to make the turn from consideration of the religion of the oppressed to the religion of the comfortable, himself included. Marginalized, minority, ignored people have no trouble with the reality toward which Kierkegaard and Tillich pointed, this living on the edge. Their lives are profoundly in jeopardy; they have no trouble identifying with the scorned, rejected, humiliated, tortured, and murdered Jesus. People from more comfortable circumstances are rarely in such jeopardy unless they deliberately choose to be so, and even then the ability to choose distinguishes them from those whose lives present no such choices. What is the message, according to Robert Coles, to the reasonably secure, indeed to the well-off, to people with bank accounts, homes, food, jobs, education, futures? What is the word of the gospels—for Coles is concerned with the Christian witness—to people like himself?

For Coles, the most ironic and damning result of wealth and privilege is the vacuousness of life. Speaking of wealthy neighborhoods, he notes,

There is great pain and sorrow in these communities, and it is not of the sort *necessarily* healed by psychotherapy because much of the pain and sorrow is not only psychiatrically connected to disturbances in family life, it is humanly connected to disturbances in human existence, to issues connected to life's meaning, or, to say it plainly, to an utter *lack* of meaning these people feel so acutely."[25]

Because privileged people like to think of themselves as in control, they ensure that worship is determined and predictable. "The format is fixed and the words and music are modulated, no extremes either from church or from those who are at worship."

It is clear to Coles that comfortable people, these "privileged ones," have largely made psychology into a new religion. In the 1950s psychiatry and psychoanalysis had become, in the hands of medically approved practitioners, means of debunking belief, or exposing statements about eternal values as masks for unconscious fears and desires. Employing a powerful set of diagnostic terms, orthodox psychoanalysts often sought to clear their patients of religion as "illusion."

Sigmund Freud provided ample precedent for this understanding of religion. In "Obsessive Actions and Religious Practices," Freud argues that one could regard "neurosis as an individual religiosity and religion as a universal obsessional neurosis." Religion gives us "fairy tales"; it is an "illusion" derived from human wishes," he wrote in *The Future of an Illusion*. Maturity and psychic health require the exposure and abandonment of such patent falsity.[26]

Coles, as we have seen, has rejected that understanding of the role of psychiatry. Ironically, he believes, psychonanalysis has become for many Westerners a new, substitute religion parading as scientific objectivity, with psychiatrists the new priests for this new religion. The great genius of Freud, Coles has recently observed, lay in his patient and careful listening, his historical method of recovery and reconstruction. To follow Freud as a cultural demigod is quite another thing.

This worship of psychology and psychiatry as new religions has reached a new level of intensity in the 1970s and early 80s, says Coles. Everywhere he traveled to interview and observe he noted a new climate of feeling, a new obsession with self-disclosure. "On a Hopi reservation (yes, *Hopi,* arguably the most persistent cultural critics this country has harbored within its midst) we found the following message, printed on a mimeographed handout: 'Something on your mind? Don't be silent. We will meet to discuss a new Hopi life. Come, and feel a lot better afterwards!'"27 Though this announcement may seem incongrous, even bizarre, in light of Hopi reticence and quiet dignity, it is by no means unusual in the larger culture.

> All the books on psychology, food, exercise, sex; all the sermons on how to win friends, on the importance of releasing tensions, on how to "cope," on how to "rear" children so they won't have "conflicts" or "problems," as if that were either possible or desirable—there is a high mound of evidence, in print, of what we are like culturally. The heart of the matter, I fear, is psychology.

People are now constantly talking about "phases" and "stages" and "patterns" and "complexes."28

The emphasis on psychology—on feeling good about oneself, on self-revelation, on "interpersonal relations," on befriending the "inner child"—affected mainstream Christianity in the 1970s and early 1980s. The work of Carl Jung made considerable impact in Catholic circles, while Abraham Maslow, Ira Progoff, and Thomas Harris (author of *I'm OK, You're OK*), to name just a few, were widely read and discussed in mainline Protestant churches. Coles finds this a deeply disturbing development. "Especially sad and disedifying is the preoccupation of all too many clergy with the dubious blandishments of contemporary psychology and psychiatry. I do not mean to say there is no value in understanding what psychoanalytic studies . . . have to offer." The issue is the way in which the language and perspective of pychology have become all-absorbing, a new gospel, a new revelation. "I am tired of all the 'value-free' declarations in the name of what is called 'social science'; tired, too, of the complexities, ambiguities, and paradoxes of our moral life being swept into yet another 'developmental scheme,' with 'stages' geared to ages." Could not the most admirable, even heroically self-sacrificing people be found psychologically troubled, in need of psycho-therapy? In answer to an interviewer's comment that it was a good thing they did not have psychotherapy in Saint Francis's time, Coles responded, "That's right! Psychiatry for Saint Francis, psychiatry for Saint Paul, psychiatry for Jesus himself!"29 From the perspective of popular psychology, Dietrich Bonhoeffer, who returned to Germany from his safe haven in New York City to plot to assassinate Hitler and suffer execution for it, was in need of therapy. What anxieties, fixations, compulsions, might he have been working out?30

Spared the kind of direct physical suffering to which "traditional" religion responds, and repelled by the ersatz religion of psychology that is practiced in private offices and in far too many churches, yet unwilling to give up the religious quest and join the secular world, Robert Coles has sought a version of the Christian faith that addresses both his privileged position and his restless nature. He has surrounded himself, so to speak, with a galaxy of thinkers and writers who nurture and encourage a particular angle of vision: Augustine, Pascal, and Kierkegaard; Tillich and Reinhold Niebuhr; Simone Weil and Dorothy Day; Georges Bernanos and Flannery O'Connor; George Orwell and James Agee. His mother, Sandra, on the most intimate family level, and what we might grandly call, following Henry James, the "New England Conscience" on the regional scale have made their contributions to shaping Coles's religious sensibility. A cluster of descriptions, surely requiring some explication, emerge from this cluster of influences: the individual's relation to the divine; Christian existentialism; "the spirit of Christian tentativeness"; struggle and suffering; Christian radicalism; self-emptying as resistance to the sin of pride.

Coles recalls, without apparent bitterness, how his mother would qualify her praise for her son's good report card with reminders about the "sin of pride, and the dangers of 'worldliness.'"[31] Coles's New Orleans psychoanalyst, Kenneth Beach, found this a disturbing insight into Coles's personality. Coles thinks not; in fact, the "sin of pride" has become a central theme in Coles's religious outlook. He is deeply drawn to those figures who have every reason to be proud of their accomplishments and yet seek to empty themselves, people like Dorothy Day and Simone Weil, like Bernanos's curé in *The Diary of a Country Priest*. He is challenged and moved by the words of Flannery O'Connor who, though an intellectual herself, "wanted to emphasize the scandal of our lives, not the psychopathology or the social malaise or the cultural impasse. . . . She wanted us to get the greatest possible distance on ourselves; hence her refusal to let us dig in and find ourselves yet another bit of solace."

O'Connor "was, all her life, 'waiting for God'—Pascal's expression, Simone Weil's. She admired them both as proud and wonderfully gifted intellectuals who knew how hard it is for anyone, certainly including themselves, to attain—to be graced by—what she called an abandonment of self."[32]

The tradition on which Coles calls is rooted in the work of Augustine, Pascal, and Kierkegaard. The intellectual and social worlds that each occupied—late imperial Rome, seventeenth-century France, nineteen-century Copenhagen—were sophisticated and compelling. But each man, in Coles's view, refused to take pleasure in systematic thinking and systems-building and defended a view of God as beyond human understanding. Human nature had been ineradicably stained by the Fall, and while we pride ourselves on our accomplishments, "thinking we are refined and sensitive . . . we step by step die spiritually." Deliverance, Coles finds Augustine saying, takes place after this burdened and divided life is completed.

This sense of humanity as essentially self-divided, inherently ambiguous, also lies at the core of Pascal's thinking, Coles believes. "Man's contradictions are not only stressed, they are insisted upon and declared ineradicable—not because Pascal was anti-intellectual or stupidly, perversely, against reason, but because he saw the mind's limits, the heart's province."[33]

Most of all, I would argue, Robert Coles has been drawn to Søren Kierkegaard as the theologian who speaks most directly to Coles's own experience of religion. The phrase "fear and trembling" recurs a great many times in Coles's writing. The Kierkegaardian irony, the mordant sense of humor, the skepticism toward human achievement expressed in the most elegant formulations, these also indicate the pervasive influence of the Danish writer on the American.

Kierkegaard, Coles reminds us, was engaged in a subtle and complex argument with Hegel over the nature of religious experience. In *Phenomenology of Mind* and other texts, Hegel attacks subjective and self-centered religion. "Hegel distrusted profoundly the private, self-absorbed man." He scorned the "frivolous, esoteric, or self-indulgent aspects of subjectivity" in the religious life, and "brusquely waved aside the claim that there is some private realm of feeling within us. . . . He viewed the seemingly personal . . . as utterly connected to the observable world. . . . Uniqueness was for him an illusion; the mind is always . . . embedded in a given time, place, nation, culture."[34]

Revealing his own distrust of contemporary popular psychology with its emphasis on self-fulfillment, Coles insists that Kierkegaard must not be understood as the polar opposite of Hegel. If Hegel did emphasize the collective and the rational elements of religion, Kierkegaard on his side must not be seen simply as the champion of total inwardness and subjectivity. In *Spirit of Christianity,* Hegel held out for the spirit, while Kierkegaard criticizes objectivity, Coles points out, with "cold, analytic force." Still, unlike Hegel, the master dialectician and synthesizer, Kierkegaard distrusted all systems of thought. Ironically, for this lonely and isolated man, the true test of an idea was its versatility in the world. What mattered was behavior.

He was a passionate theologian (as opposed to methodical phi-
lospher); so, pride for him was the sin of sins, the source of man's
continuing ability to deceive not only himself but everyone else. . . .
For Kierkegaard, quite simply, Hegel had become taken in by his
own mind's brazen willingness to account for everything. . . . The
result, an astonishing and revealing irony: abstraction piled upon
abstraction, all in the name of understanding the world, and yet no
real wisdom for anyone to take into consideration from sunrise to
sunset or, for that matter, in bed at night.[35]

Indeed, for Kierkegaard, sin, the condition of human alienation, is
fundamental to freedom. So we live in the midst of perpetual irony; our
possible futures are linked to our flawed pasts.[36]

Coles finds this irony, the continual interplay of freedom and fate,
reflected in the work of Reinhold Niebuhr, with whom he studied at
Union Seminary. Niebuhr "does not run away from modern psychiatric
knowledge, yet he sees man as more than what is contained in the
formulations of various social scientists. Ultimately he falls back on
paradox: man is fated to sin, finite as he is; yet man has freedom. . . . 'It
is within and by his freedom that man sins,' he pointed out, and he
freely acknowledges his debt to Kierkegaard in that statement and many
others."

In an echo of the passage from Kierkegaard's *Concluding Unscientific
Postscript* that began this chapter, Niebuhr writes in *The Nature and
Destiny of Man*, "The Christian doctrine of sin in its classical form
offends both rationalists and moralists by maintaining the seemingly
absurd position that man sins inevitably and by a fateful necessity but
that he is nevertheless to be held responsible for actions which are
prompted by an ineluctable fate." This fateful necessity is the human
condition, the "divided and rebel mind," as Emerson put it. One may,
indeed should, work to, improve the human condition, as Niebuhr did
in his Christian socialism or Coles in his civil rights advocacy. But no
utopias are in sight; political solutions based on modern ideology have
the unfortunate consequence of leaving millions of victims in their
wake.[37]

This same notion, the intellectual's confrontation with the sin of pride
and unremitting assault on intellectual achievement as evidence of
human deception, is clear in Flannery O'Connor. "The intellectual's
version of pride is something Flannery O'Connor knew in herself. Her
letters are exceptional in their lack of self-centeredness. She had no big
ego. . . . She mocked her own work. She loved to write in plain,
southern vernacular; no airs, ever." O'Connor helped Coles see a crucial

distinction. One can use intelligence as a gift of God without "resort to ideas as a last court of appeals, as a fundamental act of self-definition. . . . For her, the intellect was, always, but one element in life, and by no means the essence of it." One needed always to nurture the soul, which hungers not for systems, categories, theories, but for something to worship.

Resisting the sin of pride, following the example of Augustine and Pascal, Kierkegaard, Niebuhr, and O'Connor—these efforts bring us very close to the core of the religious experience for Robert Coles. After a long discussion of his feelings of creative marginality in the Catholic Church, Daniel Berrigan put the question directly to Coles: "I would like to know something about your feelings as to what it is to be a Christian in your profession. I would like to know what the Church means to you, what it offers you, and your sense of its future, if any."

Coles's reply was at first academic, almost evasive. He spoke of Freud's powerfully searching, historical mind; his lack of illusions, his ambitions. He mentioned Freud's distrust of religion, finally his lack of understanding of the religious impulse, and of the irony that Freud helped create a profession that "has itself become a sort of religion to thousands and thousands of middle-class, educated, agnostic Westerners."[38]

Then, Coles comes to the heart of the matter.

> I cannot now in a few words tell you all that Christian faith means to me, but I want to mention this: I believe self-centeredness is one of the great temptations and dangers we all have to struggle with— man's apparently inevitable inclination to worship himself, and by extension, his thinking. . . . I constantly find myself suspicious of all man-made ideologies, be they political ones or intellectual ones. To me, going into a church and getting on my knees and praying is something important and almost liberating—but at the same time it is something I don't like to talk about.

The core of the religious life, for Robert Coles, is self-emptying:

> I believe that religious faith enables man to be free of himself, to find a destiny for himself that is outside of his own inevitably narrow sphere. To me the great danger in all political activity, not to mention professional activity, has to do with this kind of egoism—call it narcissism, call it the sin of pride that is in all of us, and is exploitable and will exploit.[39]

No twentieth-century writer has spoken more directly and urgently to

Coles of the need for self-emptying than Simone Weil. References to the French Jewish intellectual who died in 1943 from tuberculosis recur throughout Coles's books and essays; recently (1987) he published an entire book exploring the themes and issues in her life and work. Coles considers her a "political and moral philosopher," a self-for-others, a Christian hero.

Perry Miller, who had already introduced the young Coles to William Carlos Williams and the American Puritans, included several works by Simone Weil in his course "Classics of the Christian Tradition," which Coles took in the spring of 1950. Miller connected Weil with Pascal, Coles recalls: "The scientifically sophisticated, skeptical mind grappling seriously with the matter of faith—and interested in doing so publicly, that is, in a literary gesture which makes others companions or adversaries. He also reminded us that writers such as Kierkegaard, Pascal and Weil are strong-minded social critics."[40]

The Coleses took their French-language copies of Weil South with them in 1960. In 1963 Coles was interviewing young civil rights workers as part of "an effort on my part to understand how and why young people became involved in social causes and political action." One student in particular began to talk with Coles not about the strains of political organizing, but about Simone Weil: Had Coles read her? What? What did he think? Prompted at first by his psychoanalytical training to see such questions as evasions, Coles still was moved by the profound seriousness of this young worker, and began an intense reading of Simone Weil. Her place in his thought and work has grown steadily since that time.[41]

Simone Weil was born in 1909 into a French professional family, a non-practicing Jewish family. A brilliant and sensitive child (she refused to eat sugar during World War I because soldiers were going without such luxuries), she received a superb education, and entered the Ecole Normale Supérieure at the young age of nineteen. In 1931 she graduated, having completed a thesis on "Science and Perception in Descartes," and began her first teaching assignment at a girls' school at Le Puy near Lyons. But her years at the Normale shaped Simone Weil not only intellectually, but politically as well. She began to read Marx and began to support the union movements in the early 1930s. Once at the girls' school, she promptly caused controversy by allying herself with the unemployed, even leading demonstrations. Labeled the "red virgin of the tribe of Levi, bearer of Muscovite gospels," Weil went through several other teaching posts in the early 1930s.

In December 1934 Weil took a job at the Alsthom Electrical Works in

Paris in order to gain some intimate knowledge of the life of French workers. A brilliant student of philosophy and ancient history, "she had already become, in her early twenties, a stern critic of intellectuals, an unrelentingly harsh critic of what she regarded as their privileged and arrogant ways."[42] After several more manual laboring jobs which taught her the slavelike status of workers and the difficulty with which any decent social relations can be built under such circumstances, Weil was rescued by her parents, who sent her to Portugal to recuperate from the strain; a physically slight person, she was already suffering from the migraine headaches that would assault her with increasing intensity.

In Portugal, Weil was struck by the extraordinary difficulty of life for the peasants. This was no new insight for the young woman already deeply, even physically, torn by the sufferings of others. What was remarkable about these people was their essential dignity: "people down and out, true, but capable, some of them, of thoughtfulness, perseverance, and an impressive kind of stoic forbearance."[43]

In 1936 Weil volunteered for military duty with the Spanish Loyalists, as civil war broke out in Spain. Stumbling into a pot of hot cooking oil, Weil had to be sent home to recover, and was spared the fascist bullets that would soon wipe out her military unit.

Traveling now, suffering from deteriorating health, Weil found herself in Solesmes, France, Easter 1938, where she experienced a conversion. Never a "joiner" for all her support of community for others, Simone Weil refused baptism in the Roman Catholic Church. Hers was a solitary pilgrimage toward God.

When the Nazis invaded France in April 1940, the Weils, along with others, fled south. Meanwhile, Simone Weil desperately wanted to be of service in the war effort (perhaps she could be parachuted into German-occupied France, to aid resistance fighters), while simultaneously pursuing her intense spiritual probings and searchings. In 1942 the Weils moved on, first to Morocco, then to the United States, but Simone Weil was unsatisfied. "She was absolutely determined to get back to Europe, to reach London, and to press upon the government of General Charles de Gaulle her scheme for behind-the-lines work with the Resistance in France."[44]

Simone Weil did travel back across the Atlantic. In London she began working for the French government in exile, studying and organizing plans for postwar reconstruction. In April 1943 she was diagnosed as having tuberculosis, and hospitalized. She was an extremely difficult patient, refusing the nutritious food, then the only treatment for the disease, along with complete rest. Like the child Simone who refused sugar out of solidarity with soldiers, the young woman refused to eat more than she thought citizens in occupied France were eating. Simone Weil died alone on August 24, 1943; she was thirty-four.

Gradually Simone Weil's reputation has grown as translations and paperback editions of her essays, journals, and aphorisms have multiplied—*Gravity and Grace, Waiting for God, The Need for Roots, First and Last Notebooks*. In his excellent 1951 introduction to *Waiting for God,* Leslie Fiedler describes Simone Weil as "our" saint, the Saint as Outsider. A Jewish intellectual, she stands at the threshold of the Church, refusing to be baptized. She seeks to complement the Christian message with insights from other religions, and resists the "patriotism of the church" by giving it, or any institution, her full loyalty. An ardent defender of workers' organizations, she refuses to join any group herself, and finds herself with few close friends, although with many acquaintances, "comrades," and admirers.

Most of all, says Fiedler, she is a hero of "our" time (that is, the early fifties) through her method and her thought. Paradox, contradiction, absurdity—these dominate Weil's essays and aphorisms. God's love is found in torture and terror; the crown of the Christian life is affliction, slavery, death; Jesus' cry of abandonment on the cross is the chief glory of Christianity; hunger is the proof of God's existence, since only God, who is materially absent from the world, can satisfy our needs. Like Camus and Sartre, Saul Bellow and Edward Albee, Norman Mailer and Lenny Bruce, Simone Weil speaks to a generation battered by depression, war, holocaust, and nuclear terror and thus hungry for spiritual depth.[45]

What in particular attracts Robert Coles, who graduated from Harvard in 1950, to Simone Weil? Here is another intellectual, like Flannery O'Connor, who distrusted the life of the mind, the workings of the intellect, and who likewise distrusted complex and satisfying systems of thought. "She examined relentlessly twentieth-century idolatrous man—the unwitting spiritual hunger and the frustrated religious impulses which, finally, obtain expression in all sorts of political beliefs, social constructs, psychological theories, scientific postulates."[46] Intellectual achievement, such as she had obtained, served all too often to cut one off from people in need and, in pride, from God. "Simone Weil's greatest achievement as an intellectual, a political and moral philosopher, may have been her slowly realized and painfully stated distrust of her own mind's brilliance. She became increasingly skeptical of her capacity of symbolization, for dense theoretical display." She knew that "man as himself subordinate to larger forces, to God, has to be reminded again and again . . . how dangerously prideful he can become."[47]

There is no denying, of course, Simone Weil's passion for justice. Already sympathetic to a Marxist analysis of class struggle while in school, she promptly took the side of unemployed workers at Le Puy where she had gone to teach in 1931. Weil began to write searching articles for a variety of leftist publications on the issues confronting France's large trade unions. She was often criticized, particularly at Le Puy, for supporting workers although herself well-paid by the town for teaching their girls, but Simone Weil was totally uninterested in personal well-being or quality of life. When her mother would travel down from Paris to visit, she would have to bring or buy food and provide coal to heat Simone's apartment. In the spacious flat which she shared with another teacher, Weil had converted the parlor into a large closet by stringing it with clotheslines, disliking the notion of having so much space.[48] She threw herself into the labor struggle in the desperate 1930s, writing letters and articles, attending conventions, speaking, leading demonstrations. She was nearly totally committed to justice, as she conceived it, for the working class.

Coles believes that Simone Weil, in her self-emptying, her selfless identification with various people struggling for justice, is a powerful role model for activists engaged in such struggle in our own time. Like the children and youth engaged in school desegregation, like the young civil rights activists (including the young man who reminded him of Simone Weil's work), she wanted very much to make her life meaningful not for herself, but for others, and thus live, as Coles put it, "close to history." In his view, she lived a moral witness, a life for others. Perhaps she was disturbed, unhealthy, pathologically self-denying; perhaps she was prickly, alternately arrogant and self-abasing, finally suicidal. Look at her life, look at her witness, Coles responds. Look at the way she calls us to challenge our own comfortable assumptions, our lives, our goals.

Robert Coles insists, correctly, I think, that psychiatric labels or indeed medical diagnoses like anorexia do little to increase our understanding of so complex a person as Weil. In this judgment he is supported by Anna Freud, with whom he had many conversations about Weil. It is far more honest to confront, as Coles and Leslie Fiedler have done, the interplay of life and thought, trying to do justice to the turns of Simone Weil's mind.

As with Erik Erikson, Simone Weil's life and work bear some remarkable resemblances to Coles's. Both come from nonpracticing, assimilated Jewish backgrounds. Both are intellectuals who have come to distrust the workings of the mind. Both are Christian socialists who deeply distrust the actual practice of socialism in the world. Both distrust intellectual systems, theories, ideologies. Both find in the poor not only objects for our sympathy and advocacy, but people of pride and dignity whose lives often have more integrity than those of the rich and privileged. Both consider themselves outsiders, alienated, wanderers, occupants of what Irving Howe once called "the homeless left." Most of all, both focus intently on the need, as they see it, to empty the self of all desire, pride, will; to be hungry, to be restless, never to be satisfied.

Simone Weil's advocacy of French laborers, her desire to serve in the Spanish Civil War, her insistence at having a role in resistance to Nazism—all these are admirable, stirring, provocative, coming as they did from a privileged intellectual, a woman destined, were it not for the mysterious quality of her character, for academic distinction. Her writing is stimulating, paradoxical, challenging, clearly revealing the brilliance of her mind despite all her efforts to renounce such brilliance. But her spiritual vision is flawed, I think, and Robert Coles is too closely bound to that same spiritual vision to see its limitations.

When Simone Weil's family fled France, first for Morocco and then for the United States, she was quite unmoved by their good fortune in escaping the death camps. She disliked Americans: "Their hospitality is a purely philanthropic matter, and it is repugnant to me to be the object of philanthropy. . . . It is more flattering, taking it all in all, to be the object of persecution." Coles interprets her as linking spiritual growth with adversity rather than with comfort. Even so, he points out, millions of Europeans would have gladly accepted such philanthropy however morally suspect, rather than face Auschwitz. Later, on the next page, Coles seeks to interpret her self-chosen death not as mental illness or the consequences of anorexia, but as "perfectly consistent with a lifetime of austerity and compassion."[49]

Later in *Simone Weil, A Modern Pilgrimage*, Coles discusses Weil's sarcastic assaults on the anti-Jewish laws of occupied France, which forbade Jews like her from holding various posts, like that of schoolteacher. Weil disputed and rejected the label "Jew," arguing that she had no identity with and no loyalty to either the religious or the ethnic dimension of the word. In *The Need for Roots*, Weil proposes insistent pressure on Jews to assimilate into French society and culture, lest their outsider status threaten the rebuilding of French community life. All this low-key anti-Semitism Coles finds repulsive and "sad." Too, he criticizes Weil for her attempts to separate God from the Yahweh worshipped by the Hebrews, seeing this effort as analogous to her dislike of the Jews for their groundedness, their physicality, their love of this world.

> She turned on her Jewishness with a vengance and got some moments of apparent satisfaction. She felt thereby closer to certain individuals, and as a scholar, she felt closer to certain people whom she admired in history: the Cathars, the Egyptians, the Greeks. . . . The Jews, on the other hand, were a catalyst for a soul absolutely bent on leaving the body—leaving a people and its past in a soaring grasp for another world. They deserved better from her. It is sad that Simone Weil did not bring her intelligent, caring comprehension to her own people, her Lord's people.[50]

I would argue that Weil's dislike of philanthropy, her rejection of Jewish identity, and her theology of renunciation all belong together.

The works of several feminist and liberation theologians, such as Rosemary Ruether, Carter Heyward, Beverly Harrison, Gustavo Guttierrez, and Juan Luis Segundo, remind us powerfully of the ways in which the early church drastically Platonized the Christian message, creating a deep fear and loathing toward material and sensual life. The mystery of the Incarnation, the fusion of material and spiritual, became lost in a dualism that equated flesh, female, nature, world, and sin on the one hand, male, spirit, divine, on the other. We are being reminded, principally by women, of the tremendous damage humanity has done to nature, to one another, and to ourselves because of this profound dualism.

In a highly intellectualized culture that was itself shot through with dualism, Simone Weil quite possibly performed the only gesture she was capable of, that of renunciation. Her vision was of the absent, distant God, for whom she constantly hungered and was never satisfied. Her God was, I think, not Jesus' God, Jesus' "Abba" about whom he told such earthy and bold stories. Despite Coles's claim that Weil "fell in love" with Jesus, she seems unmoved by Jesus' love of life, his sense of humor, love of food and wine, his associating with tax agents and prostitutes. She was interested in fleeing this world, especially in rejecting and fleeing the flesh. As Coles himself points out, Weil saw her imperialist ego triumphing over the needs of the body. Her disdain for the body is quite evident in any number of passages Coles cites in his book, including this astonishing prayer from 1942: "Father, in the name of Christ, grant me this. That I may be unable to will any bodily movement, or even any attempt at movement, like a total paralytic. That

I may be incapable of receiving any sensation, like someone who is completely blind, deaf and deprived of all the senses. That I may be unable to make the slightest connection between two thoughts, even the simplest, like one of those total idiots who not only cannot count or read but have never even learnt to speak."[51]

Quite possibly, as I say, this renunciatory stance was the only one available for her in France in the 1930s. Marxism was rigidly anti-religious, the Church generally in league with business and the government, Christian socialists few and far scattered. But Coles offers her as a witness to us today, as an exemplar of Christian radicalism. This seems to me dubious.

I believe that truly provocative Christian radicalism is renunciatory, but not of the body, but rather of the institutions that oppress "the body,"—our own bodies, the body politic, the world's body. Episcopal priest and theologian Carter Heyward has put this new emphasis on sensory theology this way:

> My body is not a shell into which and out of which God moves, leaving me either godly or ungodly. The body of humanity is not a network of flesh and blood and bones that is either visited by or not visited by God. . . . If God is worth our bother and if the life of our brother Jesus means anything worth our knowing, it is that the body is godly, the body is holy, without qualification. . . . To point to a spiritual realm "up there" and a physical world "down here" is blasphemy, a destructive assault against both humanity and divinity. Because God is here to be fed, healed, encouraged, given shelter, befriended, accepted in the person of the neighbor or not at all.[52]

It is not necessary, as I suspect Coles thinks it is, to equate such care for the body-self with narcissism and self-indulgence. That there is a tremendous amount of hedonism in contemporary culture is undoubted. What Heyward and many others call for is not the self-satisfied and selfish pursuit of pleasure. Rather, they see what Simone Weil could not, and perhaps Robert Coles will not, see, that compassion for others is incomplete without compassion for oneself, that care for others needs to be *grounded* in care for oneself. As Heyward puts it, "There is a moral imperative to love ourselves, to be tender with ourselves, to comfort and enjoy ourselves, our bodies—to grow in self-esteem, to take pleasure in who we are, delighted to realize that our bodies are members of God's body in the world. And in tending our own needs and yearnings, we are tending God's."[53] To be more body-centered in our spirituality, Heyward notes, is to understand the life of faith as *relational*. In this sense also Simone Weil does not seem to be exemplary. Her passion, while intense and real, was for communities in which she did not and could not participate—French workers, Portuguese peasants. Meanwhile, she hid her own body beneath heavy cloaks and floppy hats, had few friendships (although those she had were deep and intense), drove people away with her prickly and paradoxical comments. I would suggest, indeed, that in a very real sense Simone Weil did not want to be the person she was in this world. As a child and young person, she forbade herself all weakness, considering it a misfortune to be born female. She insisted on expressing the feminine side of her personality as little as possible, and signed her letters home from Ecole Henri IV "your respectful son." As an adult she shrank from touch and seemed particularly in flight from sexuality. Her biographer Simone Petrement recounts a story of her striking a male friend who she apparently thought was approaching her physically, although he had no such intention. One should not discount the omnipresent reality of rape in that society as in ours. But while Weil could be tender toward others, she seemed unable to accept such feelings for herself.[54] She seems to me profoundly out of touch with her body. Petrement reports that she could not stand the slightest flaw or imperfection on food. "She tried not to show these feelings of disgust that she evidently could not overcome, but Simone Antheriou [her apartment-mate] had become aware of them. So she promised to buy the best cuts of meat. Simone did not realize that these were relatively expensive cuts and thought she was eating ordinary meat."[55]

Her refusal to acknowledge her Jewishness also seems to be evidence of her denial of her full identity. To suffer as she chose to suffer was one thing; but to acknowledge her ethnic heritage meant to surrender control, to become vulnerable, and this Simone Weil could not do.

Her outsider status was powerfully resonant to intellectuals immediately after World War II, and her condition of marginality will always appeal, I think, to people caught between conflicting loyalties. But we are coming to a deeper awareness of our need to live in community, not simply to support the communities of others. Intellectuals, professionals, upper-middle-class people profoundly need care, support, encouragement, challenge just as do working-class people.

In another way also do "new occasions teach new duties," or rather prompt new insights. Simone Weil, like so many of the figures Coles admires, identifies pride as the chief sin. It may be, however, as Valerie Saiving Goldstein argued in 1960 (well before the current tide of feminist theology), that pride is a particularly male sin, or one identified with a male perspective. Goldstein points out that bioculturally males sharply distinguish themselves from mothers in order to gain selfhood. This early and continual sense of apartness leads to such male-identified traits as competitiveness, ambition, and individualism. Women, on the other hand, early on experience themselves in relationship. For Goldstein, the Protestant neoorthodox stress on sin as alienation and separation, as pride, and the call for self-emptying love is quite correct, judging by male experience. Men do require, she thinks, a good deal of self-emptying and influx of love in order to reunite them to the human condition. But women's besetting sin is not pride, but lack of self-love, a scattering and diffuseness of energy, passivity, and weakness. What so many theologians and writers, males or male-identified, take as a universal condition, the need to get out of the self, is, in Goldstein's view, a male need; women require not less self, but more.[56]

Finally, while Coles can find no reason to criticize Weil's self-sought and self-induced death, I would argue that hers was an unnecessary and indeed (to use a favorite Coles word) a "disedifying" death. Had she in fact parachuted behind enemy lines to engage in sabotage and been killed, that might have served some purpose. But her refusal to eat, despite the distinct possibility that people in occupied France were not starving, made no contribution to the war effort; no one lived because Simone Weil died. Coles has linked the suffering Jesus, who died in darkness and despair, with Simone Weil, but this seems to me to miss the point. Jesus lived a life of public witness, created a following, a movement; Jesus was murdered by his enemies and thus inspired some to continue his work. For millions of Christians, one needs to add, the mystery of the resurrection is that Jesus as Christ is still alive; the ignominious death is overcome by new life. Even if one stumbles over the resurrection (no more mysterious than any other Christian teaching that Coles thinks modern intellectuals find absurd), there is still the potent witness of the life of Jesus and his followers. Carter Heyward phrases that witness this way:

> Jesus and his friends, other outcasts, lived and taught a very simple life of faith, of expectation, and of love of neighbor and self. They bore witness to the power of love as the only necessary common ground among people who desire to experience themselves as valuable and worthwhile. . . . They were/we are called to live for the body, in the body, as one of its member bodies, to stand and act as centered selves, cultivated in appreciation of our value, our power and glory in solidarity with all others whose power and glory and dignity and worth we are willing to struggle for.[57]

But our task here has been not so much to criticize Simone Weil as to understand her influence on Robert Coles. We can use Weil to provide an opening to Coles's religious sensibility: the emphasis on *kenosis,* the identification of pride as the sin of sins, the desire to support the communities of others without experiencing the need to build community for oneself, the distrust of body, the skepticism toward ideology and intellectual systems, expressed in often elegant formulations. In the broadest terms, there is at work in both Weil and Coles an Augustinian-Jansenist-Calvinist sensibility, a culture of renunciation. I would argue that at least in the case of Simone Weil, the missing term is "love." Her love for others was compromised by her inability to love herself. It would truly be presumptuous to make a similar charge for Coles. I do think, however, that the pervasively dark, ironic view of religion he has articulated has made it difficult for him to see the genuine contributions of liberation and feminist theology and spirituality.

In 1987 Coles published two books on influential religious figures. Simone Weil is the subject of one; Dorothy Day, of the companion volume. In a variety of ways these two women share much in common. Both associated, in their early years, with leading leftist intellectuals; both converted to Catholicism; both sought to give up position and privilege in order to be, in some sense, with the poor. Both have made significant impact on Coles himself. We have already described Simone Weil's influence. As for Dorothy Day, Coles's parents read Day's *Catholic Worker* newspaper, and his mother spoke highly of her work. Coles volunteered at Saint Joseph's Hospitality House while in medical school in New York, and interviewed Day frequently in the 1970s for the book *A Spectacle unto the World.* Coles has regularly taken students to visit the hospitality houses in New York and Boston, and his sons have volunteered at the Boston houses. Now more recently he has written a book presenting the main events and themes in Dorothy Day's life.

I wish to argue, however, that Dorothy Day exemplifies a spirituality that is in some important ways an alternative to Simone Weil's, and mirrors another side of Robert Coles's own spirituality. This is, again, not to say the two do not share important themes and emphases in common; they do. I do mean to stress, frankly, their differences in order to illustrate the complexity, even the contradictions, in Coles's religious vision.

During the early 1960s, as the Coleses carried on their interviewing and as Robert Coles worked with SNCC and SCLC, they would encounter Dorothy Day participating in demonstrations and sit-ins, being arrested, carried off to jail. Just as at least one civil rights worker reminded Coles of Simone Weil's powerful witness, so more than one worker articulated the connections between the Catholic Worker movement and the nonviolent struggle in the South. One young woman put the link this way:

> I could take *The Catholic Worker,* issue after issue, and show you how the things that we were preoccupied with in St. Joseph's House are the things the people here in the Delta are preoccupied with. They leave to go to the cities because they're desperate, but they know better. They don't want to end up torn from each other, wandering in those mazes of Harlem or Chicago's South Side. They'd like to see each man able to make a living, have his farm. They'd like to keep praying, keep up all those involvements with dozens of kinfolk, neighbors, and friends—it's a community they have, geographical and blood-wise and religious and economic. They're always rescuing each other, giving each other lifts . . . with food or a "message," they'll call it, which means a prayer, a reminder that all is not that bad, because "the Lord provides"; and they don't *believe* that, they *experience* it as a living kind of truth.[58]

In the early 1970s, Coles spent over two years tape-recording his conversations with Dorothy Day; those, in addition to his correspondence and printed sources like Day's autobiography, *The Long Loneliness,* form the core of *Dorothy Day, A Radical Devotion.* As in the companion volume on Simone Weil, Coles rehearses the biography of his subject. Here he recounts Day's education at the University of Illinois, her radicalization in the years around World War I, her association with political and literary radicals in the 1920s in Greenwich Village. He describes her common-law marriage to the English biologist Forster Batterham, her growing interest in religion and in the Catholic Church, the birth of their daughter Tamar, and the end of the relationship with Batterham, who could not comprehend her attraction to an institution he deemed oppressive. Dorothy Day's encounter with Peter Maurin and the birth of the Catholic Worker movement and the *The Catholic Worker* newspaper, their constant struggles with the Catholic hierarchy on the one hand and suspicious radicals on the other— these also Coles describes. But he did not intend to write a biography, Coles insists; he means for this book, like the volume on Weil, to take up the persistent themes and issues in each life.

No theme is more central to Day's life, and none more confusing to her secular supporters, than her loyalty to the Roman Catholic Church.

Day herself has found much to criticize about the Church, beginning with its strenuous advocacy of Franco during the Spanish Civil War, its indifference and neglect toward the destitute during the Depression, its near-idolatrous support of nationalism, its fondness for pomp, display, and triumphalism. Dorothy Day was deeply aware that the Church was often Christ's worst enemy, and was fond of quoting Italian writer Romano Guardini's quip: "The Church is the Cross on which Christ was crucified."[59] Still, she insisted that she did her work at the houses of hospitality, wrote, participated in protests and demonstrations, went to jail, *because* she was a Catholic Christian. The hierarchy did not, does not, have a corner on what it means to be a Christian. She has taken sustenance and guidance from the lives of the saints, from Catholic tradition and ritual, and has refused to let the hierarchy define Catholicism for her.

More than anyone else, Peter Maurin, the French day laborer and anarchist, gave Day a new understanding of the Church. "He offered her his own relentless insistence that the spirit of the Catholic church has to be fought for—that the fate of the Church rests in each Catholic's heart and mind and soul, in each Catholic's daily deeds." The issue was, Maurin insisted, how to follow the example of Jesus in daily life.

In his many conversations with Dorothy Day, Robert Coles took note of her insistence that her conversion, and especially her meeting with Peter Maurin, marked a decisive break in her life. "Often, as I talked with her, I felt her discomfort with certain memories—discomfort, really, with her earlier life and her 'bohemian' past. She seemed uncomfortable even with the aspects of her past which persisted as strengths in her later life: the writer, the political activist, the woman prepared to break ranks with society's norms in order to uphold moral principles."

In contrast to Day's insistence on her earlier life as a "false start," Coles stresses continuities. Day's passion for justice could be seen running throughout her life, both before and after conversion. Surely another powerfully continuous thread in Dorothy Day's life was her reliance on certain books and ideas for inspiration and challenge. During her radical years, she knew Allen Tate, Malcolm Cowley, Eugene O'Neill, John Dos Passos, Max Eastman, Floyd Dell. She read Joyce and Dostoevsky and Pascal. Coles phrases her passion for reading this way:

> For Dorothy Day the connection between "art" and "life" was real, substantial, a powerful influence on her everyday actions. . . . Well before she had become a college Socialist or a Catholic convert . . .

Dorothy Day was busy searching out one book's moral message, then another's, and trying to determine whether her own life passed muster. Dostoevski would not let her sleep. Tennyson stirred her to romantic anguish. Passages from the Bible's words somehow stood out, as if meant for her.

Coles would later find that same intense application of art to life among civil rights workers in the early sixties, and makes the same application himself. This great love of literature persisted throughout Day's life. She was drawn to the great nineteenth-century writers—Dickens, Dostoevsky, Tolstoy, Chekhov—and to more contemporary political writers and activists like Orwell, Silone, Danilo Dolci, Simone Weil, Edith Stein, and Dietrich Bonhoeffer.

Dorothy Day's reliance on the Bible provides another interesting example of how her life was not quite so neatly divided between pre- and post-conversion as she sometimes liked to make out. Raised in a Protestant family, Day absorbed some of the intense Bible-centeredness of Protestant Christianity and carried that throughout her life. She occasionally faced criticism from her Catholic friends who observed that "true Catholics get their solace out of church, not reading the Bible."

Nonetheless, the Bible became increasingly central to Day from the 1930s on. Favorite passages—Romans 12, the second letter to the Corinthians, Philippians 2—provided her some comfort, but also challenge and stimulation. What does it mean to be in community? How can we be reminded of the omnipresent danger of pride? How should we bolster and encourage one another?

If the theme of reading, reading literature and reading the Bible, runs throughout Dorothy Day's life, as does the theme of her passion for justice, yet another theme is the search for community. Dorothy Day, we need to remember, had been in community before her conversion. Her intense and affectionate relationship with Forster Batterham, her connections with political radicals, her association with literary figures, these all count as forms of community. Many of these people dropped Dorothy Day, it is true, after her conversion, but from their point of view, she had violated their community. Batterham, like many other intellectuals, prided himself on his secularism and materialism and saw in the Catholic Church a bastion of privilege and superstition. For Day to go over to that institution was incomprehensible. Perhaps she was ill, mentally disturbed. "One person kept telling me I should find the best alienist in Manhattan. That was an old term for psychiatrist. I told him that I hoped God would forgive him for thinking religion was something crazy, and he got very angry with me."

But somehow, against all the weight of that community, against social pressure, against the intellectual arguments about supernaturalism and religion, Day felt the truth of the Church's claims. "I believed in Jesus Christ—that He is *real,* that He is the son of God, that He came here, that He entered history, and that He is still here, with us, all the time, through His Church, through the sacraments of the Church."

The difficulty Dorothy Day encountered was that the Catholic Church in the 1930s or through the rest of her life, was not quite the Christian community she hungered for. With Peter Maurin, she constructed community, as it were, in the midst of an alienated society, using the materials of the Church. And it is precisely the nature of the Catholic Worker community that has attracted Robert Coles, causing him to say, "The Catholic Worker is my home."

For Dorothy Day, the essence of the Catholic Worker experience was its immersion in daily experience. As Coles pointed out in *A Spectacle Unto the World,* the movement was founded by intellectuals, intellectuals work in the hospitality houses and contribute to the movement, but it is not primarily a movement of intellectuals. While not everyone there, including Day herself, could be considered a worker, the emphasis has always been on living among and serving working people, or people who would do manual work if such were available. Educated people, intellectuals, professionals, are often so taken up with words, with analysis, with plans for large-scale change. The Catholic Worker movement seeks rather a radical leveling, an emphasis on being rather than on knowing. Day insisted, in conversation with Coles, that "we are here because *we* are in need. We are here because *we* are hungry. . . . God has given us a moment to be worthy of His love."[60] The poor serve us, by reminding us that humanity and compassion are not equivalent to knowledge. And such service, Day stressed, was not simply charity. The mission of the Catholic Worker was to live in accordance with Christ's way of life.

> We are impractical, as one of us put it, as impractical as Calvary. There is no point in trying to make us into something we are not. We are *not* another Community Fund group, anxious to help people. . . . We feed the hungry, yes; we try to shelter the homeless and give them clothes, if we have some, but there is a strong faith at work; we pray.
> We are here to bear witness to our Lord. We are here to follow His lead. We are here to celebrate Him through these works of mercy.[61]

The kind of community that Day fostered and that Coles so admires is profoundly interdependent. The poor and the privileged are both encouraged to see themselves as part of the same body. For the poor to be lifted up often requires the privileged to learn humility. In all this, Day sought to build up what Saint Paul called in Philippians "the common life." Equally, the Catholic Worker community fosters a rhythm of engagement and solitude. Day herself spoke of the need for privacy, for separation as well as the need for engagement.

> A community is what Saint Paul told us—our differences granted respect by one another, but those differences not allowed to turn us into loners. You must know when to find your own, quiet moments of solitude. But you must know when to open the door to go be with others, and you must know *how* to open the door.

Coles phrases Day's rhythm of involvement and isolation this way:

> She was always trying to be alone with God, yet she lived in a community where it was hard to find even the conventional privacy of the comfortable bourgeois life. . . . Though she had both a contemplative and prophetic mind, her life was an active, essentially pastoral one: feed the hungry, house the needy, care for the sick.

Intimately linked to Day's vision of communities of interdependence is her localism. Here too Robert Coles has found much to inspire him, although he is frank about his disagreements with Day. While many radicals of the thirties saw hope only in systemic change, she and Peter Maurin chose to emphasize the building of local community, stressing the need for work as the precondition of human dignity. And although many thirties reformers enthusiastically supported the New Deal (and Coles greatly admires both Franklin Roosevelt and his political heirs like Robert Kennedy), Day was suspicious of the state as an adequate means for human liberation. Government itself, she was coming to see, because of its size, its impersonality, its distance, was part of the problem. Localism, she believed, was an effort to restore to ordinary men and women some measure of control over their own lives.

> I have just told you that we've been struggling to break away from the subjugation of plain, ordinary folks to the distant power of others, their so-called leaders. . . . We all want to surrender ourselves to some institution, some equivalent, here and now, of the Almighty, as Dostoevski kept reminding us, especially in the Grand Inquisitor scene of *The Brothers Karamazov*. If I had to be very brief about what

localism means, I would say it means a neighborliness that is both political and spiritual in nature.

Most of all, Robert Coles is deeply attracted to Dorothy Day and the Catholic Worker movement because theirs is an *engaged* spirituality; it is belief in practice. The question that Coles has struggled with—how does one live a life?—is the same one that engages Dorothy Day: "To be a witness does not consist in engaging in propaganda or even in stirring people up, but in being a living mystery; it means to live in such a way that one's life would not make sense if God did not exist." Distrustful of intellectuals and of theory, Coles prefers to look at behavior, at people's efforts to make sense out of life through their action. Here then is Dorothy Day, university-educated, well-read, a writer and speaker, a woman who nonetheless chooses to bury herself among New York's most destitute. Her actions are absurd, incomprehensible. Even those sympathetic to the work of the movement find its insistent localism, its one-by-one care of the indigent baffling because so apolitical. But to Coles these absurdities reveal a deeper wisdom. To be a mover and shaker in politics or in the academic world is to experience the temptation to power, the temptation to self-importance, and these temptations Day, like Coles, seeks to resist. The sin of pride is, for both, the sin of sins.

I have argued that Day represents the other side of Robert Coles's spirituality, an alternative to the witness of Simone Weil. Earlier I noted some of the women's similarities. But the differences seem to me more striking. Dorothy Day loved the physicality of life—the bread and soup and the hot coffee served by the gallon at Saint Joseph's. She loved her books. Most of all, she loved the men and women who came to the hospitality houses—not all of them all the time, surely, but she engaged them, touched them, fed them. She had a vision of how a life of service could nurture the self. For all her brilliance, Simone Weil, I think, had very little sense of how living for others and caring for the self are dynamically related. In Dorothy Day's case, the paradox of losing one's life in order to gain it seems tenderly and powerfully exemplified.

To put it simply, Simone Weil appeals to that self-emptying, even self-hating side of Robert Coles. She appeals to the side that loves paradox and absurdity, even gets a bit lost in it. She appeals to the prickly loner side, the critic who will not be satisfied, the restless outsider who is suspicious of all community, the wounded self who refuses healing. She appeals to the side of Coles that, having seen so much suffering and injustice, finds his own life of relative ease intolerable and feels a great burden of guilt about his privilege. She appeals to the Coles who sees in the religious life a perpetual challenge to secularism but few alternatives except loneliness and suffering.

Dorothy Day has appealed, I believe, to that side of Robert Coles which has engaged an enormous variety of human beings over several decades, and seen in them not crushed and brutalized wretches but resourceful, dignified people. Like Day, Coles believes that humanity is not equivalent to sociological or psychological categories. There is a remainder, a residuum that cannot be classified, a human mystery that is at the core spiritual, an identity that is neither class nor gender nor racial nor ethnic in nature. It is to this spiritual center that the Catholic Worker has appealed; it is that center that Coles has sought to illuminate in his work.

·7·

Loneliness and Community

*T*eaching is occupying much of Robert Coles's time, together with his current research project on the spiritual life of children. What is the connection? he was asked. "I've fed off it [the teaching] . . . it really helps me with my work. When I read those novels, and go over *Let Us Now Praise Famous Men* or Orwell, I'm sharper when I'm talking with kids."

In a position now to influence hundreds of students in courses in Harvard College and the business, medical, and law schools, Coles reflected recently on the teachers who influenced him. The big names were obvious: Perry Miller, Werner Jaeger, Reinhold Niebuhr, Paul Tillich. But there were others. He recalled his fifth grade teacher, Bernicia Avery. She was "an extraordinary Vermonter who taught me discipline, who imbued a love of American history . . . who was such a dedicated and decent human being." She "taught us Abraham Lincoln . . . what a compassionate person he was, how hard his life had been." Then there was Charles French, a teacher of history at Boston Latin. French would read the Bible aloud to his homeroom students each morning. "I remember him reading from Ecclesiastes on the sin of pride, the same thing I'd get from my mother . . . and then he'd try to connect this to our daily lives in that classroom and that school."[1]

Now more than forty years later, Coles addresses lecture halls filled with students or smaller groups in seminars. At the medical school he is teaching "Literature and Medicine," "an attempt to look at contemporary views of human nature, and the nature of social inquiry, including the ethical issues that reformist action generates." At the law school he has offered "Dickens and the Law," in which students read *Bleak House, Great Expectations, A Tale of Two Cities,* and *Little Dorrit.* Recently in the business school he offered "The Business World: Moral and Social Inquiry Through Fiction." In a course taught with Robert Kiely of Harvard's English faculty, Coles pursues "The Literature of Christian Reflection," studying John of the Cross, Teresa of Avila, Bonhoeffer,

174

Philip Larkin, Robert Frost, Emily Dickinson, Luther, Calvin, Pascal, Kierkegaard. And, together with more than a dozen section leaders, Coles teaches, each fall, "The Literature of Social Reflection," taking up Orwell, Agee, Ellison, O'Connor, Day, Bernanos, Silone, Tolstoy, Weil, Percy, Cheever, Eliot, Hardy, and Dickens, not to mention several items by Coles himself.[2]

"You teach through lives, you teach through stories . . . through autobiography, through poetry," Coles once said. His syllabi are "really my personal reading list." In his work as teacher, Coles has extended, in another form, his function as translator. As in written work, so now in lecture and seminar, Coles has sought to take a body of material, organize it, and convey it to an audience. His writing exhibits a tense interplay between absence and presence—the absence of the interviewer so that the subjects' words can come through, the presence of the interviewer in selection and arrangement. His teaching conveys the same moral intensity, angularity, that his writing does. "I just feel like you're taking my freedom away. Like you expect me to act the way you would," a young Harvard student complained. Coles apologized; "I'm sorry. I just try to give you some experiences that have touched my life, moved me. It's such a tightrope. I'm sorry."[3]

As translation, teaching, like social psychiatry (or whatever label we want to apply to Coles's writing), exists on the border between transparency and interpretation. When Coles is an inspired medium, a vehicle for stories of "others," shaped into unforgettable narratives, then he is most memorable, his work constituting major contributions to American letters. This does not always happen in the texts or in the classroom, of course. As one student noted, "There are some lectures that are just ordinary and mundane, or 'famous or well-meaning people I've known or read.'" He is at his best, in text or classroom, when he prods the reader/auditor to "unlearn," to still the impulse to categorize experience into the known and familiar, to be open to genuinely new possibilities, to mystery.[4]

By offering courses across the curriculum, courses that bring together literature, history, sociology, autobiography, Coles has exposed and criticized the rigid disciplinary boundaries in so much of contemporary academia. Even more, Coles has insisted that the issues taken up in these courses and these texts are life-concerns. The great danger of the university, at least in its humanities programs, is isolation from the ambiguity of "real life" and the arrogance that is unchallenged by immersion in life experience.

As a teacher and a writer, Coles wants to heal the split between thought and action, intellect and life. This effort takes on added poignancy when one considers that Coles himself is a fragmented, often alienated, man on the margins, "a wounded healer" in Henri Nouwen's phrase, working to heal a fragmented culture. Teaching (like writing, speaking, interviewing) has for Coles not so much an academic, knowledge-imparting function; it is rather occasionally prophetic, most frequently pastoral. These days Coles uses his Harvard lecterns as (in the best sense of the term) a "bully pulpit."

Healing requires unlearning, in Coles's view, and his harshest criticisms have been directed at fellow academics, professionals, white people (mostly men) in positions of power and influence. He has insisted that knowledge does not produce wisdom; one can be brilliant and a failed human being, "get all A's and still flunk life," as Percy put in *The Second Coming*. All too often, intellectual superiority goes hand in hand with deep character flaws—arrogance, egoism, pride.

To some readers and listeners, Coles's attacks on the intellectual establishment, sometimes verging into attacks on the life of the mind, sound oddly elitist. It makes sense for one centered at Harvard to be critical of too much intellectualizing. But for many secondary and college teachers, the problem they face is a paucity rather than an excess of cognition. A popular culture that presents human experience in seven-minute segments on television, that glorifies action, violence, revenge, and mayhem, that sells products through sex, greed, and envy—such a culture makes rational discourse, historical depth, scientific discipline irrelevant, quaint, even laughable. For people distant from major intellectual centers, defending any kind of thoughtfulness against the prevailing philistinism and narrow vocationalism is an enormous, mostly losing struggle. Coles's assault on intellectual arrogance does not do much to encourage such embattled defenders.[5]

Still, whether it is intellectual snobs who categorize and dismiss ordinary people and experience, or a philistine popular culture that debases both thought and feeling, the result is the same: The life of intellect and the life of daily experience are severed. How does Coles envision their reconnection?

When Coles says "you teach through lives" he means, I think, not only the lives described in his "documentaries," he means the lives and work of the scores of writers and thinkers on his "personal reading list." Coles has tried to infuse and interpenetrate his interviews with the insights of these intellectuals; he has placed the thoughts, lives, experiences, of his subjects in a context provided by Pascal and Kierkegaard, Dickens and Orwell, Agee and Weil. These writers have expressed, perhaps more systematically or elegantly, but rarely more powerfully, the same insights as have the miners and day laborers, Indians, Chicanos, ghetto mothers, Boston policemen and firefighters, Rio de Janeiro favela children. He has sought, contrary to what he feels is the prevailing tenor of the academy, to create a community between the published and the unpublished, the voiced and the voiceless. A shy, aloof loner, but an almost magically good listener, Coles has *created* community for us. He has demonstrated, in his books, the possible conversation between the (intellectually speaking) haves and the have-nots.

What are the limitations to this project, this linking of an idiosyncratic intellectual tradition with a vast body of social observations and interviews? The writers and thinkers Coles prefers serve as *witnesses* for him; his appropriation of them is intensely personal in nature, rather than systematic or theoretical. Coles's books on O'Connor, Percy, Williams, Erikson, Weil, Day, are thoughtful, intelligent. But they are in every case a personal "reading" of the life and the texts of these men and women. Neither biographies nor systematic analyses of thought, these books permit us to overhear conversations between Coles and their subjects.

Nothing could be clearer throughout his work than Coles's dislike of theory. "In life I fear all ideologies—political, social, psychological, and even philosophical or religious." He has much preferred to "give way to those amusing and often enough awful inconsistencies and contradictions that only the non-ideological (and very great) writer has the stomach as well as the intelligence and talent to comprehend."[6] His criticism of Lawrence Kohlberg in *The Moral Life of Children* is a more recent example of his impatience with systematic thought which, when it cannot explain experience, ignores it.[7] But Coles's critique of theory itself needs to be critiqued. He does, after all, possess a set of working assumptions, if not a theory. He believes in the descriptive accuracy of the Pauline/Augustinian view of human nature; he assumes that pride is the worst of human sins; he believes that human life can only be described in its rich historical complexity, not predicted through psychological or sociological categories; he believes in the mystery and unpredictability, the freedom, at the core of each self. Like the moral critics we spoke of earlier, Coles wishes to plunge beneath the false consciousness, the gravity, the fantasy, the net of social assumptions, and recover authentic experience, believing, as he does, that such a dimension exists.

But beyond these generalizations, how might we understand behavior? Here Coles, because of his antipathy to theory, is not very helpful. We need to take people at their word, he says; when they claim religious motivation for action, for example, we need to respect that. Surely this is true. Still, religious belief has led to a variety of contradictory actions, so we do not seem much advanced in our understanding. Is it inevitable that theory (whether in psychology, sociology, politics, religion, or literature) distances one from felt experience? Does systematic thought always isolate and alienate the thinker? Contemporary liberation theologians think not. Juan Luis Segundo, for example, has argued that simply being "open" to experience is insufficient; one needs to understand the ways in which people's very experience of their own realities is shaped. Coles's stress on the mysterious freedom in even the most hard-pressed lives requires the dialectical response of a systematic thinker like Segundo, who would point out the molding influence of media, corporations, government, educational institutions. Similarly, his insistence on the grounding of literature in real-life experience needs to be engaged, dialectically, with the poststructuralist claims about the arbitrary, constructed, ideological nature of language.8

So, on the one hand, Coles is highly critical of intellectuals for their penchant toward systematizing, and creates an intellectual community for himself and his readers by engaging certain texts and authors not critically but personally. On the other hand, the community he envisions contains the hundreds of quite ordinary people he has interviewed over the years. We have stressed how remarkably, even magically, transparent Coles is with his subjects. His own awkwardness and vulnerability, his shyness and boyishness disarm them, put them at ease. He does not come across as an important scholar and investigator; he sits on the floor, plays with the children, shares a beer on the front porch with the adults. All of this demands respect from readers, who may all too often feel quite cut off from the vast numbers of Americans in hard circumstances.

Still, we may have our doubts. Coles is rarely critical of his many subjects. Even when they voice the most outrageous prejudices, the most astounding misunderstandings, he does not often bring himself to comment. If intellectuals are regularly chastised for lacking sympathy for the working class, why were not the "middle Americans" criticized for their racism? Should not "ordinary Americans" be shown the ways in which their opinions are manipulated by media and politics? Coles seems to fear (as he said in the introduction to *Geography of Faith*) that articulate commitment to some political or social cause on his part would make him less trustworthy in the eyes of his interviewees. Still, we have the odd result that "ordinary Americans," so often (though not by Coles) condemned and ridiculed for their philistine taste and easy submission to cultural manipulation, are given new respect, while intellectuals, commonly seen as free of illusions and possessing keen critical sensibilities, are shown as dupes of their own thinking and arrogant in their characters. The terms, in short, have been reversed.

Coles's insistence on an open and nonjudgmental attitude toward his subjects leads to a curious result: Unwilling to embrace large-scale change as either feasible or desirable, fearful of small groups (of intellectuals or revolutionaries) acting as a kind of "vanguard of the proletariat" and dictating change, Coles cannot imagine (at least in his published work) the possibility of a better future. People cope, even survive, with dignity. But his pessimistic, ironic religious outlook, his sense of the permanence of flawed human nature, make him suspicious of programs for change. We obtain from Coles an increase in sympathy, but no sense of empowerment. There is in his work a remarkable paradox of sensitivity but passivity. The harassed but defiant migrant worker, the patronizing but tormented crew leader, and the hard-driving but financially pressed food grower cancel each other out.

Troubled by the divisions between intellect and experience, both in himself and in the larger culture, Coles has sought to heal that fragmentation by creating a community, a dialogue between voiced and voiceless. This is an ironic, poignant project, given Coles's own "loner" status, his years of work without assistants or companions save his wife and children, his marginal status in the psychiatric world and in the academic community. This effort to bring the world of thought into proximity with the world of ordinary experience characterizes his writing and his teaching. In both cases, I have suggested, Coles explores the frontier between transparency and interpretation.

Perhaps we are ready to acknowledge Robert Coles for what he really is. Summoning up a powerful though personal intellectual tradition, Coles brings his favorite texts and authors, together with his own considerable sensitivity, to bear on lives. He is, I think, an artist in lives. He is a social documentarist, a shaper of complex lives into narrative patterns. People have often asked him why he does not write fiction, he once observed. He cannot make things up, but given the raw materials, he is uncannily able to find the thread that runs through disparate experience. He can discern without reductionism the master metaphor that opens each life to view.

That Robert Coles should approach his work as a "poet in lives" through psychiatry is not utterly implausible, despite the prevailing scientism that dominates psychoanalysis. Recently psychiatrist Donald Spence has offered some provocative thoughts on the connections between psychoanalysis and literary criticism, which may help us understand the particular nature of Robert Coles's interpretations.[9]

Freud's favorite analogy for psychoanalysis was archeology. One digs down, through the buried layers, to the hidden treasure, the actual event. The technique of free association on the patient's part is matched by "free-floating" attention on the analyst's part, who listens with what Freud called "evenly hovering attention." Together, patient and analyst construct a narrative that recovers the original event, avoiding the traps of "screen memories" and facile interpretations.

The problem with Freud's archeological analogy, says Spence, is that it confuses two kind of truth, historical and narrative. The memories we seek to recover through psychoanalysis are largely visual; they are rich, tactile, and indescribable in words. But in psychiatry we are engaged in a "talking cure," so language is inescapable. When we speak in grammatical sentences, organize them into coherent sequences of thought, we violate the psychoanalytic rule of "nonediting." A faithful effort, says Spence, to render interior reality directly results in incomprehensible gibberish. So, Freud was naive in assuming that visual imagery can be recovered in language, through free association and "evenly hovering" attention. What psychoanalysis requires, Spence believes, is a more sophisticated interpretation theory, and calls our attention to models offered in literary criticism.

When we put experience or ideas into words, we perform a complicated translation of the "text" of the world (as we experience it) into the text of the work. When we assume the role of the reader or listener, we are obliged to reverse the order and translate the work back into common or shared experience. The ease or difficulty of that second translation, Spence points out, is linked to the author's ability to provide us clues and signals about the nature of that translation. There can never be a perfect reader's translation of the author's translation. Even more, we cannot wait until the end of the text to determine if we've done an adequate job; we are reading and translating all the time.

When we as readers rush in prematurely and assume a meaning for the text, perhaps on the basis of some clumsiness of the author, or perhaps because of some stylistic device, it is extremely difficult to clear ourselves of this preliminary interpretation if it should prove false or inadequate. Likewise in therapy, the great temptation is to rush in and provide a "reading" of the free associations being articulated. If this happens too prematurely, Spence argues, the original image may be lost forever; "Because the wrong interpretation can easily be substituted for the target image, part of the patient's past is now placed forever out of reach." Once expressed in certain form, the description *becomes* the memory.

The task of psychoanalysis then becomes the re-narrating of memory in such a way as to capture in words the dense ambiguity, the richness of that early, visual, experience. If we think about it this way, Spence believes, we can free ourselves from the notion that in therapy we are finding the single match of words with events. Not so much causal or historical, the truth of therapy is much more linguistic and narrative. Given the imaginative and interpretive nature of language, analysis needs to be much closer to poetry than history, to construction than to reconstruction.

Robert Coles's genius lies in his ability to take a vast amount of data and narrate a life story to us, in such a way as to preserve its maximum richness, complexity, and particularity. In an artful way that only seems artless in its simplicity, Coles allows the words of his informants to carry the burden of their stories, yet the selection and arrangement of those words, as well as the larger social and cultural context, is all Coles. In virtual isolation, Robert Coles has created a social document in *Children of Crisis, Women of Crisis, The Moral* and *The Political Life of Children,* in his texts for the photographic essays *Still Hungry in America, The Image Is You, The Old Ones of New Mexico,* and the volumes on Agee and Dorothea Lange, in the forthcoming work on the spiritual life of children. Like the WPA documentaries that recorded ex-slaves' lives, that transcribed folk songs, that preserved folk stories and regional customs; like the work of James Agee and Walker Evans, Dorothea Lange, and George Orwell, Coles's accounts provide an interpreted design of life from the bottom up. Through Coles's eyes, people in the United States and elsewhere in the 1960s, 1970s, and 1980s are confused, caught up in change, sometimes distrustful and suspicious, yet persistent, often courageous and resilient, given to remarkable moral insights and spiritual breakthroughs.

Consider, for example, Coles's final conversation with a group of Afrikaner children just before he was to leave South Africa. He was not relishing this encounter—having to listen to one more defense of the homeland, one more appeal to understand the unique burdens of South African whites. As he listened, Coles noticed in himself " a telltale lack of attention to what was being said; an urge to look at the watch; the yawn rising, a hard one to stifle; awareness that the stomach was empty, and craving an addict's balm, ice cream. What the hell—call it quits, get out of here; a short but sweet goodbye."

The children had talked among themselves about what would be an appropriate farewell gift for their American friend. Knowing Coles's fondness for children's paintings, their leader, Hendrick, created the scene that Coles later used on the dust cover of *The Political Life of Children*.

On the left, as Hendrick described it, is a battle, a reminder of South Africa's constant violence. In the center, the boy painted a peaceful scene from the veldt. But what was this gray structure on the right, strangely menacing in its cool and mechanical appearance? Hendrick struggled to explain himself: "I don't know what a nuclear bomb looks like. I think it's a box. I thought I'd make a reactor, or a missile pad, where the bomb is inside, and it's sent out through the roof." Coles was now paying strict attention to the boy's description of the painting.

> I thought as I was painting this: What are you doing, Hendrick, painting this? You're crazy! Then I thought—hey, we're all crazy, to have these things on our planet! Then I thought, my God almighty: if one of them goes off, everyone will die, every single one of us, probably, in South Africa! What difference will it make—where we live, and whether we're old or young. No one would be here. The colored ones would be gone, and the black ones, and the Indians— and us too, the white people! It makes you wonder! We should stop fighting! That's why I made this picture—so we could all be warned!

Once again Coles is struck by the inexplicable moral breakthrough, the sudden insight of a child so shaped by Afrikaner ideology that Coles had been ready, a few moments before, to write him off completely.

> A lifetime spent in South Africa still wouldn't be enough, with all the surprises children can offer us at unpredictable moments. . . . I catch myself, as I sit there, also realizing again, that children everywhere can stop us short with their unnerving moments of innocent good sense—even as they can also mouth all our (adult) stupid nonsense— and sometimes, one hopes and prays, give voice to our more honorable and decent thoughts.[10]

While authors prefer to give themselves the last word, the affinity between life and work that I have insisted on here requires instead that Coles provide our conclusion:

When I look back at my life, it's been a series of lucky moments that I could never have anticipated; the whole thing seems strange that I did it. I never intended to come back to Harvard and teach; I never intended to be a doctor; I never intended to be a psychiatrist; I never intended to live in the South; I never intended to become a teacher; I never intended to be a writer; I don't understand. . . . I don't know how one explains a life.[11]

This personal puzzle exactly parallels the mystery in the lives of people in crisis: "How does it come about that people can live with such pain and hunger and fear and uncertainty—only to confront us, the comfortable observers, with what at least seems to be a kind of nobility, an impressive purity of spirit?"[12]

Notes

Introduction

1. Robert Coles, *Erik H. Erikson: The Growth of His Thought* (Boston: Little, Brown, 1970), p. 58.

2. Coles, "Introduction," *Farewell to the South* (Boston: Little, Brown, 1972), pp. 8, 26.

3. Coles, *The Political Life of Children* (Boston: Atlantic Monthly Press, 1986), p. 17.

4. Coles, *Eskimos, Indians, Chicanos,* vol. 4 of *Children of Crisis* (Boston: Little, Brown, 1977), p. 57; hereafter, CC 4.

5. Coles, "The Observer and the Observed," in *Farewell to the South,* p. 378.

6. Coles, *Migrants, Sharecroppers, Mountaineers,* vol. 2 of *Children of Crisis* (Boston: Little, Brown, 1971), p. 27; hereafter, CC 2.

7. Coles, *The Moral Life of Children* (Boston: Atlantic Monthly Press, 1986), pp. 26–27.

8. George Orwell, quoted in *The Moral Life,* p. 93.

9. Interview with author, 24 October 1987, Concord, Massachusetts.

10. CC 2, p. 30.

11. CC 2, p. 37.

12. Interview with author, 24 October 1987.

13. Interview with author, 24 October 1987.

Chapter 1   The Autobiographical Impulse

1. "Open Question; An Alumni Examination," *Harvard Magazine* 89, 1 (September–October 1986), p. 172; "Children Know about Moral Hypocrisy," *US News and World Report,* 17 February 1986, pp. 61–62; "Happiness," *Vogue* 173 (January 1983), pp. 204–5; "MacNeil-Lehrer Report," September 1987.

2. *Time magazine,* 14 February 1972; interview with author, 24 October 1987.

3. Interview with author, 24 October 1987.

4. *The Confessions of St. Augustine,* translated by John K. Ryan (Garden City: Doubleday Image, 1960), 202. The importance of Augustine in the development of autobiography is considered by Janet Varner Gunn, *Autobiography: Towards a Poetics of Experience* (Chapel Hill: University of North Carolina

Press, 1982), William Spengeman, *The Forms of Autobiography: Episodes in the History of a Literary Genre* (New Haven: Yale University Press, 1980), and James Olney, *Metaphors of the Self* (Princeton: Princeton University Press, 1972).

5. Erikson's discussion of "identity crisis" may be found throughout *Identity: Youth and Crisis* (New York: W. W. Norton, 1968) and in *Life History and the Historical Moment* (New York: W. W. Norton, 1975), pp. 18–22.

6. Robert Coles, *A Study in Courage and Fear,* vol. 1 of *Children of Crisis* (Boston: Atlantic-Little, Brown, 1967), p. 4; hereafter, CC 1.

7. CC 1, p. 7.

8. CC 1, p. 8.

9. Coles, "The Observer and the Observed," in *Farewell to the South,* p. 378.

10. Coles, *The Privileged Ones,* vol. 5 of *Children of Crisis* (Boston: Little, Brown, 1977), p. 543; hereafter, CC 5.

11. "The Observer and the Observed," p. 376.

12. Ibid., pp. 393–95.

13. Robert Coles, *The Geography of Faith: Conversations between Daniel Berrigan, when Underground, and Robert Coles* (Boston: Beacon Press, 1971), p. 8.

14. Ibid., p. 12.

15. Ibid., p. 22.

16. Ibid., p. 24.

17. CC 1, pp. 30–31.

18. CC 1, pp. 17–18.

19. CC 1, p. 5.

20. Coles, "A Fashionable Kind of Slander," in *Farewell to the South,* p. 285.

21. Coles, "Serpents and Doves: Nonviolent Youth in the South," in *Farewell to the South,* p. 217.

22. CC 1, p. 5.

23. Coles, "Psychology and Civility," *Daedalus* 109 (Summer 1980), p. 137.

24. Coles, "The End of the Affair," *Katallagete* 4 (Fall 1972), pp. 47–48.

25. Ibid., p. 49.

26. Ibid.

27. Coles, *Irony in the Mind's Life: Essays on Novels by James Agee, Elizabeth Bowen, and George Eliot* (New York: New Directions, 1974), p. 5.

28. Ibid., p. 6.

29. Robert Middlekauf, "Perry Miller," in Marcus Cunliffe and Robin Winks, eds., *Pastmasters: Some Essays on American Historians* (New York: Harper and Row, 1969), p. 175.

30. Perry Miller, *The New England Mind: The Seventeenth Century* (Boston: Beacon Press, 1939), pp. 8–9.

31. Blaise Pascal, quoted in Coles, *Irony,* p. 25.

32. Coles, *Walker Percy: An American Search* (Boston: Little, Brown, 1978), pp. 8–9.

33. Coles, *Irony,* p. 6.

34. Coles, "Shadowing Binx," *Literature and Medicine* 4 (1985), p. 151.

35. Interview with author, 24 October 1987.

36. Coles, "Shadowing Binx," p. 151.

37. Ibid., p. 152.

38. Coles, "The End of the Affair," p. 49.

39. Ibid., p. 46.

40. Ibid., p. 49.

41. Ibid., pp. 49–50.

42. Interview with author, 24 October 1987.

43. Coles, "The End of the Affair," 50.

44. Interview with author, 24 October 1987.

45. Coles, *Dorothy Day: A Radical Devotion* (Reading, Massachusetts: Addison-Wesley, 1987), pp. xv–xviii.

46. Coles, "Out of the Mouth of Babes: When Ethics and Reality Collide," *Washington Post National Weekly Edition,* 2 September 1985, p. 24.

47. Coles, "The End of the Affair," p. 50.

48. Ibid., p. 51.

49. Ibid., p. 52.

50. Ibid., p. 54.

51. Coles, "Out of the Mouths of Babes," p. 24.

52. Coles, *Irony,* 5. While at Massachusetts General, Coles became interested in the psychological effects of polio on some of the young victims of that disease. This occurred when the last great polio epidemic swept the Boston area in the late 1950s, just before widespread Salk vaccine innoculation. Though studying psychiatry, Coles took his turn caring for the polio sufferers in the pediatrics ward, thus exposing himself to the disease. Out of this interest came his first publication, coauthored with Jimmy C. B. Holland, "Neuropsychiatric Aspects of Acute Poliomyelitis," *American Journal of Psychiatry* 114 (July 1957).

53. Interview with author, 24 October 1987.

54. Coles, *Walker Percy,* p. x.

55. Ibid.

56. Ibid.

57. Coles, "Character and Intellect," *American Poetry Review* 12 (September–October 1983), p. 47.

58. Ibid., p. 46.

59. Coles, "Reflections: Life's Big Ironies," *American Poetry Review* 12 (January–February 1983), pp. 15–16.

60. Richard Sennett, *Authority* (New York: Vintage/Random House, 1981), p. 5.

61. Coles, "Reflections: Life's Big Ironies," p. 15.

62. Ibid., p. 16.

63. Paul Wilkes, "Robert Coles, Doctor of Crisis," *New York Times Magazine,* 26 March 1978, p. 15.

64. Paul Tillich, *On the Boundary: An Autobiographical Sketch* (New York: Charles Scribner's Sons, 1966), p. 13.

65. Coles, "The End of the Affair," p. 56.

66. Joseph Epstein, "Dr. Coles Among the Poor," *Commentary* 54 (August 1972), p. 63.

67. Epstein, *Plausible Prejudices* (New York: W. W. Norton, 1985), 50. I am grateful to Brian Mahan for this reference.

Chapter 2   Children of Crisis: Style and Method

1. CC 4. p. 57.
2. CC 4, p. 58.
3. CC 2, p. 41.
4. CC 1, pp. 30–31.
5. CC 1, p. 24. A careful reading of the entire first volume of *Children of Crisis* is necessary to appreciate the way Coles went about finding and interviewing such a variety of Southerners. For other Coles accounts of Southern children, black and white, involved in school desegregation, see "In the South These Children Prophesy," in *Farewell to the South*, pp. 148–62; "Southern Children Under Desegregation," *American Journal of Psychiatry* 4 (October 1963); and *The Desegregation of Southern Schools; A Psychiatric Study* (Atlanta: The Southern Regional Council, 1963).
6. CC 5, pp. xi–xii.
7. CC 2, p. 32.
8. CC 1, p. 40.
9. CC 1, p. 40.
10. CC 1, pp. 40–41.
11. CC 1, p. 45.
12. CC 1, p. 46.
13. CC 1, p. 65.
14. Coles, *The South Goes North*, vol. 3 of *Children of Crisis* (Boston: Little, Brown, 1971), p. 35; hereafter, CC 3.
15. CC 2, p. 42.
16. CC 2, p. 27.
17. CC 1, p. 34.
18. CC 2, p. 36.
19. CC 1, p. 33.
20. CC 2, p. 39.
21. CC 3, p. 40.
22. CC 1, p. 34.
23. CC 2, p. 41.
24. CC 4, p. 57.
25. Judy Peace, "'What Are We Doing to Our Children?' An Interview with Robert Coles," *The Other Side* 15 (May 1979), p. 15–16.
26. CC 2, pp. 37–38.
27. CC 3, p. 38.
28. CC 1, p. 122.
29. CC 1, p. 123.
30. CC 1, pp. 124–25.
31. CC 1, p. 126.
32. CC 1, p. 133.
33. CC 1, p. 135.

34. Wayne C. Booth, *The Rhetoric of Fiction* (Chicago: University of Chicago Press, 1961), pp. 73–75.

35. CC 3, p. 64. On Coles's attempts to understand the depth of black anger see "Baldwin's Burdens," *Partisan Review* 31 (Summer 1964); "The Wretched of the Earth," *The New Republic,* 18 September 1965, and "Oppressor and Victim under Colonialism," *African Forum* 2 (Summer 1966), both on Franz Fanon; "What Can We Learn from the Life of Malcolm X?" *Teachers College Record* (May 1966); "Black Anger," *Atlantic Monthly* 221 (June 1968), pp. 106–7, on Eldridge Cleaver; "Two Minds about Carmichael," in *Farewell to the South,* pp. 257–65; and "The Rage Around Us," *The New Republic,* 17 August 1968, p. 36. Coles wrote two children's books about the bussing controversy: *Dead End School* (Boston: Atlantic-Little, Brown, 1968), on black children traveling out to suburban schools, and *Saving Face* (Boston: Atlantic-Little, Brown, 1977), on the feelings of white children when black youngsters come into "their" school. See also "Bussing in Boston," *The New Republic,* 2 October 1965, pp. 12–15, and "Northern Children Under Desegregation," *Psychiatry* 31 (February 1968), pp. 1–15.

36. CC 3, p. 65.

37. CC 3, p. 67.

38. CC 3, p. 70.

39. CC 3, p. 71.

40. CC 4, p. 61.

41. On "reader-response" theory, see, among many studies, Stanley Fish, *Is There a Text in This Class? The Authority of Interpretive Communities* (Cambridge: Harvard University Press, 1980); Steven Mailloux, *Interpretive Conventions: The Reader in the Study of American Fiction* (Ithaca: Cornell University Press, 1982); and Jane Tompkins, ed., *Reader-Response Criticism: From Formalism to Post-Structuralism* (Baltimore: Johns Hopkins University Press, 1980).

42. CC 4, p. 475.

43. CC 4, pp. 474–75.

44. CC 4, pp. 475–77.

45. CC 4, p. 478.

46. CC 4, p. 519–20.

47. CC 2, p. 25.

48. CC 2, pp. 36–37.

49. William James, *The Varieties of Religious Experience* (1902) (New York: Viking Penguin, 1982), p. 18. For Coles's reflections on James, see "Varieties of Religious Experience," in *The Mind's Fate* (Boston: Little, Brown, 1975), pp. 149–56.

50. CC 2, p. 39.

51. H. Richard Niebuhr, *The Responsible Self,* cited in William Clebsch, *American Religious Thought* (Chicago: University of Chicago Press, 1973), p. 182.

52. CC 3, p. 49.

53. James Agee and Walker Evans, *Let Us Now Praise Famous Men* (1941) (New York: Ballantine, 1966), pp. 11–12, 210.

54. CC 2, pp. 429, 438.

55. CC 3, pp. 292–93.

56. CC 4, pp. 195–96.

Chapter 3   Literary Criticism

1. Robert Coles, introduction to William Carlos Williams, *The Doctor Stories* (New York: New Directions, 1984), p. vii.

2. Robert Coles, *Dorothy Day: A Radical Devotion*, p. xvi–xvii.

3. Robert Coles, *Walker Percy*, p. xi.

4. Robert Coles, *William Carlos Williams: The Knack of Survival in America* (New Brunswick: Rutgers University Press, 1975), p. xiii.

5. Ibid., p. 20.

6. Ibid., p. 21.

7. Erich Auerbach, *Mimesis: The Representation of Reality in Western Literature* (1946) (Garden City: Doubleday Anchor, 1957), p. 36.

8. Ibid., p. 38.

9. Ibid., p. 408.

10. Nathan A. Scott, *The Wild Prayer of Longing: Poetry and the Sacred* (New Haven: Yale University Press, 1971), p. 14.

11. Auerbach, *Mimesis* p. 10.

12. Ibid., p. 404.

13. Alfred Kazin, *On Native Ground* (1942) (Garden City: Doubleday Anchor, 1957), p. 12.

14. Eric Sundquist, "The Country of the Blue," in Sundquist, ed., *American Realism: New Essays* (Baltimore: Johns Hopkins University Press, 1982), pp. 7–8.

15. Coles, *Williams*, p. 15.

16. Ibid., p. 49.

17. Ibid., p. 43.

18. Coles, introduction to Williams, *The Doctor Stories*, p. xi.

19. For an illuminating treatment of Agee and the documentary tradition, see William Stott, *Documentary Expression and Thirties America* (New York: Oxford University Press, 1973).

20. Robert Coles, *Flannery O'Connor's South* (Baton Rouge: Louisiana State University Press, 1980), 51.

21. Ibid., p. 112.

22. Ibid., p. 116.

23. Coles, *Williams*, p. 16.

24. Coles, *Walker Percy*, pp. xii–xiv.

25. Ibid., p. 8.

26. William Barrett, *Irrational Man: A Study in Existential Philosophy* (1958) (Garden City: Doubleday Anchor, 1962), p. 152–56.

27. Søren Kierkegaard, from *Concluding Unscientific Postscript*, in Robert

Bretall, ed., *A Kierkegaard Anthology* (Princeton: Princeton University Press, 1938), pp. 210–11.

28. Barrett, *Irrational Man,* p. 157.

29. Coles, *Walker Percy,* pp. 27–28.

30. Personal interview with author, 24 October 1987.

31. David Hellerstein, "On Medicine and Literature: An Interview with Robert Coles," *North American Review* 265 (June 1980), p. 14.

32. The literature on the "new" New Criticism is enormous and growing. I have found particularly helpful the following: Christopher Norris, *Deconstruction: Theory and Practice* (London: Methuen, 1982); Frank Lentricchia, *After the New Criticism* (Chicago: University of Chicago Press, 1980); and Geoffrey Hartman, *Criticism in the Wilderness* (Baltimore: Johns Hopkins University Press, 1980).

33. A good summary of the attitude toward texts taken by poststructuralist critics can be found in Giles Gunn's recent book, *The Culture of Criticism and the Criticism of Culture* (New York: Oxford University Press, 1987), ch. 3.

34. Giles Gunn, "The Moral Imagination in Modern American Criticism," in Mark Johnson, ed., *Modern American Cultural Criticism* (Warrensburg, Missouri: Central Missouri State University, 1983), pp. 31–32. Gunn elaborates on the themes of this essay in the work cited above.

35. Leo Tolstoy, *What Is Art? and Essays on Art,* translated by Aylmer Maude (London: Oxford University Press, 1930), p. 123.

36. John Gardner, *On Moral Fiction* (New York: Basic Books/Harper Colophon, 1978), p. 8.

37. See Robert A. Morace, "John Gardner and His Reviewers," 17–32, and Carol MacCurdy, "*On Moral Fiction:* The Embattled John Gardner," 135–46, in Jeff Henderson, ed., *Thor's Hammer: Essays on John Gardner* (np: Central Arkansas Press, 1985).

38. Gunn, "The Moral Imagination," 29.

39. Ibid., p. 33.

40. Josephine Donovan, "Beyond the Net: Feminist Criticism as Moral Criticism," *Denver Quarterly* 17 (Winter 1983), p. 43.

41. Iris Murdoch, *The Sovereignty of Good* (London: Routledge and Kegan Paul, 1970), p. 51.

42. Ibid., p. 65.

43. Nathan A. Scott, Jr., "The Rediscovery of Story in Recent Theology and the Refusal of Story in Recent Literature," in Robert Detweiler, ed., *Art/Literature/Religion: Life on the Borders (Journal of the American Academy of Religion Thematic Studies,* 49 [1981]), p. 152.

44. See R. W. B. Lewis, "Hold on Hard to the Huckleberry Bushes," in *Trials of the Word* (New Haven: Yale University Press, 1965).

45. William James, "What Pragmatism Means," from *Pragmatism* (1907) in John J. McDermott, ed., *The Writings of William James* (New York: Random House, 1967), p. 379.

46. Ibid., p. 382.

47. Robert Coles, *Irony in the Mind's Life* (New York: New Directions, 1974), p. 60.

48. Coles, *Flannery O'Connor's South*, p. 123.

49. Coles, *Irony*, pp. 164–65.

50. Robert Coles, "The Virtues of *Middlemarch*," *American Poetry Review* 14 (July–August 1985), pp. 41–42.

51. CC 4, p. 61.

52. Ibid.

53. Robert Coles, "Speaking of Books: *The Diary of a Country Priest*," The *New York Times Book Review*, 3 November 1967, section 7, p. 2.

54. Ibid.

55. Robert Coles, "Bernanos: The Writer as Child," *The New Republic*, 15 (April 1967), 24.

Chapter 4   Psychology, Psychiatry, and Children

1. Bruno Bettelheim, *Freud and Man's Soul* (New York: Knopf, 1983), passim.

2. Russell Jacoby, *The Repression of Psychoanalysis* (New York: Basic Books, 1983), pp. 1–2.

3. Ibid., p. 23.

4. For an interesting contemporary illustration of the tyranny of psychoanalysis, see Dan Wakefield, "My Six Years on the Couch," *New York Times Magazine*, 21 December 1987, pp. 32–33, 79, 82–84.

5. Coles, "End of the Affair," p. 55.

6. Ibid.

7. Ibid.

8. Ibid., p. 56.

9. Ibid.

10. Robert Coles, *The Political Life of Children* (Boston: Atlantic Monthly Press, 1986), pp. 3–7.

11. Coles, "End of the Affair," pp. 56–57.

12. Ibid., p. 57.

13. Coles, "Shadowing Binx," p. 154.

14. Ibid., p. 159.

15. Ibid., p. 158.

16. Robert Coles, "On Psychohistory," in *The Mind's Fate*, p. 181.

17. Robert Coles, "The Inner and the Outer World," in *The Mind's Fate*, p. 226.

18. Ibid., pp. 228–29.

19. Robert Coles, "Psychiatrists and the Poor," *Atlantic Monthly* 214 (July 1964), p. 105.

20. Coles, *Irony*, p. 1.

21. Coles, *Mind's Fate*, pp. 185–87.

22. Ibid., p. 198.

23. Ibid., p. 186.

24. CC 3, pp. 27–28.

25. Coles, *Walker Percy,* pp. 134–37.

26. Coles, *Erik Erikson,* p. 120.

27. CC 4, p. 57.

28. Coles, *Mind's Fate,* p. 117.

29. Anna Freud, from *Normality and Pathology in Childhood,* quoted in *Mind's Fate,* pp. 118–19.

30. Ibid., p. 122.

31. Personal interview with author, 24 October 1987.

32. Personal interview with author, 24 October 1987.

33. Coles, *Erik Erikson,* p. xii.

34. Coles, "The Words and Music of Social Change," in *Farewell to the South,* pp. 271–72.

35. Coles, *Erik Erikson,* p. xv.

36. Ibid., p. xvi.

37. Ibid., p. xvii.

38. Ibid., p. xix.

39. Coles, "The Artist as Psychoanalyst," in *Mind's Fate,* pp. 88, 90.

40. Coles, *Erik Erikson,* pp. 180–81.

41. Don S. Browning, *Generative Man: Psychoanalytic Perspectives* (Philadephia: Westminster Press, 1973), 147.

42. Coles, *Erik Erikson,* 33.

43. Ibid., p. 42.

44. Ibid., p. 47.

45. Browning, pp. 166–67.

46. Paul Roazen, *Erik H. Erikson: The Power and Limits of a Vision* (New York: Macmillan/Free Press, 1976), pp. 149–50.

47. Browning, pp. 155–56.

48. For a powerful statement of the need for a new public ethic, see Robert Bellah et. al, *Habits of the Heart: Individualism and Commitment in American Life* (Berkeley and Los Angeles: University of California Press, 1985). For Lasch, see *The Culture of Narcissism* (New York: Norton, 1979), and *The Minimal Self* (New York: Norton, 1984).

49. Coles, *Erik Erikson,* p. 176.

50. Coles, "Harvard Diary: Why Follow Freud?" *New Oxford Review* 52 (October 1985), p. 21.

51. Coles, "Harvard Diary: The Spiritual Life of Children; Part III," *New Oxford Review* 53 (January/February 1986), p. 17.

52. Harold Bloom has called it "the single poem that haunts all of the Transcendentalists" in "Bacchus and Merlin: The Dialectic of Romantic Poetry in America," *Ringers in the Tower* (Chicago: University of Chicago Press, 1971), p. 295.

53. See Bruce A. Ronda, "Literary Grieving: Emerson and the Death of Waldo," *Centennial Review* 23 (Winter 1979), p. 94.

54. Edith Cobb, "The Ecology of Imagination in Childhood," *Daedalus* 88 (Summer 1959), pp. 537–48.

55. For this idea I am indebted to R. W. B. Lewis.

56. Robert Ellsberg, "The Faith of Children: An Interview with Robert Coles," *Sojourners* 11 (May 1982), p. 16.

57. CC 2, p. 113.

58. Robert Coles, *The Moral Life of Children* (Boston: Atlantic Monthly Press, 1986), p. 112.

59. Ibid., p. 128.

60. CC 2, p. 109.

61. CC 2, p. 112.

62. CC 2, p. 116.

63. Robert Coles, *Still Hungry in America* (New York: World Publishing Company, 1969), pp. 85–88.

64. CC 2, p. 109.

65. CC 2, pp. 190–91.

66. Ellsberg, "The Faith of Children," p. 16.

67. Ibid., p. 12.

68. Judy Peace, "What Are We Doing to Our Children?" pp. 17–18.

69. CC 5, pp. 552–53.

70. Ellsberg, "The Faith of Children," p. 16.

Chapter 5   Politics and Culture

1. Robert Coles, "Children and Political Authority," in *Mind's Fate*, p. 245.

2. Ibid., p. 251.

3. Ibid.

4. Personal interview with author, 24 October 1987.

5. Coles, *Political Life of Children*, p. 9.

6. Ibid., pp. 13–14.

7. Ibid., p. 14.

8. This sense of the "mind of the South" is most powerfully evident in the second volume of *Children of Crisis—Migrants, Sharecroppers, Mountaineers*.

9. Robert Coles, "The South and Harvard," *Yale Review* 70 (Autumn 1980), p. 39.

10. Robert Coles, "A Psychiatrist Joins the Movement," in *Farewell to the South*, pp. 242–43.

11. Personal interview with author, 24 October 1987.

12. Coles, *Farewell to the South*, pp. 243–44.

13. Personal interview with author, 24 October 1987, and Coles, "The Words and Music of Social Change," in *Farewell to the South*, pp. 267–68.

14. Coles, "The South and Harvard," p. 40.

15. Ibid.

16. Coles, *Farewell to the South*, pp. 247–48.

17. Ibid., pp. 269, 271.

18. Personal interview with author, 24 October 1987.

19. Coles, "The South and Harvard," p. 41.

20. Coles, "Serpents and Doves: Nonviolent Youth in the South," in *Farewell to the South*, pp. 181–82.

21. Ibid., p. 203.

22. Ibid., p. 206.
23. Coles, "A Black Civil Rights Worker," in *Farewell to the South*, p. 325.
24. Coles, *The Moral Life of Children*, p. 163.
25. Coles, *Farewell to the South*, p. 189.
26. Ibid., p. 206.
27. Ibid., p. 198.
28. Ibid., pp. 291–92.
29. Ibid., p. 217.
30. Coles, *The Moral Life of Children*, pp. 173–74.
31. Paul Wilkes, "Robert Coles, Doctor of Crisis," *New York Times Magazine*, 26 March 1978, p. 4. This is apparently the man Coles names "John" in "Lookers-On and the Last Ditch," CC 1, pp. 298–314.
32. Coles, "Social Struggle and Weariness," in *Farewell to the South*, p. 235.
33. Ibid., p. 230.
34. Coles, "The South and Harvard," pp. 41–44.
35. Coles, "Strom Thurmond Country," *The New Republic*, 30 November 1968.
36. Personal interview with author, 24 October 1987.
37. Coles, "Through Conrad's Eyes," *American Poetry Review*, 13 (January–February 1984), p. 21.
38. CC 4, p. xii.
39. "A Dialogue with Dr. Robert Coles," *Chelsea* 42 (1968), p. 208.
40. CC 1, p. 332.
41. "A Dialogue," p. 215.
42. Personal interview with author, 24 October 1987.
43. "Breaking the American Stereotypes," *Time* magazine, 14 February 1972, p. 40.
44. Ibid.
45. Coles, *The Middle Americans, Proud and Uncertain* (Boston: Little, Brown, 1971), p. 11.
46. Ibid., p. 49.
47. Ibid., p. 132.
48. Ibid., p. 133.
49. Coles, "The South and Harvard," p. 46.
50. "A Dialogue," p. 216.
51. Coles, *The Geography of Faith*, p. 39.
52. Ibid., p. 42.
53. Ibid., p. 43.
54. Ibid.
55. Ibid., pp. 45–46.
56. Ibid., p. 63.
57. Ibid., p. 64.
58. Ibid., p. 70.
59. Ibid., p. 99.
60. Ibid., p. 105.
61. Ibid., p. 108.

62. Ibid., p. 110.

63. Ibid., pp. 38–39.

64. Ibid., p. 77.

65. Ibid., p. 82.

66. Ibid., p. 96.

67. Personal interview with author, 24 October 1987.

68. Robert Coles, "Books: Unreflecting Egoism," *The New Yorker,* 27 August 1979, pp. 98–105.

69. Robert Coles, "Life's Madness," *The New Republic,* 13 May 1967, pp. 25–30.

70. Robert Coles, "Freedom and its Discontents," *Triquarterly* 52 (Fall 1981), p. 29.

71. Robert Coles, "Who's to Be Born?" *The New Republic,* 10 June 1967, p. 12.

72. Robert Coles, "Harvard Diary: On Abortion," *New Oxford Review* 50 (October 1983), p. 22.

73. Robert Coles, "Harvard Diary: Further Thoughts on Abortion," *New Oxford Review* 52 (June 1985), p. 20.

74. Robert Coles, "Harvard Diary: On Women's Liberation," *New Oxford Review* 51 (January/February 1984), p. 24.

75. Robert Coles, "Harvard Diary: On Homosexuality," *New Oxford Review* 51 (March 1984), p. 24.

76. "The Good Book Versus the Textbooks," *Washington Post National Weekly Edition,* 3 August 1987, p. 10.

77. Coles, *The Moral Life of Children,* p. 246.

78. Ibid., pp. 255–56.

79. Ibid., p. 262.

80. Ibid., p. 268.

81. Ibid., p. 276.

82. Coles, *The Geography of Faith,* pp. 159, 161.

83. Ibid., p. 161.

84. Ralph Waldo Emerson, *Journals and Miscellaneous Notebooks,* ed. William Gilman et. al, 10 vols., (Cambridge: Belknap Press of Harvard University Press, 1960—), vol. 7, pp. 202–3.

85. Ralph Waldo Emerson, *The Letters of Ralph Waldo Emerson,* ed. Ralph Rusk, 6 vols., (New York: Columbia University Press, 1939), vol. 2, p. 213.

86. William James, *The Varieties of Religious Experience* (1902) (New York: Viking/Penguin, 1982), pp. 29, 31.

87. Coles, *The Geography of Faith,* p. 172

Chapter 6   The Religious Sensibility

1. In Robert Bretall, ed., *A Kierkegaard Anthology,* p. 222.

2. Coles, "The End of the Affair," pp. 47–48.

3. Coles, *The Moral Life of Children,* pp. 22–23.

4. Coles, "Harvard Diary: The Spiritual Life of Children, Part I," *New Oxford Review* 52 (November 1985), p. 27.

5. Coles, "Harvard Diary: The Spiritual Life of Children, Part II," *New Oxford Review* 52 (December 1985), pp. 24–25.

6. Coles, *The Moral Life of Children,* p. 25.

7. Coles, "The Spiritual Life of Children, Part III," *New Oxford Review* 53 (January–February 1986), p. 17.

8. In Sara Evans, *Personal Politics: The Roots of Women's Liberation in the Civil Rights Movement and the New Left* (New York: Vintage/Random House, 1980), p. 30.

9. Ibid., p. 36.

10. CC 2, p. 598.

11. CC 2, p. 579.

12. CC 3, p. 641.

13. CC 2, pp. 584–85.

14. CC 2, p. 591.

15. CC 2, p. 616.

16. CC 3, pp. 625–26.

17. CC 3, p. 631.

18. CC 3, p. 649.

19. George Abbot White, "Psychiatry and Belief: A Conversation with Robert Coles," *Commonweal* 97 (27 October 1972), p. 81.

20. Ellsberg, "The Faith of Children," p. 14.

21. Ibid., p. 16.

22. Ibid., p. 12.

23. Coles, *Geography of Faith,* p. 110.

24. Ellsberg, "The Faith of Children," p. 16.

25. George Abbot White, "The Religion of the Privileged Ones: A Conversation with Robert Coles," *Cross Currents* 31 (Spring 1981), p. 5.

26. Coles, "Freud and God," *Virginia Quarterly Review* 57 (Summer 1981), p. 382.

27. Coles, "Psychology and Civility," p. 135.

28. Coles, "Psychology as Faith," *Theology Today* 42 (April 1985), p. 70.

29. Ellsberg, "The Faith of Children," p. 13.

30. Coles, *Simone Weil, A Modern Pilgrimage* (Reading, Massachusetts: Addison-Wesley, 1987), pp. 40–41.

31. Coles, "End of the Affair," p. 47.

32. Coles, *Flannery O'Connor's South,* 160; see also Coles, "Flannery O'Connor: A Southern Intellectual," *Southern Review* 16 (January 1980), pp. 46–64.

33. Coles, *Irony in the Mind's Life,* p. 25.

34. Coles, *Walker Percy,* pp. 9, 11.

35. Coles, "But How Is Someone to Live a Life?" *Daedalus* 103 (Fall 1974), p. 311.

36. Coles, *Irony in the Mind's Life,* p. 26.

37. "*The Nature and Destiny of Man* by Reinhold Niebuhr," *Daedalus* 103 (Winter 1974), pp. 101–2.

38. Coles, *Geography of Faith,* p. 134.

39. Ibid., pp. 135, 137.

40. Coles, "Simone Weil: The Mystery of Her Life," *Yale Review* 73 (Winter 1984), p. 309.

41. Ibid., pp. 311–12.

42. Coles, *"Simone Weil,"* p. 10.

43. Ibid., p. 11–12.

44. Ibid., p. 17.

45. Leslie Fiedler, Introduction to Simone Weil, *Waiting for God* (New York: Putnam's, 1951), p. 3.

46. Coles, "Simone Weil," p. 315.

47. Coles, *Geography of Faith*, p. 137.

48. Simone Petrement, *Simone Weil: A Life* (New York: Pantheon, 1976), p. 80.

49. Coles, *Simone Weil*, p. 26.

50. Ibid., p. 62.

51. Ibid., p. 131.

52. Carter Heyward, *Our Passion for Justice: Images of Power, Sexuality, and Liberation* (New York: Pilgrim Press, 1984), p. 140. See also Beverly Wildung Harrison, *Making the Connections: Essays in Feminist Social Ethics* (Boston: Beacon Press, 1985) and the brilliant and very disturbing book by Susan Griffin, *Woman and Nature: The Roaring Inside Her* (New York: Harper and Row, 1978), especially the section "The Separate Rejoined."

53. Ibid., p. 141.

54. Petrement, *Simone Weil*, pp. 192–93.

55. Ibid., p. 81.

56. Valerie Saiving Goldstein, "The Human Situation: A Feminine View," *The Journal of Religion* 40 (April 1960), pp. 100–112.

57. Heyward, *Our Passion for Justice*, p. 143.

58. Coles, *A Spectacle unto the World: The Catholic Worker Movement* (with photographs by Jon Erikson) (New York: Viking Press, 1973), p. 67.

59. Coles, *Dorothy Day*, 51. Quotations in the following nine paragraphs come from this text.

60. Coles, "Harvard Diary: Remembering Dorothy Day Yet Again," *New Oxford Review* 50 (April 1983), p. 27.

61. Coles, *Dorothy Day*, p. 97. Quotations in the next three paragraphs come from this text.

Chapter 7   Loneliness and Community

1. Personal interview with author, 24 October 1987.

2. Course syllabi from R. C.

3. Paul Wilkes, "Robert Coles, Doctor of Crisis," p. 16.

4. Ibid.

5. See, for example, Sharon Humphries, Heidi Ravven, and Stephenson H. Brooks, "A Team Response," pp. 40–48, to Coles, "The Moral and Spiritual Imperatives of the Intellectual Life," the 1985 Associates for Religion and

Intellectual Life Consultation, in *Religion and Intellectual Life* 3 (Fall 1985), pp. 7–36.

6. Coles, *The Image Is You,* ed. Donald Erceq (Boston: Houghton Mifflin, 1969), p. 53.

7. Coles, *The Moral Life of Children,* p. 27.

8. See Juan Luis Segundo, *The Liberation of Theology* (Maryknoll, N.Y.: Orbis Press, 1976), especially Chapter 2, "In "Search of Sociology."

9. Donald P. Spence, *Narrative Truth and Historical Truth: Meaning and Interpretation in Psychoanalysis* (New York: W. W. Norton, 1982), passim.

10. Coles, *The Political Life of Children,* pp. 293–94, 300–301.

11. Personal interview with author, 24 October 1987.

12. Coles, *The Image Is You,* p. 49.

Index

abortion, 9, 133–34
"Achievement of Anna Freud, The," 92
Addams, Jane, 15
Agee, James, 6, 56, 57, 68, 74, 92, 153
  Coles's essays on, 67, 73, 181
  influence of, on Coles, 41–42, 55, 59, 66, 88, 131
  realism of, 64, 79, 80, 82
Arendt, Hannah, 97
Auden, W. H., 68–69
Auerbach, Erich, 62–63, 79
Augustine (Saint), 9, 14–15, 22, 23, 143, 153–54, 156, 185–86 n. 4
autobiographical elements, 14, 17, 19–21, 54
Avery, Bernicia, 174

Babbitt, Irving, 76
Barrett, William, 69
Batterham, Forster, 167, 169
Beach, Kenneth, 153
Beardslee, William, 136
Bernanos, George, 6, 10, 68, 130, 131, 153
  influence of, 41, 81–82, 143
Berrigan, Daniel, 1, 8–9, 10, 17–19, 127–31, 138, 141, 150, 156
Berrigan, Philip, 18
Bettelheim, Bruno, 83
Bible, 22, 62, 63–64, 71, 143, 169
Binswanger, Ludwig, 91
Bloom, Allen, 13
Bond, Julian, 119
Bonhoeffer, Dietrich, 27, 152
Booth, Wayne, 45, 48
Bowen, Elizabeth, 64, 67, 79, 150
Bridges, Ruby, 4, 39–40, 116, 119, 143–44, 150
Browning, Don, 97, 99–100

Burke, Kenneth, 76
Burlingame, Dorothy, 96

Carmichael, Stokely, 115, 120, 129–30
Catholic Worker movement, 5, 27, 133, 143, 166–67, 170–73
Catholicism. *See* Religion
children, 92–93, 102–10
"Children and Political Authority," 111
Children of Crisis, 1, 2, 4–6, 60, 73, 88, 149, 181
  content of, 7, 8, 15–17, 19, 39–40, 52, 92
  editing of, 41–44, 47
  interviews for, 18, 38–42, 113, 116, 188 n. 5
  method of, 35–58, 67, 68
  narrative strategies used in, 17, 44–55, 59
  See also titles of individual volumes
Christian radicalism, 127–31, 153, 163
Christianity. *See* Religion
civil rights groups, 7, 94, 114, 140, 149, 166
civil rights movement, 2, 4, 20, 27, 94, 117–19, 123–24, 127, 166–67
  changes in, 18, 92, 120, 140
  Coles's involvement in, 5, 7–8, 38, 114–16, 129, 149
Clinch, Nancy, 90
Cobb, Edith, 103
Coles, Jane Hallowell (wife), 1, 37, 93–94, 113, 120, 144
Coles, Philip (father), 21–22, 25, 32, 87, 142
Coles, Robert, 1–3, 13, 21–34
  as literary critic, 6, 34, 59–82
  medical training of, 25–30
  and religion, 142–73

works by, 30, 60, 70–71, 87–88
Piaget, Jean, 102, 144
political issues, 7–9, 18, 86, 111–14
  See also Radical politics
Political Life of Children, The, 1, 86, 88,
  111, 113, 181, 182
poststructuralism, 74, 77, 178
pragmatism, 68, 72, 76, 78, 140
Privileged Ones, The, 38, 110, 149
Progoff, Ira, 152
psychiatry, 29, 83, 84, 151–52
  and children, 92–93, 102–10
  Coles's disenchantment with, 2–3, 6–
    7, 28, 85, 89
  and religion, 21, 29, 56, 151
Puritanism, 23–24, 32, 143

radical politics, 130, 141
  Coles's suspicion of, 18, 120, 126–
    27, 136, 138
realism, 61–66, 73–74, 77, 79–80, 82
Reich, Annie, 84
religion, 9, 23–25, 139, 142–73
  and psychiatry, 21, 29, 56
  role of, 4–5, 133
Roazen, Paul, 99
Robertson, Pat, 136
Roosevelt, Franklin D., 171

Sachs, Hans, 97
Schneider, Herbert, 23
Schwerner, Mickey, 115
Scott, Nathan, Jr., 78
Segundo, Juan Luis, 178
Sennett, Richard, 32, 61
sentimentalism, 65, 75
"Serpents and Doves: Nonviolent
  Youth in the South," 95, 116–17
Sessions, William, 66
Silone, Ignatio, 10, 131
Simone Weil: A Modern Pilgrimage, 92,
  161–62, 177
Smith, Barbara Herrnstein, 76
Social Class and Mental Illness (Yale
  study), 89
"Social Struggle and Weariness," 120
"sociological literature," 61, 66
South, 93–94, 124

Coles's work in, 7, 16, 37–44, 87, 94,
  114–20, 188 n.5
South Goes North, The, 44, 48–51, 54,
  123–24, 146, 148
Spectacle unto the World, 166, 170
Spence, Donald, 10, 180–81
Stein, Edith, 131
Stendhal, 63
Stewart, Randall, 76
Still Hungry in America, 181
Stowe, Harriet Beecher, 64
Study in Courage and Fear, A, 16, 19–
  20, 37, 44–48, 54, 93, 121
Sullivan, Harry Stack, 71

theme, 14, 24, 30–32, 46, 70–71
Tillich, Paul, 28–30, 87, 143, 150, 153
  as Coles's mentor, 60, 81, 174
Tolstoy, Leo, 64, 75, 76, 80
Trilling, Lionel, 75, 78

Union Theological Seminary, 5, 27, 143

Vietnam War, 18
Vree, Dale, 133

Walker Percy: An American Search, 60,
  68, 72, 91, 177
Warren, Robert Penn, 8
Watters, Pat, 119
Weil, Simone, 10, 68, 77–79, 111–12,
  120, 153, 157–66, 172
  influence of, 41, 88, 131, 143
Welty, Eudora, 8
*William Carlos Williams: The Knack of
  Survival in America,* 60
Williams, William Carlos, 6, 23, 66, 74,
  79, 92
  Coles's essays on, 67, 68, 73
  influence of, 24–26, 30–32, 41, 55,
    59–61, 87, 88, 131
  realism of, 65, 80
  writings of, 24, 60, 61, 65, 67
Winters, Ivor, 76
Women of Crisis, 1, 17, 43, 55, 80, 181
women's movement, 131, 134, 140

Young, Andrew, 123

Zellner, Bob, 114
Zola, Émile, 64